Y0-BKI-588

The First Wave of Decolonization

The global phenomenon of decolonization was born in the Americas in the late eighteenth and early nineteenth centuries. *The First Wave of Decolonization* is the first volume in any language to describe and analyze the scope and meanings of decolonization during this formative period. It demonstrates that the pioneers of decolonization were not twentieth-century Frenchmen or Algerians but nineteenth-century Peruvians and Colombians. In doing so, it vastly expands the horizons of decolonization, conventionally understood to be a post-war development emanating from Europe. The result is a provocative, new understanding of the global history of decolonization.

Mark Thurner is Professor of Latin American Studies at the Institute of Latin American Studies, School of Advanced Study, University of London.

Routledge Studies in Global Latin America

Series Editors:
Peter Burke
(University of Cambridge)
Jorge Cañizares-Esguerra
(University of Texas at Austin)
Linda Newson
(University of London)
Mark Thurner
(University of London and FLACSO)

Routledge Studies in Global Latin America publishes critical, post-Area Studies scholarship that connects local histories with the global history of modernity. The editors are keen to publish in those areas where Latin or Iberian America has played a pioneering role in global history.

The First Wave of Decolonization
Edited by Mark Thurner

For more information about this series, please visit: www.routledge.com/Routledge-Studies-in-Global-Latin-America/book-series/RSGLA

The First Wave of Decolonization

Edited by Mark Thurner

Routledge
Taylor & Francis Group
NEW YORK AND LONDON

First published 2019
by Routledge
52 Vanderbilt Avenue, New York, NY 10017

and by Routledge
2 Park Square, Milton Park, Abingdon, Oxon, OX14 4RN

Routledge is an imprint of the Taylor & Francis Group, an informa business

© 2019 Taylor & Francis

The right of Mark Thurner to be identified as the author of the editorial material, and of the authors for their individual chapters, has been asserted in accordance with sections 77 and 78 of the Copyright, Designs and Patents Act 1988.

All rights reserved. No part of this book may be reprinted or reproduced or utilised in any form or by any electronic, mechanical, or other means, now known or hereafter invented, including photocopying and recording, or in any information storage or retrieval system, without permission in writing from the publishers.

Trademark notice: Product or corporate names may be trademarks or registered trademarks, and are used only for identification and explanation without intent to infringe.

Library of Congress Cataloging-in-Publication Data
A catalog record for this title has been requested

ISBN: 978-0-367-25870-2 (hbk)
ISBN: 978-0-429-29028-2 (ebk)

Typeset in Sabon
by Apex CoVantage, LLC

Contents

List of Figures	vi
Foreword TODD SHEPARD	vii
Introduction MARK THURNER	1
1. A Brief Conceptual History of 'Colonia' FRANCISCO ORTEGA	8
2. Decolonizing Customs MARK THURNER	26
3. Inventing Columbia/Colombia LINA DEL CASTILLO	48
4. Race and Revolution in Colombia, Haiti, and the United States MARIXA LASSO	77
5. Decolonizing Europe JAMES SANDERS	95
6. Second Slavery and Decolonization in Brazil BARBARA WEINSTEIN	118
7. The Lost Italian Connection FEDERICA MORELLI	133
Contributors	144
Index	146

Figures

2.1 Inca-Hispanic Royal Genealogy of Peru. Untitled fold-out insert, Jorge Juan and Antonio de Ulloa, *Relación histórica del viaje a la América meridional*, Appendix (Madrid, 1748)   30
2.2 The Country of the Incas, free of Ultramarine monarchs. Frontispiece, Mariano de Rivero and Jacob von Tschudi, *Antigüedades Peruanas*, v. 2 (Vienna, 1851)   31
3.1 *Colombia Prima or South America*. William Faden and Louis Stanislas d'Arcy de la Rochette (London, 1807)   63
3.2 *Amerique Septentrionale et Meridionale*. Pierre M. Lapie (Paris, 1819)   67

Foreword

In the 1950s, the Senegalese essayist and historian Abdoulaye Ly wrote of 'a ring of fire burning all along the Tropics.' He did so to describe the intensity with which anticolonial and antiracist activism, arguments, and uprisings were remaking the world. His is a red-hot image that shares the sense of movement and transformative power inherent in the watery allegories—'tides,' 'currents,' or 'waves'—that twentieth- and twenty-first-century commentators so often deploy to describe decolonization. These metaphors do quite a lot of work when decolonization is on the table, in part because of the baggage that weighs down the term 'decolonization' itself. It's a word that Mark Thurner, in the Introduction to this path-breaking collection, cleverly qualifies as 'a negative prefix grafted onto a venerable Latin root already burdened by two modern suffixes.' According to extant histories of the term, early variations on the verb 'to decolonize,' scattered between the 1830s and the 1950s, usually worked to explain, regretfully, why France, Great Britain, or some other Western power had to withdraw from a conquered territory or colony. Typically, there were direct ties to cost-benefit analyses or versions of white supremacist racism. 'Decolonization' became more widely used in the early 1960s when French, Belgian, and other governments rather suddenly sought to get out of lands that, just years or months before, their leaders had argued were rightfully theirs. This history helps explain why, too often, the category 'decolonization' antisepticises what it supposedly describes. Talk of 'a ring of fire' or a 'tide of History,' to the contrary, conveys the massive investment of human action and suffering at stake in various iterations of the phenomenon we call decolonization: the wide-ranging hopes and the depths of despair; the potential for tectonic shifts in human relations; and the intense efforts to ensure that, instead, things changed only so that they could stay the same. It also merits scholarly attention that decolonizations, in all their multiplicity, happened, in Ly's words, 'all along the Tropics' and that these events sundered sea-spanning lines of control. This was what he saw in the 1950s, and it's what this volume describes in the early nineteenth century.[1]

The First Wave of Decolonization takes as its title a rather dismissive qualification of what happened across Hispanophone and Lusophone Central and South America in the early to mid-nineteenth century. It does so to transform the phrase, to make the first wave's oceanic force visible, to give commentators, scholars, and activists insight into the intensity, the wide-ranging humanity, and the deeply political nature of the decolonizations that took place then and there. Such insight makes it possible to contemplate how this first wave receded before it truly transformed the world as well as why the impact and the reach it achieved largely have been erased from history and memory. This is a collection that coheres and that advances a strong thesis, a frontal challenge to existing historiographical and theoretical certainties. These reduce 'the first wave' to a precursor to the heroic anticolonial triumphs and imaginaries that, we are often told and too often presume, only really crystallized in the mid-twentieth-century 'era of decolonization.' Following Walter Mignolo, decolonial theorists have denigrated earlier anticolonial victories as state-centric elite affairs, that ensconced the values and politics of the former colonizers rather than challenged them. While recent historical scholarship emphatically rebuts such claims, revisionist historians have failed to dispel the truism that 'old' European imperialism, which the Pan-American revolutions—'American,' Haitian, and Bolivarian—ended, needs to be distinguished from 'new imperialism,' which took hold in Africa, Asia, and Oceania beginning in the late nineteenth century. This persistent analytic fiction helps obscure the resonances as well as the connections that span the modern era. The nineteenth-century history Thurner and his authors detail makes it possible to discern such echoes and links with new clarity. This book's evidence and analyses rhyme with the proposal of historians of Kenya W. R. Ochieng and Atieno Odhiambo, who counsel that 'decolonization as a theme is a much wider concept than the mere "winning of independence" or "transfer of power."' In their understanding, to speak seriously of decolonization 'entails the exploration of dreams, the analysis of struggles, compromises, pledges and achievements, and the rethinking of fundamentals.' The following pages present a 'first wave' in which exactly this was at stake.[2]

The verb 'to decolonize,' it turns out, appeared in an 1822 Peruvian publication that meditated on big questions about how a newly independent society could free itself from the deadweight of what was named 'ominous colonialism' (*ominoso coloniaje*). Which is to say that the verb was not invented, despite what a number of historians (myself included) have written, in an obscure 1836 publication by a French polemicist urging the Orléanist regime to withdraw from the formerly Ottoman ruled lands around Algiers, in North Africa, which since 1830 French forces had begun to occupy and govern. Whereas Henri Fonfrède's coinage aimed to persuade his countrymen that this venture was anachronistic, unethical, and unprofitable, José Faustino Sánchez Carrión's earlier usage sketched pathways toward a revolutionary future for his fellow citizens.

The Peruvian writer was undeniably an elite but he emphatically wrote from the position of the formerly colonized.[3]

Formerly colonized subalterns, too, and in large numbers, as every chapter in this volume demonstrates, participated directly in mass efforts to make the republican world, which independence from Spain and Portugal inaugurated, freer, more just, more equal, more democratic, and importantly, wholly new. Questions of race and racism, as was true in the mid-twentieth-century era of decolonization, were key topics in these debates. Many of these subalterns—and significant numbers of various elites, too—understood themselves in relationship to colour, notably to blackness, or to combinations of black and white. The place of 'Indians' was also multiple and important. In the 1950s, anticolonial theorist and activist Frantz Fanon insisted on the need to speak of multiple 'decolonizations.' *The First Wave of Decolonization* will make it possible for scholars of decolonizations and anticolonialisms to begin to more fully include these earlier decolonizations into their thinking as far more than stunted antecedents.[4]

Questions of state, of statehood, of state formation play out here in ways that will interest scholars—theorists and cultural critics as well as historians and social scientists—of decolonization in other eras. These chapters discuss the hopes and the political projects to build republican states, as well as the mass mobilization these inspired. Yet we also learn of federalist and other postimperial political plans. Unlike Fanon and many other twentieth-century radical anticolonialists, as well as more recent postcolonial and decolonial critics, the chapters in *The First Wave of Decolonization* attend more to what seemed possible, to whom the possibilities seemed desirable, and what they led such people—and those who opposed them—to do than to why these projects failed, or how such state-centered visions impeded other (perhaps more liberating) possibilities from taking shape. Indeed, the early nineteenth-century context, when affirming 'nations' was still quite novel and with the post-1848 weaponization of nationalisms by reactionary European elites still in the future, offers intriguing lessons that should be taken up in ongoing historiographical debates. These histories resonate with recent work on twentieth-century 'revolutionary nationalisms,' speak to ongoing discussions sparked by work on post-1945 federalist projects by historians such as Fred Cooper, and also bring to light numerous thinkers, writers, and politicians—Sánchez Carrión, for example—whose work might usefully contribute to efforts by scholars like Gary Wilder to bring previously dismissed or ignored texts and authors into debates about postcolonial and poststructuralist theory.[5]

Pushing back against what, in this volume, Lasso terms 'a historical teleology that reads this period through the retrospective lens of a future failure,' the authors of *The First Wave of Decolonization* take seriously projects and understandings, such as those around states and citizenship, that failed or disappointed. They do so to more accurately capture the complexities of the past but also to speak to questions that seem particularly pressing today. In this they tread pathways that historians and anthropologists such as Cooper, Wilder, and David Scott also have taken. The histories mapped out here make it possible to think differently, then, about histories of colonialism and anticolonialism, about race and racism, about the place of elites and subalterns in anticolonial struggle and postindependence state-making. In short, they make strong claims, as Sanders puts it, that 'the history of political modernity cannot be properly understood without reference to a vanguard, decolonizing, republican Hispanic America.' Sanders and other authors in this volume thus challenge not just Mignolo and subsequent decolonial theorists, but also claims by Dipesh Chakrabarty and certain postcolonial critics that presume that the origins of modernity are necessarily European.[6]

Historians should know, whether from reading the French historian Lucien Febvre or the French philosopher Michel Foucault, that explaining a phenomenon by virtue of its origins is almost always problematic. In this case, however, pushing back the putative birthdate of the term 'decolonize' tells us much. It makes it clear that those fighting to overcome colonial oppression really invented decolonization. It pushes us to expand the frame of existing historiographical discussions about decolonization, chronologically and geographically. Sánchez Carrión's text indicates that something really big was happening, in this case an effort to describe, analyze, and critique what he called 'the colonial system' in order to overcome its nefarious effects. Thurner tells us that the Peruvian usage of this transatlantic, eighteenth-century term, *'sistema colonial,'* described at once what was being swept away by history but also the 'debased customs' it left among the colonized in its wake. In Peru the term had circulated since the late eighteenth century and it resurged in 1813 with the Peruvian ratification of the Constitution of Cadiz, which abolished the 'colonial' distinction between American Spain and Peninsular or Iberian Spain.

In 1814, the Haitian diplomat and writer Baron Pompée Valentin de Vastey published a polemical book he titled *Le système colonial dévoilé (The Colonial System Unveiled)*. It was a direct response, as the title of an accompanying publication made clear, to the fourth volume of a five-volume 1802 publication by a former French minister of the Navy and the Colonies in which Pierre-Victor Malouet defined 'the colonial system.' He did so to celebrate how it had worked and to summon Napoléon to reestablish it on Saint-Domingue, the former French colony then still formally under French rule; in 1804, of course, the Haitian Republic declared its independence. Vastey's book is quite stunning, and recent scholars have argued that it should be considered the first systematic analysis of how European overseas colonialism functions, notably in its reliance on racialization, in this case on distinctions between 'whites' and 'blacks.'[7]

Yet the connections we can begin to imagine with Peruvian texts published around the same time are, for the historian, perhaps of greater interest. Vastey noted in 1814 that 'now that we have Haytian printing presses, we can reveal the crimes of the colonists and respond to even the most absurd calumnies invented by the prejudice and greed of our oppressors.'[8] In Peru, the likes of Sánchez Carrión and Monteagudo made similar claims. The hopes and horizons that Haitians and Peruvian imagined for their people, their countries, and for humanity, were greater still. As the pages that follow make clear, this was true of peasants and market women as well as certain writers, artists, and politicians. In its invigorating interweaving of compelling evidence and incisive analyses, *The First Wave of Decolonization* offers a novel, connected perspective on the long history of decolonization that helps us better understand the world we live in.

Todd Shepard

Notes

1. Abdoulaye Ly, *Les masses africaines et l'actuelle condition humaine* (Paris: Présence africaine, 1956), 12. On uses of 'decolonize' between 1836 and the early 1960s and related metaphors, see Todd Shepard, *The Invention of Decolonization: The Algerian War and the Remaking of France*, 2nd ed. (Ithaca: Cornell University Press, 2008).
2. See, e.g., Walter D. Mignolo, *Local Histories/Global Designs: Coloniality, Subaltern Knowledges, and Border Thinking* (Princeton: Princeton University Press, 2000); W. R. Ochieng and E. S. Atieno Odhiambo, 'On Decolonization,' in B. A. Ogot and W. R. Ochieng, eds., *Decolonization and Independence in Kenya, 1940–1993* (London: James Currey, 1995).
3. For the first identification of Fonfrède as inventor of the term, see Charles-Robert Ageron, *La décolonisation française* (Paris: Armand Colin, 1994), 5.
4. Frantz Fanon, *Towards an African Revolution*, Haakon Chevalier, trans. (New York: Grove Press, 1967), 179.
5. On post-1945 federalism, see, e.g., Frederick Cooper, *Citizenship Between Empire and Nation: Remaking France and French Africa, 1945–1960* (Princeton: Princeton University Press, 2014); and Todd Shepard, 'A l'heure des "grands ensembles" et de la guerre d'Algérie. L' "État-nation" en question,' *Monde(s). Revue d'histoire transnationale* 1 (May 2012), 113–134. On efforts to decolonize intellectual history and globalize critical theory, see, e.g., Gary Wilder, *Freedom Time: Negritude, Decolonization, and the Future of the World* (Durham: Duke University Press, 2015).
6. David Scott, *Conscripts of Modernity: The Tragedy of Colonial Enlightenment* (Durham: Duke University Press, 2004); Dipesh Chakrabarty, *Provincializing Europe: Postcolonial Thought and Historical Difference* (Princeton: Princeton University Press, 2000).
7. Baron Pompée Valentin de Vastey, *Le Système colonial dévoilé* (Cap-Henry, Haïti: chez P. Roux, imprimeur du Roi, 1814); ibid., Notes à M. le baron de V.P. Malouet, ministre de la Marine et des colonies, de sa Majesté Louis XVIII, et ancien administrateur des colonies et de la Marine, ex-colon de Saint-Domingue, etc. en réfutation de 4ème volume de son ouvrage, intitulé: Collection de mémoires sur les colonies, et particulièrement sur Saint-Domingue, etc. (Cap-Henry, Haïti: chez P. Roux, imprimeur du Roi, 1814). On Vastey,

see, esp., Marlene L. Daut, *Baron de Vastey and the Origins of Black Atlantic Humanism* (New York: Palgrave Macmillan, 2017) and the extensive commentary that accompanies the first full translation of the text into English in Baron de Vastey, *The Colonial System Unveiled*, Chris Bongie, trans. and ed. (Liverpool: Liverpool University Press, 2014).
8. Vastey, *The Colonial System*, 95.

Introduction

Mark Thurner

As Dane Kennedy notes in *Decolonization: A Very Short Introduction*, 'the first wave of decolonization occurred in the Americas' during the Age of Revolution of the late eighteenth and early nineteenth centuries.[1] Here, as Benedict Anderson famously argued in *Imagined Communities*, 'Creole pioneers' rode a series of insurrections into a receding horizon of postimperial political modernity that would eventually encircle the globe.[2] One would think that this opening continental wave would be the subject of intense scholarly scrutiny and debate in the field of decolonization studies. Curiously, the very opposite is true.

Kennedy's able survey of decolonization's global history is a case in point. Understandably, the 'meat' of his thin Oxford sandwich is the post-war Third Wave of 'the Third World' that occurred during the 'third quarter of the twentieth century.' This third wave is, the author admits, 'conventionally understood' to be the referent of 'decolonization.' A cursory internet search of books on the subject readily confirms this conventional understanding. If one enters the word 'decolonisation' with a British 's' in the Amazon.co.uk search box, the result is 682 titles. When 'Latin America' is added to that keyword only 78 titles remain, with 'Hispanic America' (the term most frequently used during the period) only 19. A closer look at those few titles reveal that only three are concerned with nineteenth-century Hispanic or Latin America. When the American spelling of the word 'decolonization' is entered on the same site, 1,638 titles result (on Amazon.com, 1,753). When 'Latin America' is added to the string, 198 titles remain (223 on Amazon.com). A closer look at these titles, however, reveals that nearly all are concerned with the post-war Caribbean, most of these former US, French, and British possessions. A survey of the contents of the several 'Decolonization Readers' in print ratifies these results: Latin America has utterly 'disappeared' from the literature in English. A similar search on Amazon.es with the Spanish word 'descolonización' yields only 108 titles, of which only two are concerned with nineteenth-century Hispanic or Latin America.

Why the dearth of titles concerned with early nineteenth-century Hispanic or Latin America or indeed the first wave of decolonization at large

(British, French, Hispanic, etc.)? As this volume makes clear, the reasons are several. Amnesia is probably first on the list. Another is that the first wave is widely seen to have been a Europhile, neocolonial affair among rival elites that effectively excluded the lower or subaltern classes. This view has been overturned by the recent scholarship on Hispanic American independence, which clearly demonstrates the opposite.[3] Yet another commonplace in the literature divides the history of imperialism or colonialism into the 'old' and the 'new' with 'Spanish empire' and 'Ottoman empire' epitomizing the former, being frequently identified, in addition to 'old,' as 'medieval' and/or 'Oriental.' This commonplace of old/new colonialism was coined in the late eighteenth century by French philosophes. Although in certain ways useful as a ready-made periodization scheme, it has obscured the long, connected or entangled histories of empire that spanned the eighteenth and nineteenth centuries. It is precisely this entangled period that gave birth to the first wave of decolonization.[4] A more stubborn but equally dubious claim has been that the modern concepts of 'colonies' and 'colonialism' and indeed 'decolonisation' are later, primarily French, German, and British inventions, and as such are 'misplaced' in Latin America. To apply these concepts to other periods and places is, it is claimed, bad history. Indeed, there is something of a consensus on this point among scholars and critics of decolonization. On what is this consensus based?

We are told that the term and concept (French, *décolonisation*) was coined in the mid-1830s by the French essayist Henry Fonfrède. A century later, the work of German emigre Moritz Bonn at LSE assisted in the establishment of the term in international political and English-language academic discourse.[5] But more than a decade before Fonfrède's supposed coinage, a Peruvian revolutionary deployed the verb 'decolonize' to argue for a radical programme of cultural change in republican Peru. The year was 1822. Writing under the pen name of 'El Solitario de Sayan,' José Faustino Sánchez Carrión argued that independence meant far more than mere divorce from the 'metropolis' and its 'colonial system'; it meant 'decolonizing customs' and 'maximizing enlightenment' among the people. How is it possible that this Peruvian revolutionary could speak to his peers of 'decolonizing the customs' established under 'the colonial system' when, we are told, such 'foreign' concepts were supposedly not yet available to him?

Apropos, Francisco Ortega opens the first chapter of this volume with a question that, he notes, is surely 'startling for some.' 'Was Hispanic America ever a colony?' he asks. As Ortega points out, this question is anything but new, having been debated in the Hispanic world off and on since the late eighteenth century. As many a historian of Latin America has noted, officially the administrative units of the 'Occidental Indies' of the Hispanic Monarchy were not called 'colonies' but instead viceroyalties, kingdoms and provinces. But, Ortega suggests, that does not mean that the concept of 'colony' was absent or irrelevant. Indeed, the evidence suggests that this and related concepts underwent a momentous transformation before, during and immediately following the first wave. As a result, Ortega concludes, the answer is 'yes and no.'

But Ortega's question is addressed primarily to doubting Latin Americanists. Another, perhaps more fruitful way to pose this question more broadly is via an approach that traces the connected (as opposed to comparative) histories of empires and the related 'waves of decolonization.' Such an approach informs this volume, which is the collective product of the London-based Global Decolonization Workshop (GDW). With initial, start-up support from the University of London's School of Advanced Study and additional support from the Global Initiative at New York University, the GDW has since 2016 regularly convened workshops of leading scholars of Iberian, British, and French empires, thereby facilitating a longer, more connected understanding of the histories of decolonization. Our questions about Hispanic America have thus been informed by a series of questions posed to other places and times. Was India ever a colony? Was Algeria ever a colony? Was Italy ever a colony? In all these cases the answer, which may be 'startling for some,' is likewise 'yes and no.' In this regard at least, Hispanic America is unexceptional. Let us briefly review these three cases.

Although a 'Colonial Office' was established in London in 1821, 'British India' was not officially created until 1889, that is, about midway into the period of Crown rule or Raj (1858–1947) that commenced after the Indian Mutiny. Like the fictitious and anachronistic 'Spanish America' (no such thing ever existed)[6] of the Anglo-American historiography on the region, the national concept of 'British India' has been retrospectively projected onto early periods, including that of indirect 'Company rule' (1757–1858). As Travers has argued, Company rule was founded on revenue collection combined with the historicist notion that Mughal India possessed an 'ancient constitution' that should be restored, to the benefit of course of the Company.[7] Although Travers traces this notion to British thought, similar concepts circulated in seventeenth- and eighteenth-century Hispanic America where, as Ortega points out in this volume, ancient constitutions and 'monarchies' were cited to deflate the claim that the Occidental Indies were dependent 'colonies' secured by 'conquest.' During the period of Crown rule, 'British' dominion and sovereignty over and within 'India' was direct and indirect. A British 'Viceroy' or, later, 'Governor-General' oversaw the rule of provincial authorities, including commissioners, governors, and 'native' princes. From 1876 to 1947, all of this was officially stamped 'Indian Empire.' Those states with British-appointed administrators were normally called 'Presidencies and Provinces' while those with hereditary rulers were named 'Princely

States.' Neither of these modalities were officially called 'colonies,' although since the 1980s a vast critical literature has revealed the 'colonial' nature of knowledge, order, and rule in such states.[8]

In the case of Algeria, the question of whether the province was a 'colony' is nearly as old as the 'Conquest of Algeria.' The term 'decolonization' was coined by the French essayist and free-trader Henri Fonfrède, who contrasted the 'Conquest of Algeria' with the Spanish 'Conquest of America.' In contrast to the profitable Spanish enterprise in the New World, Fonfrède argued that the French enterprise in the Old was unprofitable, ethically suspect, and anachronistic. It was anachronistic because the Americas had recently reversed the tide of history. The French now ignored the American history lesson. But Fonfrède was in the very distinct and unheeded minority in France. Indeed, one of the reasons his jargon—a negative prefix grafted onto a venerable Latin root already burdened by two modern suffixes—did not catch on at the time was not only that it sounded strange but that most French people including the 'Algerians' did not agree. From 1836 to 1962 the French state firmly rejected the notion that a province of France could be a colony. When in 1962 Raymond Aron finally reversed course and declared that Algeria 'was a colony and therefore historically fated to experience decolonization' he initiated what Todd Shepherd has described as an unperturbed history of French amnesia.[9] Notably, as Shepherd has pointed out, French integration or incorporation policy in Algeria was shaped by Mexican anthropologists in Paris. More to the point, Aron's intellectual about-face echoed with Fonfrède's notion, which, in turn, was derived from late-eighteenth-century arguments against colonies, whose proponents included De Pradt, Raynal, Diderot, Kant, and Herder, as well as Bentham and Smith. These same 'radical enlightenment' thinkers played a key role in the circulation of the modern, critical concept of 'colonies' around the Atlantic world, including Iberia and the Americas.[10]

We are confronted with curious historical 'facts.' Never officially 'colonies' of France and Britain, Algeria was the occasion of the 'invention' (twice) of the term 'decolonisation' while India's post-war, postpartition metropolitan diaspora became in time the travelling home of 'postcolonial theory.' The fresh memory of violent and traumatic events combined with the global valence of the French and English languages goes a long way in explaining the currency of these coins in the realm of academic discourse. Amnesia does the rest.

Such forgetting has also done its dirty work in the case of Italy. The many connections between Italy and the Hispanic world were not only dynastic and military but cultural and intellectual. In the early eighteenth century, much of Italy, north and south, was under the rule of Hispanic Hapsburg viceroys. The War of Succession changed the dynastic map, with the Bourbons now exercising rule in Spain and southern Italy as well as the Americas, well into the nineteenth century. The father of modern historicist thought, Giambattista Vico, was, for example, the royal historiographer of 'the archaeologist king' Charles III (Madrid, 1716–1778), son of Philip V of Spain, then the Bourbon King of Naples, who also held the title of Charles V of the Two Sicilies, and who later became King of the Spains and Emperor of the Indies. In the early decades of the nineteenth century, Italian republicans fought in South America for independence from Hispanic rule; they then returned to Italy to do the same, fighting wars on several fronts. As Federica Morelli shows in this volume, however, after the 1860s, anti-Hispanic Italian cultural nationalism would eventually erase its South American inspiration. This erasure obscured a historical fact that has been amply demonstrated by the literature on the Age of Revolution, namely, that the revolution was transatlantic. What this literature has failed to explicitly recognize is that the first wave of decolonization that accompanied that age was also transatlantic, and that the direction of that wave could be eastward. Parts of Europe, including Spain, Portugal, Italy, and Greece, also experienced 'revolutions of independence' and decolonization from empires during this same period. The first wave of decolonization was European, too.

The First Wave of Decolonization offers an unconventional understanding of the early history of modern decolonization. But the point is that this understanding was not and need not be unconventional. Indeed, in the past it was mainstream thinking in many parts of the world. To wit, in Chapters 1 and 2, Francisco Ortega and Mark Thurner respectively trace the late-eighteenth-century, transatlantic emergence and meanings of modern concepts of 'colony' (*colonia*), 'colonialism' (*coloniaje*) and 'colonial system' (*sistema colonial*). These concepts played critical roles in the debates about the nature and meaning of 'the revolutions of independence' producing, as Thurner notes, the 1822 Peruvian coining of the reflexive verb 'to decolonize' (*descolonizarse*). Together, these opening two chapters of *The First Wave* demonstrate that stubborn arguments to the effect that 'colonies,' 'colonialism,' and 'decolonization' are 'misplaced ideas' in Latin America are not only untenable; indeed, these transatlantic, entangled, multilingual concepts are given their first critical, on-the-ground soundings in the region, well before they become relevant to Algeria, India, or Italy. It is in part for this very reason that they remain controversial today.

In Chapter 3, Lina del Castillo demonstrates that, Benedict Anderson's arguments about 'Creole Pioneers' notwithstanding, in the early going, New World republican independence from Old World monarchies was not always imagined in limited, national terms.[11] Instead, hemispheric and federalist imaginings of an expansive, republican 'Columbia' or 'Colombia' could be appealing, and not only to cosmopolitans. Del Castillo's chapter confirms a suspicion supported by other chapters in this volume, namely, that the first wave of decolonization cannot be properly understood within the master 'empire to nation' or 'imperialism to nationalism' teleology that pervades the literature. In short, the thesis in *Imagined Communities* that 'nation-ness' was the driving force in the first wave of decolonization needs revisiting. The break up of empires could lead to supranational federations or constitutional empires that harboured within themselves nonnational political components. That national states should precariously emerge from this cauldron was not inevitable at the time, in part because there were no models to follow other than defeated or imagined ones.

In Chapter 4, Marixa Lasso argues that the burning question of 'race' was central to the transatlantic Age of Revolution and that it was in Hispanic America that this explosive question was squarely addressed for the first time in ways that anticipated subsequent struggles for decolonization elsewhere. Lasso argues that wartime approaches to this question clearly distinguished British (US), French (Haiti) and Hispanic (Colombia) trajectories after independence. In short, old arguments to the effect that with independence nothing changed in the Americas for those marked by the burden of 'race' are at best ungrounded and at worst a gross erasure of the historical struggles of subaltern actors, who were not mere pawns or fodder for Creole plots. Such views also ignore the importance of the revolutionary wars in deciding the issue.

In Chapter 5, James Sanders argues further that the global history of political modernity cannot be properly understood without reference to a vanguard, decolonizing, republican Hispanic America. This bold new republican America was intent on abolishing not only the 'colonial legacy' of Spanish rule but indeed European monarchy at large. Sanders argues that many mid-nineteenth-century Hispanic American republicans viewed Europe not as an example to follow but as the last bastion of a wretched colonialism that must be destroyed. Europe was the home of despotism and subjects; America of freedom and citizens. It was a retrograde, despotic Europe, not America, that must be decolonized if the world was to be free. Ironically, Sanders notes, postcolonial and decolonial theorists have enshrined this Europe as the model and home of political modernity.

In Chapter 6, Barbara Weinstein argues that, although in many ways distinct, the Brazilian Empire was not immune to the social pressures and political debates around race, freedom, and sovereignty that marked independence and decolonization across nineteenth-century Iberian America. However, and as the 'Second Slavery' historiography rightly notes, in vast swaths of Brazil and the US South, the slaveholding planter class did very well after independence. This fact has made it somewhat difficult to see the kinds of decolonizing developments and discourses that the new political history of Hispanic America has recently brought to light. The challenge of this case, Weinstein suggests, is not to treat Brazil as exceptional but to develop more nuanced historical interpretations that embrace the shared contradictions that the first wave generated across Iberian America.

In Chapter 7, Federica Morelli rescues the once strong but since lost connections between the South American and Italian independence movements, both of which fought wars of liberation against Hispanic rule. Morelli argues that the subsequent rise of cultural nationalism and anti-Hispanism largely erased this strong connection. In Italy and Europe at large, the Black Legend of an enduring 'Spanish despotism' was most useful for late-nineteenth-century nationalists, who came to apply the notions of despotism and inertia to the independent Hispanic American republics. These republics were now seen as failures, and the result was that pioneering Latin America was tossed into the dustbin of history.

Notes

1. Dane Kennedy, *Decolonization: A Very Short Introduction* (New York: Oxford University Press, 2016), 8.
2. Benedict Anderson, *Imagined Communities: Reflections on the Origin and Spread of Nationalism* (London and New York: Verso, 2006).
3. These old arguments are reviewed in more detail in Mark Thurner, 'After Spanish Rule,' in Mark Thurner and Andres Guerrero, eds., *After Spanish Rule: Postcolonial Predicaments of the Americas* (Durham: Duke University Press, 2003), 12–57.
4. For further discussion of the old/new colonialism concept, see Thurner, 'After Spanish Rule.'
5. For examples, see Kennedy, *Decolonization*, 1; Todd Shepard, *The Invention of Decolonization: The Algerian War and the Remaking of France* (Ithaca: Cornell University Press, 2006); and Stuart Ward, 'The European Provenance of Decolonization,' *Past and Present* 230 (February 2016), 227–260.
6. See Mark Thurner, 'The Names of Spain and Peru: Notes on the Global Scope of the Hispanic,' in Rory O'Bryen, ed., *Transnational Spanish* (Liverpool: Liverpool University Press, forthcoming).
7. Robert Travers, *Ideology and Empire in Eighteenth-Century India: The British in Bengal* (Cambridge: Cambridge University Press, 2007).
8. Notable works in this rich vein include Ranajit Guha, *Elementary Aspects of Peasant Insurgency in Colonial India* (Oxford: Oxford University Press, 1983); Bernard Cohn, *Colonialism and Its Forms of Knowledge: The British in India* (Princeton: Princeton University Press, 1996); Nicholas Dirks, *The Hollow Crown: Ethnohistory of an Indian Kingdom* (Cambridge: Cambridge University Press, 1987); and *The Scandal of Empire: India and the Creation of Imperial Britain* (Cambridge, MA: Harvard University Press, 2006).
9. Shepard, *The Invention of Decolonization*.
10. See chapters by Ortega and Thurner in this volume. On Enlightenment anti-colonialism in northern Europe, see Sankar Muthu, *Enlightenment Against Empire* (Princeton: Princeton University Press, 2003).
11. Kennedy also argues this point in *Decolonization*, 69–74, but then goes on to give only twentieth-century examples. But many more examples could be cited for the eighteenth and nineteenth centuries. Indeed, in many cases twentieth-century leaders of decolonization movements looked back to these predecessors for inspiration.

1 A Brief Conceptual History of 'Colonia'

Francisco Ortega

> [O]ne should not lose sight that this is a *colonia* that must depend on her metropolis, Spain, and it must pay with profits the benefits . . . it receives from Spain; and so it takes great skill to combine such dependency with mutual and reciprocal interest, which would cease at the moment when European manufactures and products are no longer needed in these regions.[1]
> —Conde de Revillagigedo, Viceroy of New Spain, 1831 [1789–1794]

> The vast and beautiful dominions that Spain possesses in the Indies are not properly colonies or factories as those of other nations but an essential and integral part of the Spanish Monarchy.[2]
> —Royal Order, Supreme Junta, Seville, January 22, 1809

Was Hispanic America ever a colony? The question may startle some readers. Undoubtedly, substantial parts and peoples of the region were forcibly annexed by the Hispanic Monarchy in the early sixteenth century. Furthermore, certain strains of Latin America's nineteenth-century national historiographies grew out of the conviction that the region's peoples had revolted against the colonial tyranny of the metropole. However, as the two quotes above suggest, in the decades before independence the 'colonial' status of the American or 'West Indian' possessions of the monarchy were much debated, and even today the idea of 'Spanish colonialism' remains a contested and sensitive topic on both sides of the Atlantic. In this essay, I will suggest that the contested and politicized meaning of the term 'colony' with which we are familiar today actually emerged in the late eighteenth and early nineteenth centuries.[3] At this time, 'colonia' came to be associated with an imperfect and dependent status that did injustice to the historical 'constitutions' of the American lands and peoples.

In what follows I propose to briefly trace the conceptual history of *colonia* in the Spanish-speaking world up to the years of the wars of independence. My reading aims to avoid the anachronism of projecting back in time present usages. I depart from the conviction that the meaning of *colonia* is not self-evident—nor is it in a state of becoming evident—but was instead subject to redefinition and debate at crucial moments in history. Thus, conceptual history is a necessary—though insufficient—condition to answer today's question concerning the colonial status of Hispanic America. A second necessary condition consists in tracing the emergence of contemporary categories of analysis of 'colonialism' in Latin American academic and public discourse. Only by clarifying and theorizing the gap between past historical concepts and contemporary categories, can we adequately address this important question.

The Spanish Hapsburg Indies: Perfect or Imperfect Communities?

According to the *Diccionario de Autoridades* (first official dictionary of the Spanish Royal Academy, 1729), in the early eighteenth century the term *colonia* meant 'population or tract of land peopled by foreigners brought from the Capital City or from elsewhere,' a definition which virtually repeats the Sebastián de Covarrubias dictionary (1611) and Saint Isidore's *Etymologiae* (c. 630; re-edited 10 times in the sixteenth century) and points to a long-term semantic stability. Confirming the longue durée of the term, the *Diccionario de Autoridades* adds, 'It is an entirely Latin word. Colonia . . . At that time [of the Roman empire] there were twenty-five colonies throughout Spain, which must be understood as colonies of Roman citizens. . . .'[4] Let us note that in this official definition the term *colonia* bears positive connotations as it signifies the recognition granted by the Roman Senate to notable cities within the imperial domain. The male settlers of the colonies were part of the Republic and were recognized as citizens, participating members in the political community of the empire, an inclusion that is also present in Nebrija's *Lexicon latino-hispanicum et hispanico-latinum* in 1492. The *colono*, or settler, writes Nebrija, is the citizen of the *colonia*.[5]

It is important to note that sixteenth-century legal thought offered a distinction between perfect and imperfect communities, a distinction that could arguably be construed as expressing something still present in our own comprehension of colonialism. The distinction starts from the premise, elaborated in the Aristotelian tradition, that 'a multitude of men does not suffice to constitute a community, unless those men are bound together by a particular agreement, looking toward a particular end, and existing under a particular head.'[6] According to such criteria, jurists and moral philosophers divided communities into perfect and imperfect. If a perfect community is said to be 'self-sufficient within that [political] order' and capable of possessing a political government, imperfect communities were regarded as dependent and non-political. Whereas perfect communities are 'governed . . . by a true power of jurisdiction,' imperfect ones are governed 'by the power of dominion,' since 'Human laws may properly be laid down for any perfect community, but not for one that is imperfect' (21). Furthermore, in imperfect communities, individuals 'are not united as the principal members for the composition of one political body, but merely exist therein as inferiors destined for the uses of the master, and to the extent that they are, in some sense, under his dominion' (20). If perfect community expressed the ideal within which justice and spiritual salvation could be achieved, inhabitants of imperfect communities were merely regarded as a multitude.

Colonies were subordinate parts of greater political communities—such as empires or monarchies—but their status did not preclude them from becoming perfect communities. Such a definition matched the legal status of the American dominions. The territories acquired by conquest in the sixteenth century were incorporated by royal decree as 'kingdoms and provinces' and their separation or alienation was expressly forbidden.[7] When the term *colonia* appeared in legal codes, it designated and regulated the various forms of land occupation in the territories already part of the Hispanic Monarchy or on its fringes.[8]

If the American provinces did not have an inferior legal standing within the monarchy, entire groups of its inhabitants did. Thus, the relation between the two American legal systems or republics—one for 'Indians' and the other for 'Spaniards'—carried the 'recognition of the dominion and universal jurisdiction Spaniards exerted over Indians.'[9] The point here is that dominion over Indians was not wielded by the sovereign alone but was extended with certain limitations to most Spaniards in the Indies. Moreover, such a relationship was further theorized as the consequence of native material, spiritual, and intellectual deficiencies.[10] The general representative of the Hispanic American church before the Court in Madrid, Luis Betancourt y Figueroa, explained in 1637 that of the two republics, 'the Indian is always incapable of government; the other one, the Spaniards, is always capable.'[11] At a more macro level, the administrative apparatus—for instance, Seville's House of Trade or the Royal Council of the Indies—endowed the region with a peculiar status in relation to other realms of the Crown and a very precise economic function as purveyor of precious metals, exotic goods, and forced labour.[12]

Colonia Under the Bourbons

Bourbon administrative, military, and fiscal reforms were accompanied by extensive discussions on the role and nature of American provinces within the monarchy. These debates were largely motivated by geopolitical developments reflecting a new view of European expansion which valued ultramarine territorial acquisitions as source of profit and turned them into targets of imperial rivalry and scenarios for European conflicts, such as the Seven Years War (1756–1763). All these events contributed to an intense semantic enrichment of the word *colonia* during the eighteenth century. Thus, even if eighteenth-century Spanish reformism did not alter existing legislation, reforms were grounded in a different vision of the role of the American provinces.[13]

In a key passage in *The Spirit of the Laws* (1748) Montesquieu observed the emergence of a new type of colonial regime, one which arguably substituted violent conquest and an extractive economy based on gold and silver for 'the proper subjects of commerce.'[14] The distinction acquired forcefulness in the prose of French and British commentators such as Abbe Raynal, William Robertson, and later, the Abbe de Pradt, the first two of whom derided the Spanish system of government in the Indies.[15] Even if Hispanic authors reacted angrily to the anti-Spanish rhetoric, most reform-minded thinkers took notice of the emergence of new colonial regimes in the British and French Caribbean and accepted the emerging distinction between two forms of governance. The Count of Campomanes, one of the most penetrating and influential reformers, constantly referred to the two types of colonies and modelled his proposals on the distinction.[16] The most influential economists of the period likewise drew from this same contrast.[17] Bernardo Ward's influential *Proyecto económico* (1762), for example, clarified that American provinces were not 'colonies . . . but . . . vast domains and kingdoms.' He never specified what he meant by the distinction, however. He frequently used *colonia* to refer to the American provinces while insisting that Spain's great advantage over other European nations was 'the consumption of our fruits and products in the New World.' Consequently, Ward wrote, 'it is necessary to fix the trade so that it supports our industry, extends it even further and gets rid of the contraband.'[18] The entire 'Preliminary Discourse'—with its frequent oscillations between *colonias* and kingdoms—exemplifies the coexistence of the two concepts during this moment of substantial transition. What is certain is that the mercantilist formulas both of Campomanes and Ward—prescribing American provinces to focus on supplying primary commodities while consuming manufactures produced by the metropole—progressively defined their place in eighteenth-century reformist writings. Reformists, in turn, intensified expectations about the economic potential of the colonies.

José Gálvez, Minister of Indies (1776–1787), spearheaded this new vision of America. The project for implementing the intendancies throughout the Americas sought to accentuate fiscal pressure, strengthen the capacity of the tax collection system, establish several monopolies, reform the old customs system, and create a more effective method for transferring resources to Spain.[19] Gálvez's own formula—that reforms in Hispanic America should be implemented 'under the same rules with which they were enacted in the Peninsula . . . without having to change them except in the support and promotion of industries, banned in the colonies' became a bureaucratic mantra and naturalized the view of

Hispanic America as colonies among officials.[20] Count Revillagigedo, Viceroy of New Spain (1789–1794), wrote in his account to his successor that 'one should not lose sight that this is a colonia that must depend on Spain.'[21] By then, the term *colonia* competed with official administrative denominations such as viceroyalty, captaincy, and provinces, and non-official but widely accepted terms such as kingdoms or realms and *patria*.

Three semantic features were present in the emerging concept. In the first place, the new meaning of *colonia* indicated a relation of externality with the monarchy's natural political community. This conceptual development was coeval with transformations affecting an important set of terms designating the nature of political community such as nation, *patria*, and republic. Whereas these terms evolved to designate the inclusiveness of a perfect community, *colonia* began to capture the utilitarian and subordinated or 'imperfect' condition of 'Indian' or 'Ultramarine' possessions.[22] The emerging understanding among some royal officers and reformers was that colonies belonged to the monarchy but were not part of the Spanish nation, at least not in the same way Catalonia, Aragon, and Toledo were.[23] This sense of externality to the political community would be at the core of the debates about American representation in the Cadiz *Cortes* (1810–1813).

In the second place, the mercantilist view saw European possessions abroad primarily as economic assets. These colonies were important because, if well administered, they could in theory yield fantastic profits for the mother country. In its most extreme, *colonia* designated a vicious regime of economic exploitation that suppressed the political nature of society and turned men into slaves. Finestrad summarized the situation of the French Caribbean colonies: 'The oppression and violence we see in these colonies constitute the surest forecast of their productions' (269r, p. 404). These types of colonies, also called *factorías*, set up a deliberately non-consensual regime of economic exploitation and political degradation.[24] It is not surprising to see why, despite the fantastic yields of the colonial regime and the enthusiasm exhibited by bureaucrats everywhere, the new regime remained problematic for political and legal philosophy.

Finally, the emerging meaning of *colonia* brought back the problem of the legitimacy of domination. If colonies were external to the nation, the question of the nature of the bond between metropole and colonies became a point of contention. The growing association of *colonia* with coercion and illegitimate domination, that is, with what seventeenth-century political philosophers had specified as the form of government suiting an imperfect community, was further complicated by the emergence of a conceptual matrix that put forth the Westphalian model of absolute and indivisible state sovereignty.[25] In this model, sovereignty acts through the law, an expression of the general will, which cannot be arbitrary or illegitimate. Perhaps such association was the reason some authors, such as Capuchin Joaquin de Finestrad, zealous absolutist and author of *El Vasallo instruido* (The instructed Vassal c. 1789), an irascible political treaty written in the aftermath of the Revolt of the Comuneros in New Granada (1781), were reluctant to use the term *colonia* with regard to American provinces.[26] When the word showed up in Finestrad's writings it meant settlement, except in the last chapter, entitled 'A demonstration of the natural dominion and ownership of the Kings of Spain in America.' In it Finestrad repeatedly uses the term *colonia* to designate those possessions that were acquired by illegitimate and tyrannical means and were subject to 'greed, ambition, and plunder, the usurpation by violent adventurers, pirates and bloodthirsty invaders.'[27] It is precisely in contrast to this tyranny that Finestrad argued for the just titles of Spain on America, including Papal donation (1493), and more importantly, 'the consent of the American people who assure Spain in its rights and long peaceful possession, an evident and unequivocal title of domination and natural lordship' (268r). The question of just titles remained explosive during the period and became rhetorically important during the wars of independence.[28]

However, it would be equivocal to assert an unambiguous embrace of *colonial* policy among Spanish officials. At the extraordinary Royal Council meeting that took place on March 5, 1768, Count Campomanes and Floridablanca warned that:

> To love Spain, their Mother country, your Vassals in the Indies need to unite their interests with her. As there cannot be love at such great distance, we can only promote it by making them perceive the sweetness and participation in the profit, honour and graces [of the nation]. How can they love a government whom they blame for taking all the earnings and profits while no one encourages them to love the nation; and everyone who goes from [Spain] have no other purpose than to be rich at their expense?

Campomanes and Floridablanca perceived in the emerging concept a threat to the unity of the monarchy and stressed Hispanic Americans inclusion in the nation and the consensual nature of good government. The Counts concluded: 'We can no longer hold those countries to be pure *colonias*, but significant and powerful provinces of the Spanish Empire.'[29]

Other observers pointed to the probability of an eventual separation of the colonies and proposed the creation of several independent American monarchies linked with Spain by dynastic ties. The controversial projects of the Spanish statesman Count Aranda, José de Ábalos (*Intendente* in Caracas), and Victorian de Villava (prosecutor at the Appellate Court in Charcas), and the subsequent attempt by Manuel Godoy (1808), Minister of Charles IV, to oversee the conversion of the viceroyalties into autonomous kingdoms, suggest attempts to preserve the unity of the Crown in the face of growing recognition that the enormous distance, the American provinces' wealth and the diversity of their character pushed them towards their independence.[30] Faced with such reality—that the *colonias* form their own nations—it was best to provide, according to the Memorial presumably penned by Count Aranda, for the creation of 'four nations [one for each viceroyalty] . . . tightly held together by offensive and defensive alliance for their conservation and prosperity.'[31]

Creole Narratives and Hispanic American Constitutions

Spanish Americans contested these transformations and sought alternatives. In responding to the most grievous of Madrid's directrices, they protested, sometimes violently, and rallied local narrative traditions that conceived their homelands as kingdoms. These narratives harked back to the early seventeenth century and were based in chronicles, such as the Inca Garcilaso de la Vega's two-part *Royal Commentaries of the Incas* (1609, 1617) and Fray Juan de Torquemada's *Monarquía Indiana* (1615), which offered narratives of continuity between pre-conquest native polities and the Spanish American kingdoms. These histories also presented native empires as analogous to the Roman Empire both in their classical dignity and for preparing the arrival of Christianity. Such claims effectively ratified Hispanic American provinces as recognizable realms or kingdoms within the frame of *jus gentium* and provided them with further basis for unwritten constitutions.[32]

Resistance to the reforms took place on behalf of such constitutions. It was based on the understanding that bureaucratic initiative should pass through local channels and customary laws, and that it should respect the interests and privileges of the constitutive corporations. After the General Inspection of New Spain in 1765 by Jose de Gálvez, the Crown decided to reorganize the internal structure of the viceroyalties as intendancies. Jurist Hipólito Villarroel expressed his opposition to these political reforms by pointing out that 'by divine providence, our constitution is governed by rules very different from those dictated by despotism, [and thus] the ordinances neglect the laws of the country and their imposition is an act of arbitrariness.'[33] New Spain, continued Villaroel, had its own 'constitution in accordance with those fundamental laws published and sent to observe for almost two centuries for the direction and government of America' (Numeral 49, 278). In short, by the end of the eighteenth century, the concept of *constitución* stood for the sense of a 'perfect community,' while the concept of *colonia* undermined that sense.[34]

In addition to withstanding the push for reforms, unwritten constitutions also addressed a wider discussion about the nature and meaning of human diversity. As Europeans confronted, through travel accounts and colonial ventures, the variety of people around the globe, 'race' and 'civilization' emerged as the organizing categories of a united humanity. Furthermore, a new sense of confidence led Europeans to assert their superiority and, through conjectural history, 'recast difference as a product of history, conditioned by varying economic and social situations.'[35] The world's diversity was thus temporalized so that, as Schiller famously exclaimed, it 'shows us tribes which surround us at the most diverse levels of culture, like children of different ages gathered around an adult, reminding him by their example of what he used to be, and where he started from.'[36] Ultramarine territories conformed a 'spectacle as constructive as it is entertaining' by illustrating the various stages of civilization. Conjectural history created the conditions to consider non-European territories as peopled by feeble, incapable, and historically hindered societies. European colonization, therefore, was both necessary and beneficial, a courageous act to advance the laws of progress. Increasingly Europeans acted convinced that through colonization they could, 'sell their products and instruct [natives] in trade and navigation with reciprocal utility, without depriving [native] people of their natural rights.'[37]

The discussion touched a raw nerve among Creoles whose preeminence, loyalty, and talents were threatened by these acrimonious debates about the alleged inferiority of non-European climes and inhabitants.[38] When the Mexican *Cabildo* learned in 1771 of royal officials slighting Creole faculties, it protested to the King in the strongest terms:[39]

> In Spanish America there is the same nobility of spirit, the same loyalty, the same love to Your Highness, the same zeal for the public good that the noblest, most faithful, zealous and cultivated nations of Europe can boast, and by misrepresenting these faculties as inferior with respect to other vassals, we suffer the most reprehensible injustice and undisputed insult.[40]

The *Cabildo*'s protest drew from the above-mentioned Creole narrative tradition;[41] its vehement tone was a reaction to the ongoing set of transformations that challenged New Spain's constitution as a kingdom. The defence of Creole privileges offered an alternative narrative of local viability and autonomy. Long before the political crisis of 1808, Creoles adjudged the term as an alternative for assessing the relation between the Hispanic American provinces, the monarch, and the nation. Yet, as we saw before, it also naturalized the subjugation of other social groups, such as natives who 'are, have been and will always be unable to conduct their own ecclesiastic or civil government and are thus miserable and subjected to the Spanish.'[42] Thus, if in the first case Creole narratives resisted the concept of *colonia*, by updating the narrative of native inferiority they also deepened its reach significantly.

The Popularization and Politicization of *Colonia* circa, 1808–1814

The political and legal crisis of 1808 produced a rearticulation of the concept's uses and meanings. The deepening crisis of legitimacy, the expectation of equal representation and the new laws enacting freedom of press allowed for an in-depth exploration of the conceptual possibilities. During the next six years it became so prevalent that in 1811 the author of a political dictionary described the concept as an

> Insult and inflammatory word with which despotism, superstition and the ignorance of the rights of man mistreat our fellowmen, prohibiting them from procuring products and manufactures in their country or from a foreign country: and, in a word, prohibiting them from doing as they please, separating or confederating by mere acts of courtesy, coming or making us go, obeying or commanding us, always alleging the equality of rights.[43]

The author mocked the rapid popularization of the term in public discourse, thus confirming our suspicion that the concept of *colonia* played a considerable role in shaping new political sensibilities and possibilities.

Democratic appropriation combined with intense politicization, as an already polemic word became spiteful. Even Spanish reformers became embarrassed by the term.[44] Such politicization—drawing from the three themes elaborated during the late eighteenth century, including externality to the political community, economic exploitation, and illegitimacy—intensified as the conceptual ensemble became enmeshed in the constitutional language of rights and equality. If before 1808 *colonia* was associated with the lack of an unwritten or corporative constitution, in the wake of the crisis it signified a negation of the attributes of sovereignty, representation, and moral and social cohesion. The question of sovereignty was generally discussed in Hispanic American corporations and provinces that sought to establish independent governments, while the question of political representation revolved around debates at the Cortes in Cádiz. The question of communal cohesion represented an important conceptual innovation and occurred in both scenarios. In sum, if *colonia* previously named the centripetal forces at work in the Spanish administration, after 1808 it designated the centrifugal forces within the monarchy. Given space constraints, here I will illustrate the range and importance of these forces with three examples.

Soon after Napoleon's troops invaded Spain and lured Charles IV and his heir, the future Ferdinand VII to Bayonne, during which time Joseph Bonaparte was crowned Jose I, a Spanish Constituent Assembly met in Bayonne (May 1808). Six American delegates were invited to participate in the deliberations that would approve the final version of the monarchy's first written constitution. These delegates took an active role in developing those articles that gave content to the question of representation. It is worth noting that the original wording of the title of Article 82 reads thus: 'The Spanish colonies in America and Asia enjoy the same rights as the mother country.' The title—not the content—was contested by the two deputies from Buenos Aires, José Ramón Mila de la Roca and Nicolás Herrera, who proposed to substitute the word *colonia* for that of 'Spanish American provinces' or 'Provinces of Spain in America.' For them it was a contradiction in terms to advocate political representation for *colonias*. After extensive debates, the amendment was accepted and incorporated into the final text of the constitution.[45] Henceforth the question of representation remained a heated point of contention in the constitution of the governing bodies of the monarchy. The Royal Order of January 22, 1809, cited in the second epigraph to this chapter, convened the overseas 'part of the Spanish monarchy' to participate in the central government while apportioning unequal representation to them. The chain of Spanish American responses vehemently denounced what Camilo Torres called the 'principle of degradation' by which such unequal representation was construed.[46] 'The colonial system,' claimed Fray Servando Teresa de Mier, 'degrades men so much that they cannot even be represented, as happens in Spain with women, children and the insane.'[47]

The adjective 'colonial' when conjoined to 'system' gradually acquired polemic relevance. Up to 1808 it simply described products and commerce that originated in the Indies; during the crisis and afterwards, it was also used to disparage the Spanish administrative and economic system in America. Shortly after the events of 1810—during which many cities created their local Juntas, in many cases with complete independence of Spanish authorities—the editors of Cartagena's newspaper, *El Argos Americano*, recommended abolishing the laws that were passed 'under the more rigorous system when these countries were colonial outposts.' The editors denounced the decadence in which Americans lived 'under the old colonial system,' due to total ignorance of their rights. The old system was 'strictly colonial, which is the same as saying despotic, oppressive and hostile to reason, three hundred years of gloom and wretchedness, have put America in a pitiful state.'[48] Yet, to a large extent the problem was not necessarily being a colony but the lack of autonomy and representation, something which became evident with the frequent contrasts being made with those colonies that 'had depended on Great Britain [and that] were part of that nation and yet managed their domestic affairs and made their laws, which could not be annulled even by the King himself.'[49]

Most Hispanic Americans were not lured by Napoleon's constitution and instead hastened, like their Peninsular compatriots, to set up local governments. In June 8 of 1808 the *Gaceta de Madrid* reached Mexico City with news about the abdications and the French occupation of Spain. The *Cabildo* reacted by sending to Viceroy Iturrigaray a representation declaring their loyalty to Ferdinand VII and requiring the creation of a provisional government, with the Viceroy in command. The *Cabildo* justified the request by indicating that in the absence and disability . . . [of the legitimate heir to the throne] sovereignty resides in the kingdom [New Spain] . . . [which] bears the public voice; it will retain sovereignty intact, will defend it and vigorously hold it as a sacred trust, to return it to Carlos IV or to his son the Prince of Asturias.[50]

The Appellate Court quickly reacted against the declaration of sovereignty. The prosecutors stated that:

If a subordinate or colonial people like this one of New Spain meddles to appoint such guardians, it would be usurping the right of sovereignty which it has never used and it is not in its competency to use; and if it does by itself and for itself, it is an act of division and independence which is prohibited by law.

Another civil prosecutor of the case added that 'I cannot convince myself that in these circumstances anybody could acknowledge as legitimate the sovereignty of this colonial people.' He closed the case by stating that 'America, acquired by the Catholic Kings by the privileged right of conquest, is a veritable *colonia* of our old Spain.'[51]

On the other hand, independence-minded Americans could no longer regard *colonias* as esteemed settlements within empire but as the intolerable experience of a political negation. As Mark Thurner notes in this volume, in 1822 a polemical letter by José Faustino Sánchez Carrión, republished in Lima's *La Abeja Republicana*, exemplified the republican critique of 'the colonial system.' Sánchez Carrión's defence of the republican ideal offered a sustained and original reflection on the negative effects of an '*ominoso coloniaje*,' ominous colonialism. The term *coloniaje* would soon exercise a lasting presence in the region.[52] Spanish colonialism had given Peruvians a 'second nature' without personhood ('*no tiene persona*'), property or the impulse of freedom.[53] The only way to render him a person again was to 'decolonize [his degraded] customs.'[54] Moreover, such 'degradation is the origin of political emancipation.'[55]

Conclusion

By the early nineteenth century, *colonia* could designate overseas establishments that were not an integral part of the metropolitan nation, were internally divided, and that required guardianship for survival. A key element of such *colonia* status was the presence of what were deemed to be ungovernable, internal fissures. Alexander von Humboldt, for example, saw Spanish America as a land where 'Conquest . . . and the slave-trade . . . brought together the . . . strange mixture of Indians, whites, negroes, mestizos, mulattoes, and zambos . . . accompanied by all the perils which violent and disorderly passion can engender.' The violent coexistence of heterogeneous elements is what defined 'the odious principle of the colonial system.' It was a principle that 'had burst forth with violence.'[56] Spanish Liberals, many of whom opposed equal representation in Cádiz or independence for Spanish Americans, found this narrative of disorder and violence useful. Álvaro Flórez Estrada insisted that 'Spanish America is not in a position to aspire to be free today' due to its essential lack of social cohesion.[57] She must remain a *colonia* to avoid

> a civil war, all the more frightening as the hatred that rules amongst the various races is greater and more inveterate. This heterogeneity of individuals, greater than in any other part of the globe, makes it more difficult to secure rights and carry out transactions; it makes civil war more bitter, and reconciliation and the establishment of a solid government more difficult.[58]

Humboldt's and Flórez Estrada's arguments offered old and novel elements. On the one hand, they extended the familiar argument that perfect communities had developed a moral bond among themselves. The mere coexistence of mutually hostile peoples—as in *factorías*—rendered them a multitude, not a political community. The coexistence of social groups whose particular wills were in permanent conflict, prevented the production of a general will and its essential corollary, the law. In other words, colonies, like imperfect communities, were self-destructive; they had to be administered from without and they required special laws; neither sovereignty nor authority could emanate from them.[59] Hispanic American republicans, the first self-proclaimed anti-colonialists in the history of decolonization, counterargued that communities were not defined by the homogeneity of their people but by their love of republican freedoms. They also insisted that such love developed stronger and more virtuous moral bonds among American citizens than any found in the European monarchies.[60]

And so, we return to the question with which this chapter opened: Was Hispanic America ever a colony? The answer is 'yes and no.' During the late eighteenth and early nineteenth centuries 'colonia' was transformed from a univocal and not very controversial term (*colonia* as foreign settlement) into a field of contention. By the early nineteenth century, some Hispanic Americans used 'colonia' and 'colonial' in critical ways to describe and evaluate relations between the metropole and its possessions, while others preferred older terms such as 'kingdoms' and 'provinces.'

Notes

1. Conde de Revillagigedo, *Instrucción reservada que el Conde de Revillagigedo dio a su sucesor en el mando Marqués de Branciforte sobre el gobierno de este continente en el tiempo que fue su Virrey* (México: Agustín Guiol, 1831), 364, 90–91.

2. Supreme Junta, Real Orden, Seville, January 22, 1809.
3. The argument advanced here builds on my previously published work: 'Colonia, nación y monarquía. El concepto de colonia y la cultura política de la Independencia,' in Heraclio Bonilla, ed., *La cuestión colonial* (Bogotá: Universidad Nacional de Colombia, 2011), 109–134; 'Ni nación ni parte integral. "Colonia" de vocablo a concepto en el siglo XVIII iberoamericano,' *Prismas. Revista de historia intelectual* (2011), 11–30; 'Entre constitución y colonia, el estatuto ambiguo de las Indias en la monarquía hispánica,' in Francisco Ortega and Yobenj Aucardo Chicangana, eds., *Conceptos fundamentales de la cultura política de la Independencia* (Bogotá: Universidad Nacional de Colombia, 2012), 61–91; and 'The Conceptual History of Independence and the Colonial Question in Spanish America,' *Journal of the History of Ideas* 79:1 (2018), 89–103.
4. Real Academia de la Lengua Española, *Diccionario de Autoridades* (Madrid: Joachim Ibarra, 1729), v. 2, 419.
5. Antonio de Nebrija, *Vocabulario Hispano-Latino* [1513], Mónica Vidal Díez, ed. (Coruña: Universidade da Coruña, 2015), 101.
6. I follow the argument of Francisco Suárez in *De Legibus* (1612). Quotes from Selections from Three Works. *De Legibus, ac Deo Legislatore*, 1612; *Defensio Fidei Catholicae, et Apostolicae adversus Anglicanae Sectae Errores*, 1613; *De Triplici Virtute Theologica, Fide, Spe et Charitate*, 1621, James Brown Scott, ed. (Oxford, UK: Clarendon Press, 1944), v. 2, 19, 86.
7. The veto is made explicit in Book 3, Title 1, Law 1 of the *Recopilación de Leyes de los Reynos de las Indias* (Madrid: I. de Paredes, 1681).
8. See Rafael Altamira y Crevea, 'Texto de las leyes de Burgos de 1512,' *Revista de Historia de América* 4 (1938), 66; Juan de Solorzano's *Política Indiana* (Madrid: Carrera, 1648) and Manuel Josef de Ayala's *Notas a la Recopilación* (Madrid: Cultura Hispanica, 1945[1795]) follow the same usage..
9. Antonio León Pinelo, *Recopilación general de las Leyes de Indias* [c. 1660], 3 vols. (México: UNAM-Porrua, 1992), v. 2, Libro 7, Título 13, 'De los tributos, demoras y tasas de los indios.'
10. Juan de Solorzano described natives as suffering from 'capitis diminution' and qualifies them as 'miserables.' See *De Indiarum iure. Liber III, De retentione Indiarum* (Madrid: CSIC, 1994 [1639]), 118–127. Paulino Castañeda Delgado, 'La condicion miserable del indio y sus privilegios,' *Anuario de Estudios Americanos* 28 (1971), 245–335. Also see Caroline Cunill, 'El indio miserable: nacimiento de la teoría legal en la América colonial del siglo XVII,' *Cuadernos intercambio sobre Centroamérica y el Caribe* 8:9 (2011), 229–248.
11. Luis de Betancourt y Figueroa, *Derecho de las Iglesias metropolitanas y Catedrales de las Indias: sobre que sus Prelacías sean prohevidas en los Capitulares de ellas, y naturales de sus Provincias* (Madrid: Francisco Martinez, 1634). Reissued as *Semanario Erudito, que comprehende varias obras inéditas, críticas, morales, instructivas, políticas, históricas, satíricas, y jocosas de nuestros mejores autores antiguos y modernos. Dadas a la luz por don Antonio Valladares de Sotomayor* (Madrid: Don Blas Roman, 1789), Tomo XXII, 108.
12. Argentine legal scholar Ricardo Zorraquín Becú underscores that despite its legal autonomy the Indies was in a state of dependency on 'el reino y de la comunidad castellana.' Furthermore, the Indies as a collective body did not participate in the Cortes or in Council of the Indies until the early nineteenth century. See 'Condición política de las Indias,' in *Memoria del Segundo Congreso Venezolano de Historia* (Caracas: Academia Nacional de la Historia,

A Brief Conceptual History of 'Colonia' 21

1975), 389–476. For a different view, see Mario Góngora, *Studies in the Colonial History of Spanish America* (New York: Cambridge University Press, 1975). For the context of these debates, see Víctor Tau Anzoátegui, 'Las Indias ¿provincias, reinos o colonias? A propósito del planteo de Zorraquín Becú,' *Revista de Historia del Derecho* 28 (2000), 77–137.

13. A cursory look at the accounts of government by Viceroys and Governors (the so-called, *relaciones de mando*) in the newly created Viceroyalty evinces a forceful will to transform the domain to yield higher returns in the relationship with the metropolis. See Germán Colmenares, ed., *Relaciones e informes de los gobernantes de la Nueva Granada* (Bogotá: Fondo de Promoción de la Cultural del Banco Popular, 1989), v. 1. For an overview, see Allan Kuethe and Kenneth Andrien, *The Spanish Atlantic World in the Eighteenth Century: War and the Bourbon Reforms, 1713–1796* (New York: Cambridge University Press, 2014), 68–97, 271–304.
14. Montesquieu, *The Spirit of the Laws*, Book 21, 'Of Laws in Relation to Commerce, Considered in the Revolutions It Has Met with in the World,' Chapter XXI, 'The Discovery of Two New Worlds and in What Manner Is Europe Affected by It,' in *The Complete Works of M. de Montesquieu* (London: T. Evans, 1777), v. 2, 72.
15. See Guillaume Thomas François Raynal, *Histoire philosophique et politique des établissements & du Commerce des Europeens dans les deux Indes* (Geneve: J.L. Pellet, 1782); William Robertson, *The History of America* (London: W. Strahan, 1777–78); and Dominique-Georges-Frédéric Dufour de Pradt, *Les Trois ages des colonies ou de leur état passé, present et a venir* (Paris: Giguet, 1801).
16. See *Reflexiones sobre el comercio español a Indias* [1762], ed. Vicente Llombart Rosa (Madrid: Instituto de Estudios Fiscales, Ministerio de Economia y Hacienda, 1988).
17. See Gerónimo de Ustariz, *Theorica, y practica de comercio, y de marina* . . . (Madrid, 1724), José del Campillo y Cossio, *Nuevo sistema de gobierno económico para la América* . . . *escrito en 1743* (Madrid: Benito Cano, 1779), and Bernardo Ward, *Proyecto económico en que se proponen varias providencias, dirigidas á promover los intereses de España, con los medios y fondos necesarios para su plantificación* (Madrid: Por D. Joachin Ibarra, 1779).
18. Bernardo Ward, '*Preliminar,*' *Proyecto económico* (Madrid: Ibarra, 1779), xv.
19. Of course, this should be qualified by insisting that the reforms were not as successful as the reformists had hoped. See Luis Navarro García, *Intendencias en Indias* (Sevilla: Escuela de Estudios Hispano-Americanos, 1959); and Horst Pietschmann, *Las reformas borbónicas y el sistema de intendencia en Nueva España. Un estudio político-administrativo* (México: Fondo de Cultura Económica, 1996).
20. *Informe y Plan de Intendencias para el reino de Nueva España presentado por el Visitador D. José de Gálvez y el Virrey Marqués de Croix, y recomendado por el Obispo de Puebla y el Arzobispo de México* (1768).
21. de Revillagigedo, *Instrucción reservada*, 90–91.
22. The phenomenon is related to José María Portillo's account whereby the nation and the monarchy ceased to coincide during the period. See his *Crisis Atlántica. Autonomía e independencia en la crisis de la monarquía hispana* (Madrid: Marcial Pons, 2006).
23. Portillo further noted that 'With very few exceptions, any Spanish thinker thought as self-evident that the Monarchy's extra-European possessions—with

the exception of the Canaries—were part of the monarchy, but not of the nation. The nation, even without a substantive political definition, was a matter only of Europeans.' *Revolución de nación: Orígenes de la cultura constitucional en España 1780-1812* (Madrid: CEPC, 2000).
24. Factoría was an old term for a trading location. See Sebastián de Covarrubias, *Tesoro de la lengua castellana o española* (Madrid: L. Sanchez, 1611).
25. Historians have traditionally located the turning point in the emergence of the contemporary concept of sovereignty in the writings of Bodin, Hobbes, and Rousseau. See, for instance, Daniel Philpott, *Revolutions in Sovereignty: How Ideas Shaped Modern International Relations* (Princeton: Princeton University Press, 2001). The debate has recognized the importance of the conquest of the Americas and the subsequent issues concerning commerce and settlement. See, for instance, Srinivas Aravamudan, 'Hobbes and America,' in Daniel Carey and Lynn Festa, eds., *The Postcolonial Enlightenment: Eighteenth-Century Colonialism and Postcolonial Theory* (New York: Oxford University Press, 2013), 37–70. Most of the existing literature is limited to Northern European Protestant authors. When Iberian sources appear, they do so either as the antithesis of modernity or in the guise of precedents to our contemporaneity (such as Vitoria). Without dismissing the importance of Locke or Hobbes, Ibero-American authors drew from other sources, such as Jacques Bosuet, to address respective challenges. See François-Xavier Guerra, 'Políticas sacadas de las Sagradas Escrituras: La referencia a la Biblia en el debate político, siglos XVI-XIX,' in Mónica Quijada and Jesús Bustamante, eds., *Elites intelectuales y modelos colectivos. Iberoamérica, siglos XVI-XIX* (Madrid: CSIC, 2002), 155–198.
26. The recent work by Philippe Castejon corroborates this point. See ' "Colonia" y "metrópoli" la génesis de unos conceptos históricos fundamentales (1760–1808),' *Illes Imperis* 18 (2016), 166.
27. Joaquín de Finestrad, *Vasallo instruido en el estado del Nuevo Reino de Granada y en sus repectivas obligaciones* (c. 1789), Margarita González, ed. (Bogotá: Universidad Nacional de Colombia, 2000), 264v–265r, 398.
28. See Sagredo Baeza, Rafael, ed., *De la colonia a la república: Los catecismos políticos americanos, 1811–1827* (Madrid: Ediciones Doce Calles-MAPFRE, 2009).
29. For a more detailed analysis, see Richard Konetzke, 'La condición legal de los criollos y las causas de la independencia,' *Estudios Americanos* 2 (1950), 31–54. The existence of these divergent views of America was evident in the transformations undergone in the institutional design governing the Indies. See Óscar Álvarez Gila, 'Ultramar,' in Juan Francisco Fuentes and Javier Fernández Sebastian, eds., *Diccionario político y social del siglo XIX español* (Madrid: Alianza Editorial, 2002), 681.
30. See 'Dictamen reservado que el excelentissimo Señor Conde de Aranda dió al Rey sobre la independencia de las colonias inglesas después de haber hecho el tratado de paz ajustado en París el año de 1783,' and 'Representación del intendente Abalos dirigida a Carlos III, en la que pronostica le independencia de América y sugiere la creación de varias monarquías en el Nuevo Mundo' (1781). Both are reproduced in Carlos Muñoz Oráa, *Dos temas de historia americana: La independencia de América (pronóstico y proyecto de monarquías). La sociedad venezolana frente a la Intendencia* (Mérida, Venezuela: Universidad de los Andes, 1967), 34–49. The 'Proyecto de don Manuel Godoy para el gobierno de las Américas (1808)' is included in Ernesto de la Torre, *La Constitución de Apatzingán y los creadores del Estado mexicano*, 2nd ed. (Mexico: UNAM, 1978), 107–111. For an overview of the literature,

see Manuel Teruel Gregorio de Tejada, 'Monarquías en América,' *Espacio, Tiempo y Forma* (2005–2006), 247–270.
31. 'Memoria secreta presentada a Carlos III después de firmado el tratado de Paris de 1783,' in Manuel Lucena Giraldo, ed., *Premoniciones de la Independencia de Iberoamérica* (Madrid: Doce Calles, 2004), 77.
32. As Antonio Annino points out *jus gentium* regulated land occupation. If natives had lived in *policía* at the time of European conquest they constituted perfect communities, a political domain with its own constitution integrated into the empire. Otherwise, Spanish occupation was a mere expansion of the conquistadors' space. *Silencios y disputas en la historia de Hispanoamérica* (Bogotá: Universidad Externado de Colombia, 2014), 221. For a discussion of these narratives in Peru, see Mark Thurner, *History's Peru: The Poetics of Colonial and Postcolonial Historiography* (Gainesville: University Press of Florida, 2011).
33. Hipólito Villarroel, *Enfermedades políticas que padece la capital de esta Nueva España; en casi todos los cuerpos de que se compone y remedios que se le deben aplicar para su curación si se quiere que sea útil al Rey y al público* [c 1787–1787] (México: Porrúa, 1999), 278.
34. For a conceptual history of constitution in the region, see 'Constitución,' in *Diccionario político y social del mundo iberoamericano. La era de las revoluciones, 1750–1850* (Madrid: Centro de Estudios Políticos y Constitucionales, 2009), v. 1; also see Beatriz Rojas, 'Constitución y ley: viejas palabras, nuevos conceptos,' in Erika Pani and Alicia Salmerón, eds., *Conceptualizar lo que se ve. François-Xavier Guerra historiador, homenaje* (México: Instituto Mora, 2004), 291–322; and Francisco A. Ortega, 'Ariadne's Thread: Navigating Postcolonial Spanish America's Labyrinth Through Constitution Building in New Granada (1809–1812),' in Kelly Grotke and Markus Prutsch, eds., *Constitutionalism, Legitimacy and Power: Nineteenth-Century Experiences* (New York: Oxford University Press, 2014), 225–240.
35. Daniel Carey, *Locke, Shaftesbury, and Hutcheson: Contesting Diversity in the Enlightenment and Beyond* (New York: Cambridge University Press, 2005), 188. Also see Daniel Carey and Sven Trakulhun, 'Universalism, Diversity, and the Postcolonial Enlightenment,' in Carey and Festa, eds., *The Postcolonial Enlightenment*, 240–280. A good account of these debates in Spanish America is David J. Weber, *Bárbaros: Spaniards and Their Savages in the Age of Enlightenment* (New Haven, CT: Yale University Press, 2005).
36. Friedrich Schiller, 'What Is, and to What End Do We Study, Universal History?' in *Poet of Freedom* (New York: The Schiller Institute, 2015), v. 2, 258.
37. Pedro Rodríguez, Count of Campomanes, *Apuntaciones relativas al comercio de las Indias para resolver la cuestión por él suscitada* (1788), manuscript in Biblioteca de Palacio Real, Madrid, *Miscelánea de Manuel José Ayala*, II/2867, f.13. For extended commentary on this text, see José Muñoz Pérez, 'La idea de América en Campomanes,' *Anuario de Estudios Americanos* 10 (1953), 209–264; and Ramón Ezquerra, 'La crítica española de la situación de América en el siglo XVIII,' *Revista de Indias* 22 (1962), 87, 159–286.
38. The discussion produced a heated debate about the inferiority of the American continent. See Antonello Gerbi, *The Dispute of the New World: The History of a Polemic*, Jeremy Moyle, trans. (Pittsburgh: University of Pittsburgh Press, 1973).
39. The secret report stated that 'the spirit of Spanish Americans is submissive and weak, as they go well with dejection: but if they are lifted by licenses or jobs they are exposed to great errors: for that reason, it is convenient to keep them under control.' For more, see David Brading, *The Origins of Mexican*

Nationalism (New York: Cambridge University Press, 1985), 30–32. And Peggy Korn, 'The Problem of the Roots of Revolution: Society and Intellectual Ferment in Mexico on the Eve of Independence,' in Frederick B. Pike, ed., *Latin American History: Select Problems* (New York: Harcourt, Brace and World, 1969), 101–107.

40. Reproduced in Juan E. Hernández y Dávalos, ed., *Colección de documentos para la historia de la guerra de independencia de México de 1808 a 1821*, 6 vols. (México: José María Sandoval, 1877), v. 1, 452.
41. See Antony Higgins, *Constructing the Criollo Archive: Subjects of Knowledge in the Bibliotheca Mexicana and the Rusticatio Mexicana* (West Lafayette: Purdue University Press, 2000); Anna More, *Baroque Sovereignty: Carlos de Siguenza y Góngora and the Creole Archive of Colonial Mexico* (Philadelphia: University of Pennsylvania Press, 2013); Margarita Eva Rodríguez García, *Criollismo y patria en la Lima ilustrada, 1732–1795* (Buenos Aires: Miño y Dávila Editores, 2006).
42. Luis de Betancurt y Figueroa, *Derecho de las Iglesias metropolitanas y Catedrales de las Indias* (Madrid: Francisco Martinez, 1637), 66.
43. *Diccionario razonado. Manual para inteligencia de ciertos escritores que por equivocación han nacido en España* (Cádiz: En la Imprenta de la Junta Superior, 1811), 18.
44. Few Spanish liberals defended the term during the constitutional period (1810–14). For an instructive exception, see Valentín Foronda, *Carta sobre lo que debe hacer un príncipe que tenga colonias a gran distancia* (Philadelphia, 1803; Cádiz 1812).
45. In *Actas de la Diputación general de españoles que se juntó en Bayona el 15 de junio de 1808, en virtud de convocatoria expedida por el Gran Duque de Berg, como Lugarteniente general del Reino, y la Junta Suprema de Gobierno, con fecha de 19 de mayo del mismo año* (Madrid: Imprenta de J. A. García, 1874) 114. As Antonio-Filiu Franco Pérez points out, it was only in the third revised version that the assembly 'officially admitted representation from the Indies and Philippines and created a constitutional section recognizing these territories.' See Antonio-Filiu Franco Pérez, 'La 'Cuestión Americana' y la Constitución de Bayona (1808),' *Revista Electrónica de Historia Constitucional* 9 (2008).
46. Responses include: Mariano Moreno, 'Representation of the Landowners and Farmers' (Buenos Aires, September 30, 1809); Camilo Torres, 'Representation of the *Cabildo*' (Bogotá, November 1809); José Amor de la Patria, 'The Christian Political Catechism Prepared for the Instruction of the Peoples of South America' (Chile, ca. 1815); Fray Servando Teresa de Mier, *Idea of the Constitution Given to the Americas by the Kings of Spain Before the Invasion of Ancient Despotism* (Mexico City, 1812).
47. Fray Servando Teresa de Mier, 'Segunda carta de un americano al Español,' *El Español*, London (1812), 2, 14. Quoted in *Cartas del Dr. Fray Servando Teresa de Mier (bajo el seudónimo de un americano) años de 1811 y 1812* (Monterrey: Tipografía del Gobierno, 1888), 330.
48. In 'Reflexiones sobre nuestro estado,' *El Argos Americano*, Cartagena, 4, October 8, 1810, 17–18.
49. 'Correspondencia del Sr. P. Carta segunda.' *El Argos Americano*, Cartagena (June 1811) 34, 25.
50. 'Acta del Ayuntamiento de México, en la que se declaró se tuviera por insubsistente la abdicación de Carlos IV y Fernando VII hecha en Napoleón; que se desconozca todo funcionario que venga nombrado de España; que el virrey gobierne por la comisión del Ayuntamiento en representación del

virreinato, y otros artículos,' in Juan E. Hernández y Dávalos, ed., *Colección de documentos para la Historia de la Guerra de Independencia de México* (México: José María Sandoval, 1877), v. 1, 199, 14–15.
51. 'Exposiciones de los fiscales contra las opiniones de los novadores,' in Hernández y Dávalos, ed., *Colección de documentos* (December 14, 1808), v. 1, 260, 11–15.
52. 'Remitidos,' *La Abeja Republicana* (January 11, 1823), 5, 86.
53. 'Cartas remitidas por el Solitario de Sayan,' *La Abeja Republicana* (August 15, 1822), 4, 45–46.
54. Ibid., 53.
55. 'Señor Editor,' *La Abeja Republicana* (November 24, 1823), 33, 307.
56. Alexander von Humboldt and Aimé Bonpland, *Personal Narrative of Travels to the Equinoctial Regions of America, During the Year 1799–1804*, Thomasina Ross, trans., 3 vols. (London: Herny G. Bohn, 1853), v. 3, 275.
57. Álvaro Flórez Estrada, *Examen imparcial de las disensiones de la América con la España, de los medios de su reconciliacion, y de la prosperidad de todas las naciones* (Cadiz: Manuel Ximenez Carreño, 1812), 52–53.
58. Ibid., 66.
59. The 1837 Spanish Constitution established that Cuba, Puerto Rico, and the Philippines would be governed by special laws, depriving them of representation in the Cortes and suppressing the democratically elected city and provincial councils. Governors were appointed by Madrid and retained supreme power. For more, see Josep Maria Fradera, *Colonias para después de un imperio* (Barcelona: Edicions Bellaterra, 2005).
60. Vicente Rocafuerte, *Ensayo político: El sistema colombiano, popular, electivo, y representativo, es el que más conviene á la América independiente* (New York: En la imprenta de A. Paul, 1823). Simón Bolívar argued similarly in his 'Letter from Jamaica' (1815). For a general discussion, see Rafael Rojas, *Las repúblicas de aire: utopía y desencanto en la revolución de Hispanoamérica* (Madrid: Taurus, 2009).

2   Decolonizing Customs

Mark Thurner

> Al declararse independiente el Perú, no se propuso solo el acto material de no pertenecer ya a la que fué su metrópoli, ni de decir *alta voce*: ya soy independiente: sería pueril tal contentamiento. Lo que quiso, y lo que quiere, es: que esa pequeña población se *centuplique*: que esas costumbres se *descolonizen*: que esa ilustración toque su *maximum*: y que al concurso simultáneo de estas medras, no sólo vea nuestra tierra empedradas sus calles con oro y plata, sino que de cementerio, se convierta en patria de vivientes.
>
> —El Solitario de Sayan (1822)[1]

Scholars routinely assume that the noun and idea of decolonization (*décolonisation*) was invented in southern France in the mid-1830s vis-à-vis 'the Conquest of Algeria.'[2] What these same scholars fail to realize is that Henri Fonfrède's coin manifested a self-interested, guilt-ridden, free-trader argument that only made sense in the wake of the first wave of decolonization in the Americas. Fonfrède contrasted the high human cost and unprofitability of the 'Conquest of Algeria' for France with the (for Spain) relatively cheap and highly profitable 'Conquest of America,' pointing out that the French cost in lives and profits and ethical standards was excessive. But there was an earlier, rather different and more active usage of the concept of 'decolonize.' It was not a metropolitan idea that attempted to persuade rulers, generals and merchants to invest taxes, soldiers and capital more wisely and ethically but instead a bottom-up notion that could only make sense in the 'ex-colony' where it was necessary to attack the 'customary' effects on the people of 'the colonial system.'

This active notion of decolonizing in the ex-colony was coined not in France or Algeria but in Peru in 1822. The author of the coin was José Faustino Sánchez Carrión, a provincial intellectual from the Andean highlands north of Lima. In a polemical letter published in Lima newsprint under the pen name 'El Solitario de Sayan,' Sánchez sharply reminded his compatriots that Peru's recent declaration of independence (1821) meant much more than simply breaking with the 'metropolis.' The deeper purpose of independence from 'the colonial system' was to 'decolonize customs' so that the population could flourish and the people's 'enlightenment' reach its 'maximum' potential. How could such a seemingly radical concept as this—possibly the first active call to 'decolonize' culture in modern world history—appear in a supposedly backward and 'royalist' Peru where, as the scholarly literature insists, the very concepts of 'colonialism' and 'decolonization' were not yet available?

Historians of colonialism and decolonization insist that real 'decolonization' (in name and deed) was not possible or even desirable for at least another century, and then only or primarily in Europe. This European concept was, it is argued, not taken up by 'anti-colonial nationalists' in the colonies until the middle decades of the twentieth century.[3] In a similar vein, today's 'postcolonial' and 'decolonial' critics alike remain deeply sceptical about the decolonizing potential of nineteenth-century Latin American thought and practice, which they routinely dismiss as 'liberal' if not 'neo-colonial.' In the 'postcolonial' theory narrative, which breezily universalizes the 'post-war' chronology of French and British decolonization in Africa and Asia, Latin America is an anomaly. In the more recently invented 'decolonial' idiom or 'option' trendy in the last decade in Latin American cultural studies, it was generally held that a 'racist' and 'colonialist' or 'Occidentalist' mentality among Creoles and Mestizos prohibited Latin America's 'Creole pioneers' from even imagining let alone acting upon, meaningful decolonization.[4] The notion that Latin America was never really 'colonial' or 'postcolonial' was also readily affirmed by a phalange of 'revisionist' historians, who insisted that the 'common' or modern sense of 'colony' as economic and political dependency is foreign to the region. For these critics and scholars, 'colonialism,' 'postcolonialism' and 'decolonization' are misplaced ideas in Latin America.[5] The 'colonial' concept and the 'colonial question' were, they argue, invented after the fact by Creole nationalists seeking to create unifying pasts and later by Marxian *dependentistas* who would connect the 'national liberation' struggles of the late twentieth century with the 'Third Wave' of the 'Third World' (a concept coined in 1952).[6] In short, there is today a motley consensus around the notion that Hispanic American independence was a Europhile affair that was *not* inspired by a struggle against 'colonialism.' The region only became legitimately 'anti-colonial' in the twentieth century, first in Marxist thought in the 1930s and then when leftist national liberation movements in the 1950s through the 1970s sought to realize that thought by joining the post-war 'Third Wave' of decolonization.

In what follows I challenge this motley consensus. I do so by tracing in broad strokes the late eighteenth-century emergence of the modern concept of 'colonial system' in Atlantic and Peruvian discourse. This concept informed the polemics that gave rise to the Peruvian coining of the reflexive verb 'to decolonize' (*descolonizarse*).

The Transatlantic Emergence of the Modern Colonial Concept

Sánchez Carrión's polemical coinage was surely singular but it did not fall upon deaf ears. The active negation or reversal of 'to colonize' (*colonizar*) could ring in Lima's learned ears precisely because for decades the modern notion of 'colonies' (*colonias*) and the adjective 'colonial' had been circulating widely in French, English and Spanish discourse.[7] Reviewing Spanish dictionaries and discourse of the period, Francisco Ortega notes in a previous publication and again in his contribution to this volume, that from the sixteenth to the eighteenth centuries the meaning of the Greco-Roman term 'colonia' remained stable in Hispanic discourse.[8] During this period, 'colonia' normally named an isolated settlement of 'colonos,' or settlers, in a foreign land, sent out from a mother city or 'metropolis.' This apparently stable, classical meaning begins to shift rapidly in the late eighteenth century, however. Beginning in the 1770s, 'colony,' 'colonie' and 'colonia' are similarly deployed to refer to 'the Indies' (East and West) in general and to the 'countries' of the Indies, understood not as isolated enclaves or settlements but now as integral, natural and cultural entities. This modern or generic concept of 'colonies' as 'countries' was both commercial and political in nature, and it circulated widely. Notably, this modern concept appeared in print in official Spanish language periodicals read by educated or 'enlightened' Peruvians, including the *Mercurio de España* (1784–1830), the *Mercurio Peruano* (1791–95), the *Gaceta de Lima* (1793–94), and the *Verdadero Peruano* (1812–13). In these journals the relatively new notion of Peru as 'country,' invented earlier in the eighteenth century, was developed.[9]

Two influential 'foreign' works stimulated the emergence and circulation of the modern concept of 'colonies' in enlightened Hispanic and American discourse. The first published work to do so was Raynal and Diderot's bestselling compendium of philosophical history and travel writing, *Histoire philosophique et politique des Etablissements et du Commerce des Européens dans les deux Indes*, the first edition of the nearly fifty appearing in Amsterdam in 1770. The second was Robertson's more succinct *History of America* (1777). The French word 'colonie' appears everywhere in the pages of the *Histoire philosophique* where the Spanish Indies, including the vast Viceroyalties of New Spain (Mexico) and Peru, are readily glossed as 'colonies Espagnoles.' The neological adjective 'colonial' also makes its appearance here.[10] In his *History of America*, Robertson likewise employs the term 'colonies' with profusion, opting for 'Spanish colonies' to designate Hispanic America, including Peru.[11] Although censored, these works were nevertheless eagerly culled, provoking debate across the Hispanic world and influencing Spanish Bourbon policy thinking among such powerful reformist functionaries as José de Galvez and José Antonio de Areche.

Raynal and Robertson's widely cited (and despised) works provoked a tide of criticism among those who read in their attacks on Spain and her 'Indias' or 'colonias' an amateur litany of hearsay and half-truths. Among the dozens of works that sharply criticized these armchair philosophical histories was the well-known rebuttal of the exiled Catalonian Jesuit, Juan Nuix. His *Riflessioni imparziali sopra l'umanità degli spagnoli nell'Indie, contro i pretesi filosofi e politici, per servire di lume alle storie dei signori Raynal y Roberston* (Venice, 1780) was promptly translated and published in Madrid in 1782. Nuix's animated critique exposed numerous errors of fact and interpretation. Lacking credible primary sources or relevant experience, the French and Scottish authors had based their accounts on unreliable and hyperbolic travel accounts and missionary memoirs. The result was, to say the least, rather bad history by Hispanic standards. As Jorge Cañizares-Esguerra has amply demonstrated, those standards were at the time among the most rigorous and academic in the world.[12] Nevertheless, the key point here is that to dispute this bad but nevertheless prestigious and popular history, Nuix found himself reluctantly engaging the 'colonial' lexicon of his intellectual foes, referring at one point to the Spanish Indies as 'our colonies.'[13] Rising to the charge that Spain had ruined her 'colonies,' Nuix championed all of Spain's America as 'one single Colony' (*una solo Colonia*) founded upon 'commercial advantage' (*la ventaja del comercio*) and united under a single Sovereign.[14] Noting Britain's recent loss of its relatively small, poorly managed and exploited North American 'colonies,' Nuix concluded that 'no other European Colony has been maintained for so long a time, and with such glory' than Spain's America.[15]

Nuix's defence of Spain and its 'Colony' was one of many critiques directed against what was later called the 'Black Legend' and, later still, 'the dispute of the New World.'[16] Exiled Jesuits in Italy, many of Catalan origin, played critical roles in these debates, which ran into the twentieth century. But as Nuix's widely cited text suggests, the defence of the Spanish Indies against British, Dutch and French critics had the unintended but perhaps inevitable effect of increasing the likelihood that the 'kingdoms and provinces' (reynos y provincias) of the 'Indias' would be discussed in the Spanish language as 'colonias.'

Enlightened Peruvians routinely rebuked the notion that Peru was merely a 'colony' but they did not reject the term altogether. For example, in a commentary appended to an essay on mathematics in Peru, the academic editors of the *Mercurio Peruano* (1793) noted 'that these sciences are cultivated in Peru rather more than those who imagine this country to be a sad and isolated Colony, think . . . They should know that among us dedication to the exact sciences is fanatical.'[17] When the editors of the *Mercurio* frowned upon the foreign notion that Peru was 'a sad and isolated colony' they rejected not only the idea that Peru consisted of an 'isolated' Spanish settler colony in a 'savage' land far removed from civilization but also that Peru was dependent upon others for her culture and knowledge.

A longstanding Peruvian historiographical and artistic tradition had firmly established the vanguard hybridity of Peru's modern 'Empire,' understood to have sovereign Inca origins that, under providential auspices, was united with the leading currents of high Mediterranean civilization at the time, namely, the Holy Roman Empire and the Catholic Crown of Hispania as manifested in the royal personage of Charles V and I of Spain. Following Charles, the 'Roman' and Hispanic Hapsburg and Bourbon 'Emperors of the Indies' were thus depicted in Peruvian and Spanish historiography and iconography as a modern, mestizo continuation of the ancient, sovereign dynastic line of the Inca or 'Peruvian Emperors' (see Figure 2.1).

In addition, building upon earlier intellectual work in Peruvian cosmography by Francisco Antonio Cosme Bueno and Pedro de Peralta Barnuevo, Unanue and his associates at the *Mercurio Peruano* had scientifically described Peru as a vast and fertile 'country' (país) endowed with universal natural and human attributes. Rejecting Montesquieu's crude environmentalist scheme as inapplicable to South American climes,

Figure 2.1 Inca-Hispanic Royal Genealogy of Peru. Untitled fold-out insert, Jorge Juan and Antonio de Ulloa, *Relación histórica del viaje a la América meridional*, Appendix (Madrid, 1748).

Source: Courtesy of the John Carter Brown Library at Brown University.

Unanue marshalled an array of statistical, observational and experimental data to argue that Peru's verticality meant that the vast 'country' contained all the world's climes. As a microcosm of creation, Peru's clime 'influenced' the precocious and adaptable 'genius' of her native and transplanted sons.[18] Such a vast, diverse and enlightened country of native genius with a long and distinguished history of civilization could not be a 'sad and isolated Colony.' This notion was ratified in the decades during and after Peruvian independence, producing a vision of Peru as a rich country with a deep Inca past, now free of 'the heads' of Hispanic rule (see Figure 2.2).

If a place like Peru was to be considered as such, however, then the meaning of 'Colony' would have to be enlarged, and indeed it was. As noted, by the 1790s a more generic usage of 'Colony' came to designate not only an isolated settlement of colonists but indeed an entire 'country' in 'the Indies' with all its diverse inhabitants and natural features. A notable letter by a *Mercurio Peruano* subscriber, printed in the April 20 and 24 editions of 1794, is illustrative of this shift. Making use of the emerging, Bourbon language of 'colonial commerce' à la Raynal and Robertson, the author in question refers to trade between Spain and Peru

Figure 2.2 The Country of the Incas, free of Ultramarine monarchs. Frontispiece, Mariano de Rivero and Jacob von Tschudi, *Antigüedades Peruanas*, v. 2 (Vienna, 1851).

Source: Courtesy of the John Carter Brown Library at Brown University.

as 'commerce between the Metropolis and its Colony' and he further speculates, mostly in critical and conservative fashion, on the political and social consequences of this commerce.[19] The author notes that

> times had changed . . . The Maritime Postal Service, established in 1764, has cut the distance between America and Spain by more than 20 leagues . . . The subdivision of vast territories in proportional and well-governed departments, the abolition of the Repartimiento, the extinction of the Private Encomienda, and most notably the magisterial stroke of Free Trade, are more political miracles made by our Sovereigns.[20]

This passage is a reference to the better-known Bourbon political economic reforms, designed to carefully diversify commerce and more tightly govern and tax the 'Reynos y Provincias' of 'las Indias' or 'las Americas.' These material 'miracles' were achieved by opening new ports and customs houses to the Indies trade, creating new administrative units and posts and applying new or increased levies on an array of goods, labour and services. The reforms significantly boosted the volume of trade, profits and paperwork.

As this letter demonstrates, modern notions of 'colony' and 'metropolis' could now be used to publicly describe past and present commercial relations between Spain and Peru. Ironically perhaps, such new notions of metropolis–colony relations provided semantic and material grounds for a strong political reinvention or twisting of older notions of natural and constitutional rights. Thomas Paine's *Common Sense* was a good example of this twisting. Paine would ingeniously recycle naturalist notions of primitive liberty often associated with Rousseau although, as Hispanic commentators noted, with deeper origins in Francisco Suarez or indeed Thomas Aquinas, now adding a modern 'colonial' twist to the old story of rights. In 1811 at least two Spanish translations of *Common Sense* appeared, one of these likely done by the Peruvian revolutionary Manuel José de Amunátegui under the pen name of a 'Peruvian native Anselmo Nateiu.' This Peruvian translation was published privately in London in 1811 and reprinted in Lima in 1821.[21] For Paine, the imagined original society of natural freedom before the rise of kings was a solitary and pure 'Colony' blissfully detached from the corrupt world of 'despots.' Paine thus upends the traditional idea that a 'colony' was a dependent settlement issued by a city or a prince. He also parts company with Rousseau, who does not use the term 'colony' in this sense. Paine's original and free 'Colony' was autonomous and natural, dependent upon no one. 'Every man' had 'by natural right' a 'seat' in the 'parliament' of this free 'Colony.' In this and other ways Paine anticipated the arguments of Abbe De Pradt, which as we shall see would soon play a key role in the Spanish and Peruvian revolutions of independence. Here, Paine concedes that 'small islands' might for a time be held as dependent 'colonies' of foreign 'governments' or 'princes.' This concession, no doubt, was a veiled reference to the Caribbean islands. But Paine insisted that very large, continental territories such as those found in North and South America were wholly unnatural dependencies, since they far outstripped their old European 'metropoles.' The natural order of things, Paine wrote, was that big America be free of little England. 'It is evident that they belong to different systems. England to Europe, America to itself.'[22]

In the ensuing, early nineteenth-century decades of war and political crisis, the old notion of 'system' (*sistema*) would be modified by the new sense of 'colonial' to create the enduring and suitably vague concept, still alive in Latin America today, of 'colonial system' (*sistema colonial*). At the same time, the related and equally vague but highly useful term of *coloniaje* (colonialism, colonial rule or period of colonial rule) appears across the region. These broad concepts would shape the course and discourse of events in early nineteenth-century Peru. As is well known, the Napoleonic occupation of the Iberian Peninsula generated a momentary succession crisis, unleashing a wave of unrest characterized by new appeals to old 'constitutional' rights across the early nineteenth-century Hispanic world. Aided by the British, the besieged court of the Portuguese Braganzas set sail for Brazil. The Bourbon King of the Spains and Emperor of the Indies was retained in southern France while succession to his legitimate heir, the young Prince Ferdinand, was held in abeyance. Meanwhile, in Madrid Joseph Bonaparte was proclaimed Jose I, King of the Spains and Emperor of the Indies. The Bonapartist interlude elicited both acquiescence and Catholic defiance in Spain and America, marked by pledges of allegiance to the displaced Prince Ferdinand and renewed defences of constitutional rights of earlier origin. The immediate result on both sides of the Atlantic was a precarious and de facto autonomy from Bonapartist Madrid marked by instability and conflict. Protected by the British and other mercenaries, representatives of the pro-Ferdinand forces headed for Cadiz, proclaiming the Constitution of the Spanish Monarchy in 1812. In theory, the new constitution placed Peninsular Spain and Overseas Spain (previously called 'Indias Occidentales' or 'America') on a level plane, undoing what were now identified as old 'colonial' hierarchies.

In the wake of these sweeping events, the concept of 'sistema colonial' appeared in print in Peru once again, notably in the February 18, 1813, edition of the *Verdadero Peruano*. The *Verdadero Peruano* was a short-lived, enlightened periodical supported by the reformist Viceroy of Peru, Don Jose Fernando Abascal. It resumed on a more modest scale the brilliant work of its well-known predecessor, the *Mercurio Peruano* (1791–95).[23] Its most illustrious contributor was the sagely Unanue, Professor of Anatomy at the University of San Marcos and editor of Peru's widely consulted annual statistical survey. The February 18 edition of

VP reprinted the final pages of Unanue's last annual *Compendium of Statistics of Peru* (1797), also called the *Political, Ecclesiastic and Military Guide to the Viceroyalty of Peru*. It is in the editors' commentary on Unanue's final report that the term 'sistema colonial' appears.

> It may be supposed that the Colonial System of Peru came to an end in the last century and with this last edition of the Guide. In this year of 1813 a new era commences with the swearing in of the constitution of the Spanish monarchy. Within one or two decades, her beneficent laws will be well established and then it will be possible to compare the colonial picture offered by this statistical compendium with that presented by liberty and civil equality and all the other excellent prerogatives that this Overseas Spain now enjoys, and which we hope will cement the peace, union and true love of patria without which no state may flourish. The thirteen years that have passed since the end of the colonial system and the beginning of the new government are full of extraordinary developments in all branches of public administration.[24]

Nowhere does the term 'sistema colonial' appear in any of the many annual editions of Unanue's official statistical guide to the Viceroyalty of Peru. The use of the term is evidently retrospective, and it represents an historical judgement that now made sense since the 'new government' (*nuevo gobierno*) established by the Constitution of 1812 had 'levelled' the terms of the former 'colonial' relationship between Spain and America, now considered equal columns of the 'Spanish Monarchy.' Notably, for the editors the 'colonial system' had come to an end circa 1799, that is, a dozen years or so before the Cadiz Constitution.

Like all other periodicals published in Lima during these heady years, the *Verdadero Peruano* was fully committed to the Constitution of 1812.[25] Still, the title of the journal is itself noteworthy, since it strongly asserts the 'true' name of 'Peruvians' at the very moment in which the name of Peru is eclipsed by the name of 'Overseas Spain.' The constitution created a unified, global 'Spanish Nation' (*nación española*) of citizens and, for the first time, a 'Spanish Monarchy' (*Monarquía española*). America became, as Unanue noted in the *Verdadero Peruano*'s inaugural Prospectus, *la España Ultramarina* (Overseas Spain) and all its citizens, including Indians and most *castas* or mixed groups (after heated debate, those of African descent were denied citizenship although in Peru this limitation was not necessarily observed in all cases), were now 'Spaniards.' The new constitution was, in Unanue's words, a 'heroic act of great wisdom' that went well beyond all ancient and modern precedents, creating the world's first global, unified nation of civil equals among metropolitans and ex-colonials, uniting 'two worlds ruled by a single order.'[26] This new global order of the Spanish nation, ratified and sworn across Peru by

1813, called for a more enlightened and expansive form of patriotism. The *Verdadero Peruano* responded with enthusiasm to this global call.[27]

The concept of *sistema colonial* resumes its public career in Peruvian letters soon after independence in 1821. In the decade between 1812 and 1822, a restored Ferdinand VII resumed absolute powers, ordering expeditionary armies of 'pacification' to sail against armed American insurgents. Many of these American patriots rejected both the Constitution of 1812 and the restored King Ferdinand. The southern patriot army of liberation that declared Peru's independence was among those who remained defiant. Commanded by the *rioplatense* General José de San Martín, the official voice of the Peruvian campaign was Bernardo Monteagudo, a bold and brilliant 'mulatto' intellectual born and educated in Upper Peru (present day northern Argentina and Bolivia). Monteagudo would have none of the 'liberalism' of the Constitutional Spanish Monarchy declared in Cadiz. For him as for his rival Sánchez Carrión, it was the old emperor in new clothes. As Monteagudo wrote in *El Pacificador del Perú*, the official periodical of San Martin's campaign:

> In one palm [Spain] offers a liberty of frenetic sacrifices, and with the other she hands us extermination. She sanctions premature reforms for herself, although unfit for a people who have loved slavery and fanaticism, and dictates hateful restrictions for America, who has her own destiny. In short, she threatens us with national indignation, forgetting that our [resistance] is only that more terrible . . . For us, the celebrated Constitutional Monarchy has never left the sixteenth century . . . Hypocrites! . . . We would rather die a thousand times than belong to Spain or have anything in common with Spaniards.[28]

This defiant declaration was followed by an excerpt from the Bolivarian *Gazeta de Bogotá* of Colombia, where Spanish military repression of the patriots was particularly severe. Spanish troops sent by the restored Ferdinand VII to 'pacify America' were, the Gazeta editors noted with satire, no different than

> what they were under the despotic regime . . . The constitutionalists fight to strip us of our rights and meanwhile they are furious when we do not wish to receive the name of Spaniards, which they dispense with such loving generosity . . . They forget that, separated from them *by reason and by force*, we cannot and do not wish to call ourselves anything other than Americans.[29]

Three weeks later, *El Pacificador del Perú* pronounced that the cruel war with Spain left no alternative: 'la Independencia o la muerte.' Independence or death![30]

At this critical moment, Monteagudo reached for the 'moral' weapon of 'philosophy.' On the eve of taking Lima, *El Pacificador* reprinted an excerpt from Dominique-Georges-Frederic Dufour De Pradt's *De la Revolution actuelle de l'Espagne* (1820), translated to Spanish in the same year as *De la Revolución actual de España*.[31] The occasion of De Pradt's book was the 1820 declaration of military officers. Citing the Constitution of 1812, those officers had impeded the execution of Ferdinand VII's royal orders to set sail for America to 'pacify' the armies of independence. 'The Spanish army,' Pradt wrote, had effectively 'proclaimed American independence' when it 'refused the King's orders to march against her.'[32] This enlightened act sealed the fate of 'the colonial order.'[33]

In *Des colonies et de la révolution actuelle de l'Amérique*, (Paris, 1817), De Pradt had advanced his argument that the global 'colonial order' (*l'ordre colonial*) or 'system' (*systeme colonial*) was doomed by the American revolutions. Quickly translated into English and Spanish, De Pradt's book on the revolution of the colonies circulated around the Atlantic world.[34] In its Preface, De Pradt acknowledges Raynal but notes that 'the colonial order' had changed dramatically in the years 'between Raynal and us.'[35] De Pradt also distinguishes between 'old and new ages of European colonies' (*l'état ancien et moderne des colonies européennes*).[36] It was, apparently, the first time that these concepts had appeared in print in French, English and Spanish, and with reference to all the Americas.[37]

Clearly 'inevitable' by 1817, in 1820 'absolute independence' across the Americas was for De Pradt an undeniable 'fact.'[38] The 'absolute separation' of America from Europe would return the world to 'the natural state' in which 'the Author of Nature' had arranged it. The old 'colonial system' would give way to 'the American system.' *El Pacificador del Perú's* excerpt notably included these lines:

> The American System is complete and will be perfected . . . The old order is finished. . . . Things will return to the state of nature in which they were originally placed, but which political events had violated . . . America will exist for America, Europe for Europe . . . Each will be his own master. This was the will of the Creator, that will now be carried out . . . An independent America will by necessity make all other colonies independent as well.[39]

In the same way that Mexico would be returned to the Mexicans, De Pradt now called on the English to 'hand over all English India to the Indian soldiers (cipayos).' If 'freed from subjugation to the 24,000 English soldiers among them, you will see how quickly India acquires her liberty!'[40] The semantic reach of *sistema colonial* was thus extended across the globe. This global system of European colonialism had met its match in the new 'Sistema Americano,' however. In the original French and in the Valencia Spanish translation, De Pradt explains why the 'American system' would bring an end to the 'colonial order' not only in America[41] but around the globe. The 'reason' for the worldwide spread of the 'American system' was not only that such an order was 'natural' but that old territorial 'colonies' ruled by foreign sovereigns were now out of step with the emerging commercial and national or 'natural' order.[42] In short, the 'colonial system' would wither away because it was both unnatural and backward.

> Spain no longer has any interest in the sovereign and territorial possession of America, only in its prosperity. This truth is bitter for Europe and has taken a long time to arrive but finally it has sprung roots. With the example now in view of an England that has gained much in losing America, it is now clear that the interests of a metropolis consist not so much in the possession of a colony than in its prosperity. Extending this principle to all colonies, it is natural and easy to infer that Europe no longer has any interest in possessing her colonies but only in increasing their prosperity. If the governments of Europe would stop wasting time on affairs that produce no utility . . . they would see that the possession of colonies is prejudicial, not only to the colonies but also to the [European] governments, and that the most convenient thing for both parties is independence.[43]

De Pradt favoured a global future of independent states that included both constitutional and naturalized monarchies as well as republics. He thus proposed, 'if there was still enough time,' that the Bourbon King of Spain select princes from his own line[44] who might settle and rule in Mexico and Peru as naturalized kings, following the example of the Braganzas of Portugal who had relocated to Brazil. For De Pradt, the future of European royalism (*realismo europeo*), which he defended against the 'horrors' and 'despotism' of the misguided French Revolution, was also at stake. Independence for the colonies could, in his view, guarantee a future for endangered European royalism. Rather than squander limited resources on armies and subsidies for colonies that were not worth the expense and would in any case soon become independent, De Pradt advised European dynasts to send their enlightened sons west, to the colonies. These arguments were consistent with Monteagudo's latest plan to convince Spaniards in Lima that, first, their cause was lost and, second, that the best option for Peru was to recruit a suitable European prince ready and willing to occupy 'the Peruvian throne.' A similar independence plan was pursued by patriotic monarchists in New Spain or Mexico.

The Peruvian Debate on 'Colonial' Customs

For Peruvian revolutionaries like Monteagudo and Sánchez Carrión, the notion of *sistema colonial* was not only a grand historical concept useful for describing the old order that was now being swept away by the

American revolutions. Although Peru had recently 'recovered its natural independence' it was still marked by a stubborn inheritance of 'debased customs' readily traced by both men to 'the colonial system.'[45] This was the more immediate sense of 'colonial' that marked 'ex-colonial' Peruvian attempts to define the form of government they would now adopt. As Monteagudo and others anticipated, this 'colonial legacy' or, as historians and social scientists later dubbed it, 'colonial heritage' or 'problem,' would continue to haunt the Peruvian Republic for decades, if not centuries.

Sánchez Carrión's charge to 'decolonize customs' was born of a debate that sought to decide what form of government independent Peru should adopt. In this polemic, the more pressing, domestic notion of an implanted 'colonial system' is registered repeatedly. Indeed, it appears in the very same letter of 1822 wherein Sánchez Carrión's coinage makes its print debut. The purpose of the letter was not only to rebut the constitutional monarchy position defended, in this instance, by the cleric and Patriotic Society member Jose Ignacio Moreno, but to attack and dismiss the very framing of the debate as it was formulated by Monteagudo. The question, clearly informed by well-known ideas then associated with Montesquieu and Rousseau, was worded as follows: 'What form of government was most adaptable to the Peruvian state, given its extension, population, customs and grade on the scale of civilization?'[46] Monteagudo apparently refused to admit the unsigned letter of 'el Solitario de Sayan' to be read before the Society, noting that only bonified members were invited to partake in the debate. Sánchez Carrión despatched his letter to the friendly editor of a Lima newspaper called *El Correo Mercantil, Político y Literario*. It was quickly reprinted in the newly founded polemical rag of a group of partisans, *La Abeja Republicana*.

La Abeja Republicana was created by embattled republican allies of Sánchez Carrión who sought to 'contener a los despotas' (restrain despots). In truth, its unabashed purpose was to attack and slander the ideas and personal character of Bernardo Monteagudo.[47] Monteagudo was openly detested by *Abeja* writers, who flatly accused him of 'inquisitorial' and 'tyrannical acts.' *Abeja* writers also did not hide the fact that for them Monteagudo was an unruly and 'despotic' mulatto foreigner given over to personal excesses.[48] Ironically perhaps, Monteagudo's 'tyrannical acts' would today be considered radical if not routine acts of decolonization. These measures included stripping Spaniards of their property and forcing them to leave Peru. Monteagudo also ordered the removal of their titular names, images and aristocratic seals from public display, replacing these with 'national' or Inca ones. Indeed, Monteagudo made sustained 'war' on Spaniards and Spanish 'colonial customs' for reasons not dissimilar to those that motivated Sánchez Carrión. Writing later from Chilean exile in defence of his actions, Monteagudo explained that 'it would mean nothing to make war on the Spaniards if we did not also wage war on the vices that they legated to us.' But none of that mattered to *La Abeja* writers.

The third issue of *La Abeja* featured a vengeful 'epitaph' for Monteagudo, now branded as 'The Honorary Inquisitor of State, protector of idiots and serfs.' But Monteagudo was no inquisitor and his followers no idiots: they included the best minds in Peru. Monteagudo himself masterminded and composed many of Peru's most memorable and brilliant independence decrees, including those often assigned by historians to (because signed by) San Martin.[49] Although he clearly favoured the enlightened, historicist camp associated then with Montesquieu and later with the supporters of Simon Bolivar in Peru such as Benito Laso,[50] in his 'Inaugural Oration' Monteagudo sought to strike a balanced and pragmatic tone, seemingly both for and against Rousseau's more provocative, anti-Enlightenment theses, which the Swiss 'citizen' had presented to the Academy at Dijon. Did progress in the sciences contribute to the corruption of customs? Were the enlightened mere courtesan buffoons? Or could they truly represent and foment enlightenment and virtue among the people?

Setting the finer points of Rousseau's provocative attack on enlightenment aside, Monteagudo concluded that, under the circumstances, 'experience would decide the matter.'[51] Monteagudo had learned first hand that bold and sudden 'changes of language' made by revolutionary decree may not have the desired effect on the populace.[52] Stubborn customs 'perpetrated by the colonial system of the Peninsula' predisposed Peruvians, he argued, to the seductive appeals of demagogues and arrivistes (a thinly veiled reference to Sánchez Carrión).[53] 'Confirmed by experience,' these living 'colonial customs were the deeper cause of our problems.'[54]

It is important to note that Montesquieu had argued that the republican form of government worked best in small states, and Rousseau added that resource-poor states (like his own) were more likely to produce the virtues necessary for republicanism. The ideas of both men were rooted in part in older notions and narratives of the heroic Greek city-states and the 'despotic' and 'decadent,' rich Oriental empires that had threatened them. However, they were also strongly influenced by modern notions that routinely associated America with noble savagery and Spain with the Oriental empires. Thus, Montesquieu compared America to Asia and Africa, all suffering under the yoke of 'Asiatic slavery.'[55] Adding insult to injury, Rousseau argued that despotism was doubly favoured in hot and sparsely populated countries (such as Peru). As a vast and mountainous territory located in 'the torrid zone' with, after Conquest, a supposedly sparse population, the writings of these authors led many to conclude that Peru was ill-suited to the republican form of government. Peru's customs were likewise widely considered vice-ridden or 'servile' and its 'grade on the scale of civilization' was at best 'semi-barbarian.' Indeed, most European thinkers of the period assumed that 'enlightenment' and 'civilization' were extremely scarce in Peru. It was also then widely held that the republican form of government required 'virtuous' citizens and 'moral' customs, normally found, according to the Frenchman, only at the upper 'grade' of civilization or, conversely for the Swiss Rousseau, at a primitive, community level uncorrupted by the miseducation and vanity of 'despotism.' All of this indicated that monarchy and not the republic was most 'adaptable' or suitable to Peru.

But the debate in Lima was rather more than a Peruvian dubbing of a French fantasy. To be sure, Montesquieu and Rousseau were frequently cited as authorities by the opposing Peruvian camps. These figures of rhetoric served not only or necessarily as sources of ideas (as is routinely claimed) but as strategic artillery, useful to those who sought to deploy their names to carve out distinctive and meaningful positions that appealed to local conditions and circumstances. As Elias Palti notes, while informed by old concepts and European debates, the political and conceptual problem of selecting the correct 'form of government' in the Americas required 'technical' expertise and local knowledge of history, geography and customs.[56] That expertise and knowledge came from enlightened Peruvian figures such as Unanue, whose considered views contrasted with those of Montesquieu and Rousseau.

The very forum that elicited Sánchez Carrión's coin to 'decolonize customs' was the occasion for Monteagudo to unveil his own remedy for the very same problem, namely, how to extirpate the 'colonial customs' that blocked the full realization of Peru's true potential. Monteagudo's 'war' on 'colonial' custom was multifaceted, but its centrepiece was the rapid assembly of 'a mass' of useful knowledge 'for the people.' The instrument of this useful knowledge was the *Sociedad Patriótica*, a select, enlightened society of Peruvian patriots who represented 'the general will of the people.' Such societies were not only created in Peru. Societies of the same name and purpose were created in Caracas in 1810 and Buenos Aires in 1811. The double charge of the Peruvian Patriotic Society was not only to augment the people's 'natural' enlightenment and felicity with more and better knowledge. More importantly, the charge was to 'imprint in their hearts the sublime truth' of 'popular sovereignty and the general will.' This 'sublime truth' had been 'announced by philosophy from the throne' not of the prince, but 'of reason.'[57] In short, Peruvian enlightenment would not be at odds with the 'general will' of popular sovereignty announced by Rousseau. It was not enough to enlighten the people with better knowledge of truths. Everyday customs would also have to be 'perfected.' In ex-colonial Peru, perfecting meant 'decolonizing.' It was a grand, collective task of mind and heart that, moreover, could not be met by 'the solitary man' (another thinly veiled reference to 'el Solitario de Sayan,' Sánchez Carrión). Monteagudo's Sociedad Patriótica was the collective vessel of this grand, historical work.[58]

Sánchez Carrión was not invited to join Monteagudo's select Patriotic Society. Sidelined, he adopted the 'solitary' outsider position, reminiscent of Rousseau. In truth, his position was hardly solitary: it reflected a concerted putsch to oust Monteagudo, embodied in *La Abeja*. *La Abeja* painted the Patriotic Society as a farce that would create a new aristocracy. Sadly, *La Abeja* propaganda against the Society and its 'Order of the Sun' later became the accepted version of events in Peruvian historiography. What is clear, however, is that Monteagudo's project was as anti-colonial or decolonizing as that of *La Abeja*.

Citing 'the author of the social pact,' in his fiery letter Sánchez Carrión dismissed absolute monarchy as a 'political heresy' unworthy of 'the dignity of man.' Constitutional monarchy, he added, was no better since it, too, was 'the rule of one.' Such rule could never produce anything other than 'despotism.' Rejecting the very terms or framing of the question posed by Monteagudo to the plenary of the Sociedad Patriótica, Sánchez Carrión argued that the question could only elicit predictable responses that would miss the crux of the matter. The real question was how best to guarantee natural 'liberty' so that Peru could 'maximize' its true potential. The most adaptable form of government was not that which 'accommodated the present situation' since that was the baneful 'result of Spanish conquest.' Instead, the debate should take aim at the establishment of a 'permanent' order that could guarantee those 'natural rights' (liberty, property, security) that would allow all Peruvians to 'increase population a hundredfold, decolonize customs, and maximize enlightenment.' In short, 'if the question is how to reach our maximum potential, monarchy is clearly unadaptable since it fits our present, degraded situation.' Peruvians were, he added, 'weakened and accustomed to the colonial system, whose education had given us a second nature.' Under the proposed Peruvian monarchy, we would only make 'excellent vassals and never citizens' since, and here Sánchez Carrión echoes the Orientalism of Montesquieu, 'a throne in Peru would likely be more despotic than those in Asia.' Why should Peru's form of government be based on this debased, 'second nature' born of the 'colonial system?' The most 'adaptable' form of government was therefore not monarchy but the republic.

In a second letter published in *El Correo* in August 1822, Sánchez Carrión makes critical use of the related term '*coloniaje*' (colonial rule or colonialism). This interesting term begins to circulate with some frequency in the first decade of the nineteenth century. By the middle decades of the nineteenth century it became the standard gloss in Peruvian historical writing for 'the epoch of Spanish domination.' Here Sánchez Carrión uses the term to reluctantly compare ('*entrar en comparación es muy odioso*') the Peruvian 'situation' with that of other 'colonies,' in this case those of British America. Most comparisons between British and Spanish *coloniaje* or colonialism made during this period (and beyond) argued that the Spanish were by far the more 'despotic' overlords. Conditions for liberty were thus more advantageous in the Anglo North, and this notion explained why the British colonies had declared their independence first. Notably, Sánchez Carrión's view was quite the opposite: British colonialism in the North was harsher. In the Hispanic South, the people were accustomed to exercising liberty on a local level and as a result were better prepared for a republican life of liberty. He was thus optimistic that the new Peruvian Republic would rapidly overcome the servile 'customs' it had inherited under the 'colonial system.' Moreover, the task of decolonizing customs would be made easier by the fact that all the Americas north and south were now united in the epic task of 'shedding the humiliating colonial costume.'

Shedding the Colonial Costume

But was it so easy to shed this 'humiliating colonial costume' in Peru, many now asked? Monteagudo came to see the project of 'perfecting' colonial customs as a prolonged war complicated by those ardent demagogues (like Sánchez Carrión) who promised quick fixes without solid bases. To 'suddenly demand new customs' before establishing 'the precedence of a series of contrary actions' against old 'colonial' habits of the people, was to 'make a monstrous stew . . . of high-sounding democracy and colonial debasement.' In such a stew, the people only alternate between 'acting like a slave' and 'commanding like a tyrant.' They seek to 'preserve their old prerogatives' under the colonial regime while at the 'first cry of an ambitious demagogue all cry for equality, without understanding or desiring it.'[59]

Despite these dangers, the federal approach to government and society promised a possible solution to the vexing problem of customs in ex-colonial 'countries' like Peru. In philosophical terms, the federal approach sought to wed the basic form of society (the family) with that of government, that is, in contemporary parlance, to marry 'the social world' to 'the political world.' Sánchez Carrión held that Peru was naturally and historically federal in its local political organization. Consequently, existing municipalities and provincial counsels of 'colonial' origin could serve as the solid building blocks of republican government. In short, the republican 'form of government' in its federalist variation could work in Peru not because it had succeeded in another ex-colonial society in the Americas (British America and the emerging United States), but because it was best suited to Peruvian social and political reality. Similar federalist visions of republican government would emerge in the Rio de la Plata, Mexico, Central America, and Brazil. Notably, De Pradt had also argued that 'the revolution in Spain' (of 1808–20) that brought an end to 'the colonial system' was 'the most important event the universe has ever seen,' precisely because 'in it we see verified the complete reunion of the social world and the political world.'[60] It was this same naturalist ideal of a perfect 'reunion' of the social and the political that, in different ways, inspired both Monteagudo and Sánchez Carrión. Referred to routinely with such phrases as 'los derechos naturales de la Sociedad' or 'los preciosos derechos de la Libertad, igualdad, y mejor estar, que con la vida concede la naturaleza a todo hombre,' these rights were understood by both men to be 'la verdadera legitimidad de los Gobiernos.'[61] Reclaiming and defending those rights would mean that in Peru the collective, historical task of 'decolonizing' or 'waging war' on colonial customs would need to be both sudden and ongoing.

As I noted at the outset of this chapter, scholars and critics of various persuasions have missed the critical relevance of the modern concept of 'colonial system' for early nineteenth-century Hispanic American independence. Many of the same critics have similarly missed not only the existence of serious decolonization projects in the region during the early republican period but the very possibility of imagining it. I hope to have demonstrated here that such views are in the case of Peru unfounded. I would suggest, however, that Peru was not solitary in this regard. Nor did the impetus to 'shed the colonial costume' fade across the region in the decades after independence. On the contrary, the spectre of the 'colonial legacy,' which as Lina del Castillo points out in the case of Colombia was a powerful 'invention' with a consequential material and intellectual history, was a repeating and motivating motif of nineteenth-century politics and thought across the region. In Peru, heated and actionable debates on colonial customs were not only registered in Lima in the 1820s. They raged in word and deed up and down the country for much of the nineteenth century, and indeed returned with a vengeance in the twentieth century. Federalist and republican approaches to political community and customs resonated not only among elites but in unsuspected ways in nineteenth-century Andean peasant communities, creating openings for hybrid forms of citizenship contingently erected upon colonial 'republican' precedents of local government, as Sánchez Carrión had indeed foreseen.[62] Recent research in intellectual history and historical anthropology has uncovered similarly dynamic and innovative approaches to the challenges of ex-colonial, federal republicanism across Hispanic America.[63] In short, we are witnessing yet another effort to 'decolonize customs' of thought both within the academy and beyond. We may thank Sánchez-Carrión and Monteagudo for blazing the trail.

Notes

1. *La Abeja Republicana*, n. 4 (August 15, 1822), facsimile edition, 1971 (Lima, Ediciones Cope), 53. With prologue and notes by Alberto Tauro. Emphasis in original. The letter appears to have been written on March 1, 1822, and sent to the editor of *Correo Mercantíl, Político y Literario de Lima*. It was reprinted in *La Abeja* as 'Carta al Editor del Correo Mercantíl y político de Lima sobre la inadaptabilidad del gobierno monárquico al Estado Libre del Perú, empezada a publicar en el N. 17.'
2. See, among others, Dane Kennedy, *Decolonization: A Very Short Introduction* (New York: Oxford University Press, 2016) and Todd Shepard, *The Invention of Decolonization: The Algerian War and the Remaking of France*

(Ithaca: Cornell University Press, 2006). The author was Henri Fonfrède. His collected works were published in 1846 as *Questions d'Economie Publique* (Bordeux: Chaumas-Gayet, 1846). Chapter 9 of this collection is entitled 'De la Decolonisation de Alger.' The editor notes that the pieces were written between 1833 and 1835 and originally published in *Le Memorial bordelaise* (Bordeaux).

3. On the European invention of 'decolonization' and its supposed subsequent dispersion to 'other parts of the world,' see Stuart Ward, 'The European Provenance of Decolonization,' *Past and Present* 230 (February 2016), 227–260.
4. For the 'decolonial' narrative or option, see Walter D. Mignolo, *Local Histories/Global Designs: Coloniality, Subaltern Knowledges, and Border Thinking* (Princeton: Princeton University Press, 2000). 'Creole pioneers' is Benedict Anderson's coin in the revised, second edition of *Imagined Communities: Reflections on the Origin and Spread of Nationalism* (New York and London: Verso, 1991).
5. A highly influential text in the 'misplaced ideas' vein was Jorge Klor de Alva's 'The Postcolonization of the (Latin) American Experience: A Reconsideration of "Colonialism," "Postcolonialism," and "Mestizaje",' in Gyan Prakash, ed., *After Colonialism: Imperial Histories and Postcolonial Displacements* (Princeton: Princeton University Press, 1994), 241–277. Another was Walter Mignolo's *The Idea of Latin America* (Oxford: Blackwell, 2005). Klor de Alva's and Mignolo's arguments are sophisticated variations on the older, dependentista and world-systems veins of Latin American cultural criticism. Perhaps the iconic text of this tradition is Roberto Schwarz's *Misplaced Ideas: Essays on Brazilian Culture* (London and New York: Verso, 1992). For a critique of Schwarz and this vein of thinking, see Elías Palti, 'The Problem of "Misplaced Ideas" Revisited: Beyond the History of Ideas in Latin America,' *Journal of the History of Ideas* (January 2006), 149–179.
6. See Annick Lempériere, 'La cuestión colonial,' *Nuevo Mundo/Mundos Nuevos* (February 2005), 8.
7. By their nature, official dictionaries always follow far behind vernacular usage, and therefore should be used with caution as indicators of change. The word 'coloniaje' (colonialism), for example, does not appear in a Spanish dictionary until 1895 but it was widely used in Hispanic America since the 1820s. 'Descolonizar' does not appear in any Spanish dictionary until 1992, when it was finally accepted by the Real Academia Española.
8. See Francisco Ortega, 'The Conceptual History of Spanish American Independence and the Colonial Question,' *Journal of the History of Ideas* (January 2018), 89–103.
9. On the invention of 'país' or country in Peruvian discourse, see Mark Thurner, *History's Peru: The Poetics of Colonial and Postcolonial Historiography* (Gainesville: University Press of Florida, 2011).
10. The *Dictionaire critique de la langue française* (1787) entry for 'COLONIAL, -ALE' reads: Neologisme: qui concerne la Colonie. 'Le Ministere voulut que les Habitans pussent doner leur voix dans les Assemblees colonials. Rayn.' The first appearance of the Spanish adjective 'colonial' (meaning 'of the colonies') in a dictionary is 1825 (Nuñez de Taboada, 344) although there is no doubt that it circulated in public discourse since at least 1812.
11. William Robertson, *History of America* (London: Strahan, Cadell and Balfour, 1777).
12. For an extended critical discussion of eighteenth-century Hispanic historiography, Nuix and the exiled Catalan Jesuits, see Jorge Cañizares-Esguerra, *How to Write the History of the New World: Histories, Epistemologies, and Identities in the Eighteenth-Century Atlantic World* (Palo Alto: Stanford University Press, 2001).

13. Ibid., 80.
14. Ibid., 144.
15. Ibid., 238.
16. See Julián Juderías, *La leyenda negra y la verdad histórica: Contribución al estudio del concepto de España en Europa, de las causas de este concepto y de la tolerancia política y religiosa en los países civilizados* (Madrid: Imprenta de la Revista de Archivos, Bibliotecas y Museos, 1914), and Antonello Gerbi, *La disputa del Nuovo Mondo. Storia di una polemica, 1750–1900* (Milan: Adelphi, 2000 [1955]).
17. 'Apéndice de la Sociedad,' *Mercurio peruano* (1793), v.7, f. 25.
18. See Thurner, *History's Peru*.
19. *Mercurio Peruano* (April 24, 1794), n. 345, f. 265. The letter appears to have been written by Francisco de Paula de la Mata Linares. It provoked a Peruvian debate on the risks of uniting the 'nations' of Spaniards and Indians in Peru, thereby anticipating the Cadiz constitutional debates of 1810–13.
20. *Mercurio Peruano* (April 24, 1794), n. 344, 258–259.
21. See Víctor Peralta, 'La pluma contra las Cortes y el Trono. La prensa y el desmontaje del liberalismo hispánico en el Perú, 1821–1824,' *Revista de Indias* LXXI:253 (2011), 729–758.
22. Thomas Paine, *Common Sense* (Philadelphia: Robert Bell, 1776), 92.
23. On Peruvian periodicals of the period, see Victor Peralta, 'Prensa y redes de comunicacion en el Virreinato del Perú, 1790–1821,' *Tiempos de América* (2005), n. 12, 113–131.
24. *Verdadero Peruano* (February 18, 1813), n. XII, 214.
25. Peralta, 'Prensa y redes,' 118.
26. *Verdadero Peruano* (February 18, 1813), 4–5.
27. Ibid., 6.
28. *El Pacificador del Perú* (Huara, April 20, 1821), n. 2.
29. Ibid., n. 2.
30. Ibid. (Barranca, May 10, 1821), n. 4.
31. The wording of Monteagudo's excerpt differs somewhat from the Valencia translation, published in 1820 by José Ferrer. The Valencia translation includes a critical commentary on De Pradt's many errors and biases.
32. Dominique-Georges-Frédéric Dufour de Pradt, *De la Revolución actual de España y de sus consecuencias* (Valencia: Ferrer de Orga, 1820), 181–182. The commander of the expedition was arrested by fellow officers.
33. The constitutionalist uprising of 1820 led by Coronel Rafael de Riego restored the Constitution of Cadiz only until 1823, when a French punitive expedition backed by the Triple Alliance restored Fernando VII. The Spanish movement set off similar movements in Portugal, Naples and the Piedmont. Further afield, constitutional movements in Germany, Russia and Greece also challenged absolutism, with mixed results.
34. De Pradt's *De las colonias y de la revolución actual de la América* (1817) was printed in Bourdeaux by Juan Pinard and *The Colonies and the Present American Revolutions* (1817) in London by Baldwin, Cradock and Joy.
35. De Pradt, *Les colonies*, v.
36. Ibid., 11.
37. The terms 'colonial system' and 'colonial order' do not appear in Raynal's *Histoire philosophique*.
38. De Pradt, *De la Revolución actual de España*, 183.
39. *El Pacificador del Perú* (Barranca, June 10, 1821), n. 7. See somewhat different wording in the translation of this excerpt in De Pradt, *De la Revolución Actual de España*, 184–185. Monteagudo's translation is closer to the original, *La revolution actuelle de l'Espagne, et de ses suites* (Paris: Bechet Ainé, 1820).

40. De Pradt, *De la Revolución actual de España*, 223.
41. Although Mexico and Cuba were not yet fully independent in 1820, in part because 'Mexico was Spain's greatest and most profitable Colony' and because together 'Mexico and Cuba provided Spain with most of its colonial wealth,' de Pradt predicted that Mexico and the remaining 'island colonies' of the Caribbean would soon follow the example of South America. Peru was already free in a de facto sense. This judgement of de facto independence was now used to boost San Martin's strategy, which was to convince the remaining royalist Spaniards that their cause was lost. De Pradt had also recommended that Spanish or European princes be sought and placed on independent, national thrones in Peru, Mexico and Cuba, which he proposed be conjoined with Puerto Rico as a united 'kingdom.' See De Pradt, *De la Revolution actuelle*, 168–169, 172.
42. De Pradt, *De la Revolución actual de España*, 13–14.
43. Ibid., 219–220.
44. Ibid., 15.
45. Bernardo Monteagudo, *Oración inaugural de la Sociedad Patriótica de Lima* [January 13, 1822] (Buenos Aires, 1824).
46. '¿Cuál es la forma de gobierno más adaptable al estado peruano, según su extensión, población, costumbres y grado en la escala de la civilización?'
47. This purpose was obvious to Monteagudo, who noted that *La Abeja* had 'proclaimed contrary ideas under the apparatus of triumph, its trophy being the liberty to slander' and its purpose 'to aggravate resentments.'
48. Monteagudo's sudden fall from grace occurred when San Martin sailed to Guayaquil to meet with Simon Bolivar. Monteagudo's local enemies, Sánchez Carrión chief among them, conspired and publicly accused the First Minister of tyranny and censorship. In a local putsch organized by Lima elites led by José de la Riva Agüero, these 'liberals' stripped 'the mulato foreigner' of his power and had him ridden out of the country. With Monteagudo in exile in Chile, Sánchez Carrión rose to Secretary of the Constitutional Congress and principal author of Peru's first constitution (1823). He was later named Supreme Court Justice.
49. Like San Martin, Monteagudo was not 'Peruvian' in the narrow sense that came to prevail in post-independence Lima and coastal environs, although he had a claim to being 'Peruvian' in the continental or Andean sense of the word that prevailed in the late eighteenth century since he appears to have been born in Tucuman when that city was part of what was then called Upper Peru (Alto Peru). Upper Peru was part of the Audiencia de Charcas of the Viceroyalty of Peru until 1776 when it was incorporated into the new Viceroyalty of Rio de la Plata. Monteagudo studied in Chuquisaca (Sucre), Upper Peru in what is today Bolivia. It was there that he formed many of his revolutionary ideas.
50. For contextual analysis of the historicist views of the Peruvian Bolivarians, see Thurner, *History's Peru*, ch. 4.
51. Monteagudo, *Oración inaugural*, 11.
52. For discussion of these decrees, see Mark Thurner, 'After Colonialism and the King: Notes on the Peruvian Birth of Contemporary History,' *Postcolonial Studies* 9:4 (2006), 393–420.
53. In his *Memoria sobre los principios políticos que segui en la administration del Peru* (Santiago, 1823), 4, Monteagudo uses the term 'sistema colonial' to refer to the three centuries of Spanish rule in Peru.
54. Monteagudo, *Oración inaugural*, 8–9.
55. Montesquieu, *El Espíritu de las Leyes* (Mexico: Editorial Porras, 2003), 256–257.

56. Elías Palti, '*La Abeja Republicana*: La democracia en el discurso de la emancipación,' in Carmen McEvoy, Mauricio Novoa and Elías Palti, eds., *En el nudo del imperio: Independencia y democracia en el Perú* (Lima: Instituto de Estudios Peruanos, 2012), 99–118.
57. Monteagudo, *Oración inaugural*, 8–9.
58. Ibid., 14–16.
59. Monteagudo, *Memoria*, 13–14.
60. De Pradt, *De la Revolución actual de España*, 163.
61. *El Pacificador del Peru* (April 20, 1821), n. 2, and (May 20, 1821), n. 5.
62. See Mark Thurner, '*Republicanos* and *la Comunidad de Peruanos*: Unimagined Political Communities in Postcolonial Andean Peru,' *Journal of Latin American Studies* 27:2 (1995), 291–318.
63. For a review of this historiography, see Mark Thurner, 'After Spanish Rule: Writing Another After,' in Mark Thurner and Andres Guerrero, eds., *After Spanish Rule: Postcolonial Predicaments of the Americas* (Durham: Duke University Press, 1997).

3 Inventing Columbia/Colombia

Lina del Castillo

'Do Columbia and Colombia, as words, mean the same [thing]?' This is an interesting question. After all, the Spanish-language place name Colombia is only one vowel away from the English-language Columbia. But as we shall see, these names reverberate in ways that go far beyond mere grammatical coincidence. During the first wave of decolonization in the Americas, cosmopolitan actors imagined a Colombia/Columbia not of national but instead hemispheric, and still broadly republican, scope. The entire Western Hemisphere would be an independent federal republic named Columbia or Colombia, with elected 'Incas' and 'Amautas,' and with its capital in Panama, not the District of Columbia. Not until 1819 did 'Colombia' name a singular republic in the northwest corner of South America. That republic was still impressive in scale, claiming sovereignty over what is today Panama, Colombia, Ecuador, Venezuela, and parts of Brazil, Peru, Guyana, Costa Rica, and Nicaragua. In short, the names of Columbia/Colombia remind us that, contrary to Benedict Anderson's narrative, decolonization was not always limited to national horizons.[1] Projects to form large federations of republics were also pursued. This continental ideal, and the humanitarian universalist principles that 'Columbia/Colombia' represented, left a long legacy in the Western Hemisphere.

As Mark Thurner notes in the introduction to this volume, 'decolonization' enters the English academic lexicon via German and French in the middle decades of the twentieth century. Today, when Anglophone scholars discuss 'decolonization' they almost universally refer to the postwar 'Third Wave' of the 'Third World.' Nevertheless, recent historical surveys of decolonization have begun to recognize the importance of the 'first wave' also known as the Age of Revolutions. Indeed, it was during this period that the term was coined, first in Peru and then in France. This first wave ended European monarchical rule over a vast swath of territories in the Americas between 1776–1826.[2] And yet, as Reuben Neptune has recently noted, even though the Anglophone republic forged out of British North America starting in 1776 was obviously the first modern political community that needed to 'decolonize,' this fact has been trivialized, if noticed at all, especially after 1945.[3] To better see how the emerging community of the United States could form part of the first wave across the Americas, it is worth considering the early, connected history of the names of Columbia and Colombia. Doing so reveals how actors imagined the political transformations of this first wave on a hemispheric scale.

By revisiting the image of Christopher Columbus invented in the late eighteenth century, we may appreciate why 'Columbia/Colombia' became the chosen name for the hemisphere. 'Colomb' and 'Columbus' were different spellings of the name given to the Genoese explorer who sailed as Admiral under the auspices of the Crown of Castile and Aragon. While the first, 'Colomb,' is the French spelling, 'Columbus' is the Anglicized spelling familiar to English-speaking audiences. By the eighteenth century, both names referenced a new historical figure. This refashioned Colomb/Columbus was separated out from the other Conquistadors of the day. The Admiral from Genoa became a uniquely modern and virtuous genius who embodied a revolutionary vision of global commerce. According to this eighteenth-century version of history, the Admiral was rewarded by the monarchy for his discoveries by being hauled off in chains. This hyperbolic story cursed the Spanish with the original sins of conquest: violence, opprobrium, and ignorance.

Former British North Americans adopted this emerging eighteenth-century historical narrative about Columbus and placed him among the pantheon of founding fathers of the United States of America. In doing so, they reworked British North American history into a new narrative that broke with foundations based solely on British colonialism. The history of the United States avenged the history of the tragic hero, Columbus. This measured distance allowed the United States to assert continued cultural affinity with British cousins while denouncing the opprobrium of monarchical rule, not under the British, but rather under the long-standing enemy, the Spanish. Early republicans in the United States breathed new life into the discoverer of the New World by naming an array of places including cities, rivers, universities, and literary societies after him. The poets who allegorized 'Columbia' from the United States expanded its reach beyond national borders to encompass the entire New World. Several entrepreneurial cosmopolitan actors were enraptured by poetic visions of an expansive geography for Columbia. Rather than seek out an imperialist 'manifest destiny' for the United States, these actors offered an alternate, imaginable if utopian possibility: a federal, hemispheric government with the emerging 'sister republics' to the south.[4]

The connected history of the name 'Colombia' was entangled with the career of a contemporary figure whose life and vision were inspired by the figure of Columbus: the Venezuelan-born, cosmopolitan revolutionary Francisco de Miranda. Miranda fought on the side of the Spanish Monarchy against the British in the Caribbean theater of the American

Revolutionary War. The signing of the Treaty of Paris in 1783 that ended the American Revolution coincided with Miranda's falling out with the Spanish Monarchy. He thus toured the United States from 1783–1784 as an exile at a time when an Anglo-American 'Columbian' identity was in the air. The people he encountered inspired him to take the 'Columbian' project to its logical, continental or 'New World' level. He tirelessly lobbied potential European and American allies—of the North, South, and Caribbean regions—susceptible to the continental, American ideal. Miranda's own persecution at the hands of the Spanish Monarchy further pushed him toward finding ways to transform Spain's continental possessions in the New World into an independent 'Colombia'—the French-inflected, Spanish-language version of the name.

The successes and humiliations that Christopher Columbus supposedly suffered at the hands of the Crown of Castile and Aragon now appeared to prefigure Miranda's own experience as an exile pursued by the Spanish Monarchy for treason. Spurned, Miranda now courted investors in Britain, the United States, and France to back a plan to liberate Spain's America. To do so, Miranda evoked the by then well-known and tragic figure of Columbus through his use of 'Columbia/Colombia' to refer to the continent he wished freed from the Spanish Monarchy. Miranda's remarkable 1790s plan included forceful transfer of Spanish Louisiana to the French Republic. Republican neighbors would facilitate a three-pronged attack on Spain's possessions, with Miranda leading forces on Coro, British forces taking Buenos Aires, and the United States invading Panama. After Napoleon serendipitously reacquired the Louisiana Territory from Spain and then sold it to the United States on the eve of Haiti's independence, the plan was significantly edited. Only Coro and Buenos Aires were attacked. Both these military missions, in turn, ended in utter failure by 1806. Napoleon's occupation of Iberia between 1807 and 1808 nevertheless convinced some investors and mercenaries that Miranda's vision was realizable; timing was key. When Simón Bolívar came calling at Miranda's Grafton Street, London home in 1810, Miranda had gathered the wherewithal to launch Venezuela's First Republic, then only the first component of a greater Colombia.

With the failure of the First Venezuelan Republic in 1812, Bolívar's best survival strategy was to turn Miranda over to the Spanish authorities. As Miranda lay disgraced and dying in a Cadiz prison, some of his acquaintances in the United States, including William Thornton, architect of Washington's Capitol building, put forward a remarkable plan modeled on Miranda's vision. The idea was to create a federated republic uniting North and South Columbia, with Panama as its capital. Not everyone was on board with this plan. Bolívar decided to make Miranda's Colombian project his own, tweaking it for what he understood to be on-the-ground realities. In 1815, as Thornton published his constitution for a hemispheric Columbia and Miranda languished in Cadiz, Bolívar found himself exiled in Jamaica trying to regain momentum for independence. From that British colonial island, Bolívar articulated a vision for world audiences wherein several republics would emerge from Spanish possessions in America. He named one of these Colombia. Colombia would unite the former Captaincy General of Venezuela with the former Viceroyalty of New Granada. The Colombian Republic formed in 1819 and confirmed by constitution in 1821 realized Bolívar's aspirations.

Reducing the scope of the territory encompassed by the name of Colombia did not mean Bolívar had abandoned the continental dream that the name had until then evoked. The Amphictyonic Congress he envisioned for 1826 was modeled on Miranda's vision for a Columbian/Colombian federation with its capital in Panama. The idea now was to bring together representatives of all republics in the hemisphere to address common concerns, highlighting foreign threats and trade opportunities. Modeled on an eighth-century Greek 'league of neighbors' and recognizing the proven value of the Isthmus for connecting the hemisphere, the Congress in Panama would bring to fruition the hemispheric dream of Miranda. Growing controversy over the meaning and implications of hemispheric unity partially explains the difficulties the Colombian Republic's officials encountered with the organization of the Amphictyonic Congress. Bolívar himself was tentative about creating a federation that included the United States, yet he ultimately agreed to do so, despite growing tensions with the republic to the north. Despite the influence of men like Thornton who favored unity and collaboration, others in the United States, especially those who feared that the 'sister republics' would pressure the United States to abolish slavery, were adamantly opposed.

Columbus Decolonizes Columbia, 1770–1785

The historical figure of Christopher Columbus invented in the eighteenth century offered a unique origin myth for the early republican United States and for the rest of the New World. This new Columbus encapsulated the ingenuity, modernity, and individualism required for the discovery of the New World. Columbus also was History's grand martyr, condemned to oblivion by an ignorant and corrupt Spanish Monarchy that refused to recognize his pioneering genius. The Columbia that served as allegory for the United States in the late eighteenth and early nineteenth centuries thus sought to right the wrongs of the Spanish past. It therefore necessarily encompassed a world beyond the United States. The martyr's namesake of 'Columbia' would serve as an 'Empire of Liberty' free from the monarchical ignorance that had destroyed Columbus and condemned the land he 'discovered' to tyranny, slavery, and abuse.[5] Because the imperial tyrant in the story was Spain and not Britain, this new Anglo Columbia would not negate continued cultural ties to Britannia. Rather than seek to decolonize its colonial culture, the United States would maintain close, if tense, relations with the British until the onset of the Civil War.[6]

The first to invent the historical character of a modern genius for Columbus were neither the British nor the Americans but the French philosophes.[7] Drawing upon sixteenth-century Black Legend accounts that were highly critical of Spain and its Empire, the French philosophes offered a heroically tragic picture of the man they called 'Colomb.' In the sixteenth century several writers, most notably the Admiral himself, his son, and Bartolomé de las Casas sought to link the designs of Divine Providence to the Admiral's name. 'Ypo Ferens' or 'Christoferens,' as the Admiral was reportedly baptized, meant 'bearer of Christ.' Columba, the Latin word for 'dove,' spelled 'colombe' in French, was used to associate the Admiral with the Holy Spirit. Later, eighteenth-century philosophes refashioned the providential ring of the Admiral's name to serve a new teleology: Colomb's unique contribution to modernity as discoverer of the New World and victim of Spanish cruelty and ignorance.

Guillaume Thomas François Raynal (1712–1796), better known as the Abbé Raynal, brought together an array of collaborators and contributors, most notably Denis Diderot, to produce what came to be one of the most widely read books in the Republic of Letters: the *Histoire philosophique des établissements et du commerce des Européens dans les deux Indes*, generally referred to as *Histoire des deux Indes*.[8] The first edition printed in Amsterdam is dated 1770, and was published in French in six volumes. It identified the historical figure and significance of Christophe Colomb as

> Un homme obscur, plus avancé que son siecle dans la connoissance de l'astronomie & de la navigation, sembloit veiller à l'agrandissement de l'Espagne. Christophe Colomb sentoit comme par instinct, qu'il devoit y avoir un autre continent, & que c'étoit à lui de le découvrir. Les Antipodes, que la raison même traitoit de chimere, & la superstition d'erreur & d'impiété étoit aux yeux de cet homme de génie, une vérité incontestable.[9]

In the hands of Diderot and Raynal, Colomb became a unique individual who bravely challenged commonly held yet erroneous ideas about the world. Raynal underscored how gatekeepers to the Spanish monarchs 'le traiterent long-temps avec cette hauteur insultante que les hommes communs, quand ils sont en place, ont pour les hommes de génie.'[10] Only Colomb's enthusiasm, perseverance and courage, joined with the arts of prudence and management, would finally win over the doubting handlers of the Catholic Monarchs of Castile and Aragon.

The French Enlightenment narrative of Colomb's 'discovery' of the New World ultimately pitted the rational, enthusiastic, prudent genius of the Genovese Colomb against the incompetence, indolence, capriciousness, and barbarity of his Spanish contemporaries. In short, Colomb was the brave individual 'qui avoit ajouté aux yeux de l'Europe étonnée, une quatrieme partie à la terre, ou plutôt une moitié du monde à ce globe si long-tems dévasté & si peu connu.'[11] Raynal and Diderot call upon their readers to react with surprise and outrage at the fact that Colomb never enjoyed public gratitude for his astounding discovery. Instead, Americ Vespuce, a Florentine 'quoiqu'il ne fit que suivre les traces d'un homme dont le nom doit être placé au-dessus des plus grands noms' was honored as namesake for the New World.[12] For Raynal and his co-authors, the injustice Colomb suffered could be considered a 'présage fatal de toutes celles dont ce malheureux pays devoit être le théâtre.'[13] Colomb's sorry fate was thus transfigured into a harbinger of the fate that the New World would suffer under Spanish rule.

The *Histoire des Deux Indies* remarkable popularity (48 editions) set the stage for subsequent historical works that sought to create a modern, tragic hero out of a Colomb who cried out for redemption.[14] In the 1780s alone over 100,000 copies were in circulation throughout the world.[15] In the United States by 1795 sales totaled roughly 25,000 copies, making it one of the bestselling works of its time.[16] Raynal and his collaborators produced two subsequent editions in 1774 and 1780 that introduced substantial changes to the text, but the narrative on Columb remained stable.

Scottish historian William Robertson's *History of America*, originally published in London in 1777, echoed Raynal in its portrayal of the unique, lone genius who faced the 'obstinacy of ignorance but with what is still more intractable, the pride of false knowledge.'[17] Writing in English, Robertson followed a long tradition that had Anglicized the Admiral's name as Christopher Columbus. Robertson cast Columbus' parents as an honorable, but poor family of seafarers who recognized their son's unique curiosity and fomented his love of learning through lessons in Latin, geometry, cosmography, astronomy, and drawing.[18] Robertson's mature Columbus was much like the man described by Raynal: an intrepid, enterprising, ambitious, modest yet enthusiastic genius who wished to test his theory of reaching India by sailing west. Early negotiations between Columbus and several European monarchs describe the Admiral as patient, courteous, circumspect, and irreproachable in his morals, and 'exemplary in his attention to all the duties and functions of religion.'[19] These qualities of character superseded the humble origins of Columbus, and for Robertson they explained why Columbus won the respect of the Crown of Castile and Aragon. Robertson also echoed the injustice served upon Columbus described by Raynal, lamenting how,

> By the universal consent of nations, AMERICA is the name bestowed on this new quarter of the globe. The bold pretensions of a fortunate impostor have robbed the discoverer of the New World of a distinction which belonged to him. The name of Amerigo has supplanted that of Columbus; and mankind may regret an act of injustice, which, having received the sanction of time, it is now too late to redress.[20]

At the very least then, Columbus' name demanded recognition. Poets and writers in the fledgling United States saw a way to honor the tragic Columbus through the allegorical female figure of Columbia, a poetic name that rhymed with Britannia and carried the same number of syllables. Columbia would come to represent a new presence in the world, one that promised freedom, virtue, and scientific ingenuity.

Joel Barlow's *The Vision of Columbus* was among the first poems penned in the United States that offered a new history for 'the life and character of that great man, whose extraordinary genius led him to the discovery of the continent, and whose singular sufferings ought to excite the indignation of the world.'[21] Concerned that Robertson's history had yet to reach broad audiences in America, Barlow disseminated the Scot's history lessons on Columbus through poetry.[22] As Steven Blakemore has recently argued, Barlow sought to convey in poetic language the progressive drive of a history that produced an American Revolution that promised a utopian future of republican ideas and institutions.[23] The American Revolution became in Barlow's hands an evolving phenomenon that would free the world. And notably for Barlow, Columbia was not limited to the United States.

By 1807, as Napoleon's troops invaded Iberia, Barlow's famous poem was revised, significantly expanded, and shorn of any allusions to the critical role that the French Monarchy had played in New World independence. The poem was renamed 'The Columbiad.' Barlow's poetry produced a redeemed Columbus who enjoyed a God's-eye view of his legacy, one encompassing the entire Western Hemisphere. Columbus' postmortem consciousness took in the New World from the Orinoco, which 'checks great ocean's wave' to Quito's plains that 'o'erlook their proud Peru,' to the Darien's isthmus checking 'the raging tide' and onward to where 'Ontario hears his Laurence roar,' where the 'tenfold Alleghanies meet the day,' and finally 'Where Maine's bleak breakers line the dangerous coast.' This New World, gazed upon by the Mariner, was none other than 'Columbia, from thy patriarch name.' Barlow's romantic Columbus sheds tears when, from beyond the grave, he overhears how 'In quest of peace great Montezuma stands, A sovereign supplicant with lifted hands, Brings all his treasure, yields the regal sway . . . But treasures, tears and scepters plead in vain.' Lamenting the suffering unleashed by Cortes, Columbus asks for divine forgiveness, and Hesper whispers in his ear that his labors have not been in vain. The American Revolution would undo the damages done and free the world that Columbus had called into being.[24]

Barlow was by no means the first to use the anglicized term 'Columbia' to refer to the New World. The first known recorded instance emerged in the *Gentleman's Magazine* in the 1730s as part of a playful and poetic critique of Britannia's control over New World possessions. By the late eighteenth century, the name of Columbia began to resonate. During and in the wake of the American Revolution, Kings College in New York became Columbia University. An array of cultural magazines adopted the name of Columbia in their titles. The capital of the new republic bore the names of its two founding fathers, Washington and Columbus. Robert Gray's discovery and naming of the Columbia River staked out the territorial claims the United States made on the Pacific Northwest.[25] In 1776, African American poet Phillis Wheatley was among the first to use the allegory of Columbia to refer to the newly independent republic, anticipating Barlow by nearly a decade.[26] In short, as the American Revolution was consummated, 'Columbia' became an alternative name for the United States of America, and yet it also pointed to something far greater. Bartisik-Vélez has argued that these representations of Columbus made him an appealing figure for an early Anglo-American republic bent on expansion into Spanish territories.[27] However, for a short but significant period, roughly from 1780s until about 1819, rather than an Anglo-Saxon Columbia imperiously taking over Spanish America, several cosmopolitan actors from North and South America envisioned a sisterhood of republics embraced by a continental, federalized Columbia/Colombia.

Miranda's Continental Colombia

In 1783, Francisco de Miranda fled the Caribbean theater of the American Revolution after allegedly disobeying orders from his Spanish commander, Bernardo de Galvez, for joining his superior, General Juan Manuel Cajigal y Odoardo, in defeating the British at New Providence Island in the Bahamas. Although the naval victory was clear, the maneuver had diverted forces from Galvez's plan to attack the British stronghold of Jamaica. Galvez's obsession with launching a strategic attack on Jamaica reflected an anxiety plaguing Spanish officials after 1779, when the Spanish Crown decided to aid the United States in the American Revolutionary War. The Crown worried the British would seek revenge by using their presence in the Caribbean to instigate rebellion in Hispanic dominions. News about the rebellions raging along the Andes in South America from 1780–1783 fanned fears of British involvement. Governor Galvez came to see the taking down of Jamaica as of paramount importance. Francisco de Miranda, who spoke English fluently and had himself brokered a cushy commercial deal with British officials and merchants in Jamaica, also understood the strategic value of that island. The British ultimately valued Jamaica much more than the 13 colonies of continental North America. These circumstances suggest Miranda and Cajigal may have had their own reasons for launching an attack on New Providence Island in the Bahamas, diverting forces away from Jamaica. Galvez was furious, charging Miranda with treason.

With letters of recommendation in hand and resentment at his recent persecution fresh in his mind, Miranda left Cuba for the United States.

From June 1783 until December 1784, Miranda encountered the continental, republican 'Columbia' conjured by historians, poets, and scholars. The people he met included Phyllis Wheatley, the African-American poet who had allegorized the United States as 'Columbia' in 1776.[28] Miranda also met with the leaders of Yale, Brown, Harvard, Dartmouth, and Kings College, the last of which had been renamed Columbia by stipulation of the New York State Legislature on May 1, 1784.[29] The friendships Miranda struck up in the United States during this period included 'the famous poet John Trumbull, author of the poem 'McFingal,' 'The Progress of Dulness,' and other works in the [Hudibraico] style, which bring him unbounded honor.'[30] Although Miranda's diary of travels through the United States does not mention meeting the poet Joel Barlow, it does effusively describe his long literary conversations with John Trumbull. At the time of this fortuitous meeting, Trumbull had just returned from a trip to Philadelphia with his good friend and fellow 'Hartford wit,' Joel Barlow where they tried to secure federal copyright protections on their work.[31] By then, Barlow had developed a draft version of *Vision of Columbus*, which he delivered during the conferral of his Master of Arts degree in 1781.[32] As Barlow struggled for recognition of his epic poem, another Hartford wit, Timothy Dwight, penned the verses to his song, 'Columbia,' in 1777. Dwight published these verses in 1783, as Miranda toured the United States. Dwight's verses created a place inspired by a Columbus who now represented science, freedom, and virtue.

> Columbia, Columbia to glory arise
> The queen of the world, and the child of the skies!
> Thy genius commands thee; with rapture behold,
> While ages on ages thy splendors unfold.
> Thy reign is the last, and noblest of time,
> Most fruitful thy soil, most inviting thy clime;
> Let the crimes of the East ne'er encrimson thy name,
> Be freedom, and science, and virtue, thy fame.[33]

Columbia was thus shorn of the crimes of the East, offering pure virtue, science, and freedom to the world. Miranda, whose vast library included several books on Columbus, including two copies of William Robertson's *History of America*, would have been sympathetic to this emerging Columbian vision for the Western Hemisphere.[34]

The social circles Miranda plugged into while in the United States proved fortuitous for his personal needs and political aspirations. Historians have long noted how Miranda's letters of introduction allowed him to hold meetings with the highest echelons of American society, including George Washington, Henry Knox, and Alexander Hamilton. Less well-known, yet nevertheless important figures proved essential for Miranda's livelihood and very survival. Not only did Joel Barlow later rent to Miranda his London abode from June 1789 to September 1791, he also saved Miranda from the French guillotine in 1793 when he was tried for treason against the French Republic.³⁵ In short, Miranda's tour of the United States brought him into the company of people who envisioned a liberated, republican Columbian ideal that was continental in scope and included Spain's possessions in the New World. This vision proved contagious.

Once on the other side of the Atlantic and closely pursued by agents of the Spanish Monarchy, Miranda developed an important relationship with the sympathetic court of the Russian Empress Catherine the Great. Miranda recorded in his diary his long conversations with Catherine II, noting how, when he mentioned to her that Robertson's *History of America* was prohibited from circulating in the Spanish dominions, she exclaimed that for such an insult the entire Spanish Academy ought to be consigned to the Inquisition.³⁶ The Empress clearly was familiar with Robertson's history. She also seemed familiar with the Inquisition, an institution that by then had become synonymous with Spanish suppression of ideas through torture. Catherine the Great believed Miranda innocent and oppressed, not unlike the genius Columbus that Robertson and others had eulogized. The positive impression Miranda left in Russia transferred easily back to Edinburgh via the letters of introduction Miranda obtained there. From Dr. Guthrie, British surgeon in Russian service to Dr. Dunchan of Edinburgh, we see clearly the extent to which Miranda's reputation was staked on the Black Legend of an obscurantist and inquisitional Spanish Monarchy, a legend cultivated by her imperial rivals:

> Permit me to introduce to your acquaintance a most liberal and enlightened Traveler from a part of the Globe where you would least expect, a Mexican nobleman who in spite of every gothic barrier to knowledge which the Holly tribunal can invent has found secret means to come at it and now travels for additional instruction.³⁷

En route to Edinburgh, Miranda was warmly received by King Gustavus III of Sweden, where he visited Masonic temples and, despite efforts to remain incognito, made the headlines.³⁸ A Dutch gazette noted how Spanish diplomats in Sweden had received a direct order from Madrid to arrest a certain 'Count Miranda,' who it was said was a Spaniard by birth in the service of Russia, suspected of high treason.³⁹ Miranda deftly turned the Crown's persecution in his favor by amplifying existing prejudices toward Spain. Miranda refused to turn himself in, claiming that the noble purpose of his travels was 'to remove certain absurd prejudices resulting from his defective education' under Spanish tyranny.⁴⁰

Miranda's travels seeking refuge from persecution increasingly radicalized his position against the Monarchy. Letters and diary entries regarding Miranda's meeting with Prince Charles of Hesse dated March 1788 reveal how Miranda wedded his plan to overthrow Spanish rule in America with the mythic figure of Colomb/Columbus. They also suggest that by doing so Miranda was plugging into existing expectations and understandings of what 'Columbia,' or, in this case, 'Colombia' could mean as a providential place in the world. Miranda recorded in his diary the favorable predictions that the Prince of Hesse gave for the liberating endeavor Miranda proposed. Miranda's papers also include his notable letter to Prince Hesse penned in French that national historiographies often refer to as Colombia's birth certificate, for it is the first document that refers to Spanish America by the name 'Colombia.' Miranda, graciously indebted to the Prince, wrote in French 'Si l'Horoscope favorable que la coeur genereux de votre A. voulut bien former pour la malheureuse *Colombia*, pourroit jamais avoir lieu, je ne manquerois pas de lui communiquer des Nouvelles.'[41]

In any case, Miranda's Francophile marriage of the persecuted genius Admiral 'Colomb' to Spanish America via 'Colombia' proved auspicious. The horoscope Prince Charles Landegrave de Hesse gave the region predicted that Miranda's cause would be fulfilled within 8 to 10 years, and he wholeheartedly embraced the justice of the cause.[42] Such portents from the Hessian prince were encouraging. After all, when Miranda was in the United States, he had learned of the critical role Hessian troops played in the American Revolution.

Miranda's plan for a sprawling, republican Colombia with Panama as its capital emerged in the early 1790s when he courted investors and imperial agents for the cause. Miranda's decision to join the cause of the French Revolution, for instance, was staked on the promise that republican France would aide in the liberation of Spanish America. This scenario encouraged Miranda to pursue a strategy that would include turning over Spanish Louisiana to France.[43] A violent French take over of Louisiana with the help of the republican United States would wrest the supply chain of New Orleans away from the Spanish Monarchy, ensuring the success of coordinated, surgical attacks on Panama, Coro in Venezuela, and Buenos Aires in Argentina. This plan likely emerged out of Miranda's experiences fighting on the Spanish side against the British in the American Revolution. His on-the-ground expertise of Spanish supply chains and lines of defense and attack convinced an array of French functionaries and investors, most notably the French ambassador to the United States, Edmond-Charles Genêt.

In the wake of the Tupac Amaru II rebellion and the Comunero revolt in the Andes in the 1780s, Miranda convincingly argued that discontented South Americans would welcome an auxiliary naval and military force that could facilitate the formation of an independent government. Miranda was himself purveyor of information on these rebellions that the Spanish Monarchy worked so hard to keep under wraps. Miranda likely learned of the revolts from his mentor, Cajigal, who received the 'happy news' of the capture and imminent execution of Tupac Amaru via the Viceroy of New Granada in July 1781 when serving as Governor of

Cuba.[44] Prominent diplomats and leaders with whom Miranda shared his plan to liberate Spain's possessions in the New World included men such as General Knox of the US military, US diplomat John Turnbull, and British Prime Minister William Pitt. They were interested, to say the least. After unfurling maps of the Western Hemisphere for William Pitt, demonstrating the plan of attack, the Prime Minister was enthralled and begged Miranda for more information on the Tupac Amaru and Comunero rebellions in South America.[45]

The state Miranda proposed to liberate and establish was far-reaching. It would be bounded on the 'East by [the] Atlantic coastline, the Brazilian and Guianan boundaries and the Mississippi River'; on the North, by the '45 degree parallel from [the] source of [the] Mississippi to Pacific Ocean'; and on the West by the 'Pacific coast . . . south to Cape Horn.' It would also include the 'Islands within 10 degrees [of the] Western coast [of the] jurisdiction of [this] vast state.' And finally, to the 'East, only Cuba.'[46] The name for this sprawling swath of territory had yet to be finalized, and Miranda experimented with variations depending on the audience. While South America tended to dominate Miranda's exchanges with the British in the 1790s, the term Columbia/Colombia also offered a useful reference in his conversations with them. When negotiating with potential investors and allies in the United States and in Spanish America, Miranda's use of Columbia/Colombia increased significantly.[47]

Miranda's flexibility in naming this new polity was matched by his flexibility in terms of the type of government that would rule it, at least in the early 1790s. The conflict between Britain and Spain over colonizing the northeast corner of North America at Nootka Sound in 1790 seemed to augur well for Miranda's plan.[48] At this early stage, Miranda was open to the possibility of adapting a British model of constitutional monarchy to the South American setting via Quechua nomenclature, which he drew from the classical account of Inca Garcilaso de la Vega, *Los Comentarios Reales de los Incas*, which was widely read both in Spanish (a revised edition was published in Madrid in 1723) and in highly abridged translations on both sides of the Atlantic. The two chiefs of the Executive branch would be known as 'Incas,' while elected provincial assembly leaders would be called 'Curacas' (Quechua for hereditary chiefs and governors). Ordinary legislators would be called 'Amautas' (the Quechua term for learned men), and the supreme military leader would be the 'Hatunapa,' or 'great captain.'[49] British investors and politicians seemed open to a constitutional monarchy even if headed by authorities royally wrapped in Inca authority.

For the increasingly radicalized French republicans, Miranda tweaked the plan. He convinced several cosmopolitan republicans that the French reacquisition of the Louisiana territory ceded to Spain in the wake of the Seven Year's War would further the cause of liberty. The Republic of France would, after all, share a border with the new, federal Republic of the United States. Attempts to expand France into the New World would reinvigorate Old World France's own republican institutions by diminishing the centralizing grasp of Paris. Genet, inspired by Miranda, promoted the Louisiana plan while serving as French ambassador to the United States. Miranda's associates, who included Stephen Sayre, Gilbert Imlay, and Joel Barlow, worked to raise a Franco-American force in the Ohio Valley that would sail down the Mississippi to capture New Orleans.[50] George Rogers Clark would lead another troop to help loosen Spain's hold on Louisiana, Florida, and Mexico.

Despite significant investment in the scheme to retake Louisiana, plans never got off the ground. One problem was that the French Revolution was growing increasingly radicalized. After Louis XVI was beheaded for treason in 1793, England sought to attract Spain in a coalition of forces against France. Relations were tense at best between the two powers, and an attack on Spanish dominions in America at the time proved unwise. Miranda's best hope for financial and political support for a coordinated takeover of Louisiana and attack on Spain from the French side was in the Girondin faction's (a moderate republican group) continued dominance of the National Convention. General Dumouriez' defeat at Neewinden marked the beginning of the decline of the Girondin's influence in the French National Convention. Growing French radicalization caused several Girondin to flee France or suffer the guillotine. On the other side of the Atlantic, Genet's overaggressive efforts to rally US support for an attack on the Ohio River Valley further undermined the plan. US leaders feared they would compromise their official stance of neutrality vis-à-vis Spain if they engaged in this attack. Seven years, the rise of Napoleon, and the dramatic escalation of the slave insurrection in Saint Domingue would have to pass before Miranda's geopolitical calculations could inadvertently come to fruition. Seeking to regain control over France's most prized colonial possession, Napoleon negotiated with Spain the transfer of Louisiana back to the French, as he sent 60,000 troops to Saint Domingue under the command of his brother-in-law, Charles Leclerc. By 1803 these efforts had come to naught. Napoleon cut his losses by offering French Louisiana to the United States at a bargain price. President Jefferson accepted the deal, nearly doubling the territorial reach of the United States.

Amidst these dramatic geopolitical transformations, Miranda found himself on the wrong end of another treason trial, this time in France.[51] The same General Dumouriez who had defected to the Austrian side now accused Miranda of treason against the French Republic. To escape the guillotine, Miranda's anti-monarchical and pro-republican credentials needed to be airtight. The American poet Joel Barlow, whose republican credentials were impeccable, eloquently defended Miranda. Republican friends in Britain also came to his defense. Miranda was freed. The experience appears to have consolidated Miranda's vision of 'freeing' the New

World from Spanish Monarchy and turning it toward republicanism. As the freed Miranda made his way back to London, Saint Domingue's revolt became openly anti-colonial, winning independence in January of 1804.

By August Miranda found himself back in London, where he scrambled to convince British patrons that the time was ripe for attack. He contacted British mapmaker William Faden to build the cartographic arsenal he needed to plot a coordinated attack on South America. The attack would include Commodore Sir Home Riggs Popham, Prime Minister William Pitt, Henry Dundas, and Lord Melville, who served as the political head of the Royal Navy at the time.[52] Lord Melville guaranteed Miranda that if the expedition went forward its only purpose would be to assure the independence of South America.[53] Miranda took what he could get, despite obvious interests on the part of the British to expand its trade in the region while also seeking viable maritime routes that could facilitate its growing colonial presence in India. In this regard, Buenos Aires offered an intriguing South Atlantic route. With the US republic expanding exponentially and Haiti asserting its independence from France, the time seemed ripe for a British-supported overthrow of Spanish rule in the New World. Miranda's 1790s plan for a three-pronged attack nevertheless had lost one of its prongs by 1804 when the United States rejected the invitation to send a naval expedition to Panama. Miranda was left to coordinate a maritime attack on Coro with Popham commanding the siege of Buenos Aires.

Despite official rejection by the United States of Miranda's plan, unofficial excitement and collaboration with Miranda surely existed. Upon arriving at New York on November 9, 1805, Miranda traveled down the Eastern Seaboard to meet with many of his acquaintances made during his 1780s tour. These meetings included Aaron Burr, who had his own plans for revolution in Louisiana and the West.[54] By December of 1805, Miranda had surreptitiously met with President Jefferson and Secretary of State James Madison. Miranda claimed tacit approval, which seems to be confirmed given that his outfit sailed on with weapons, munitions, and several American mercenaries. Two weeks before setting off to Venezuela, Miranda sent Jefferson a geographical treatise on Chile with a note of thanks for 'the happy predictions that you pronounced on the luck that *our* beloved Colombia will surely have in our times.'[55]

On March 24, 1806, the Colombian ideal turned openly militant on Haitian shores. After arriving on the *Leander* to the newly independent nation that abolished slavery, Miranda hoisted the new tricolor Colombian flag, thereby making clear his intention to liberate all Spanish America. Haitian presses agreed to print 2,000 copies of five different texts, each promising to recover 'our glory as Colombian Americans.' Miranda then held a swearing-in ceremony in Jacmel, Haiti, which required all volunteers to take an oath of loyalty to 'the army of Colombia.' The volunteers swore

> to be true and faithful to the free people of South America, independent of Spain and to serve them honestly and faithfully against all their enemies or opposers whatsoever and to observe and obey the orders of the supreme government of that country legally appointed, and the orders of the General and his officers sent by them.[56]

Many of these recruits were US citizens. Miranda, however, was not asking them to renounce their American citizenship. On the contrary, the oath they took included a clause clarifying that their actions on behalf of Colombia were evidence of American allegiance.[57]

After raising the Colombian flag at La Vela de Coro, Miranda distributed handkerchiefs with portraits of Popham, who was on his way to liberate Buenos Aires. Other handkerchiefs boasted images of George Washington and of Miranda himself. Christopher Columbus made it onto flags with British colors, signaling ties to the British who helped sponsor liberation.[58] These Anglophile images together with the piles of printed broadsides and declarations Miranda produced for this Colombian enterprise made explicit the transatlantic and hemispheric roots of the endeavor. Despite these efforts on behalf of a continental Colombian ideal, Miranda's mission was by all accounts a disaster. Spanish colonial authorities had long been privy of Miranda's plans, and the fighting itself yielded little more for Miranda's Colombian army than casualties due to disease or friendly fire.[59] Sir Home Popham's 1806 attack on Buenos Aires, on the other hand, initially met with some success and approval by a surprised King George III who immediately recognized the value of trade with a Buenos Aires under British control.[60]

Nevertheless, by the following year, and despite reinforcements, the British were forced to withdraw from Buenos Aires. Despite these failed attacks, the Colombian ideal was not yet dead. If anything, the problem was one of timing. In 1807, as Napoleon set his sights on Iberia, Miranda returned to London with renewed vigor. Upon arrival, he found that mapmaker William Faden had commemorated the continental ideal with a map entitled 'Colombia Prima or South America' (Figure 3.1).

Miranda thus built on this growing effervescence in London and set his sights on developing a print culture that would support a continental Colombian ideal. As the printing press rolled out Miranda's newspaper, *El Colombiano*, in 1810, spreading information about the effects of the abdication of the Spanish Kings at Bayonne, Caracas officials deemed Miranda a persona non grata.[61] They gave a young Simón Bolívar, one of the diplomats from the Caracas junta, direct orders that he not contact Miranda. What Caracas officials sought was continued loyalty to Ferdinand VII while asserting autonomy given the dire circumstances of the Spanish abdication to Napoleon at Bayonne. Bolívar ignored these.

Figure 3.1 Colombia Prima or South America. William Faden and Louis Stanislas d'Arcy de la Rochette (London, 1807).

Source: Reproduced with permission of David Rumsey Map Collection.

After a thrilling visit with Miranda, Bolívar was convinced independence was the best path forward. The *Morning Chronicle* printed Bolívar's invocation for the need for complete independence from Spain, not just for Venezuela, but for all American peoples. 'El día, que no está lejos, en que los venezolanos . . . alzarán definitivamente la bandera de la independencia y declararán la Guerra a España. Tampoco descuidarán de invitar a todos los pueblos de América a que se unan en confederación.'[62] Taken with Miranda's vision and connections in London, Bolívar invited Miranda to return to Venezuela once more. The return proved auspicious, culminating in the formation of the First Republic of Venezuela.

The new congress voted in favor of complete, unconditional independence from Spain and passed a new constitution on December 21, 1811. Within the articles of that document, we see how Miranda convinced fellow Venezuelans to consider forming alliances with other places on the Colombian/Columbian continent:

> In like manner and under the same principles [of union among the Venezuelan Provinces], shall be admitted and incorporated, any other of the provinces of the Columbian continent, (before Spanish America) which may be desirous of uniting therewith, under the necessary conditions and guarantees, in order to strengthen the union, by the addition and connexion of their integral parts.[63]

The English-language passage above translated Article 129, Chapter 5 of the Spanish-language constitution, one that renamed Spanish America the 'continente colombiano.' By 1810, Columbia and Colombia referred to the same thing: a Spanish American continent that nevertheless would be new in the world because of its independence from Spain. Changes in spelling reflected linguistic differences, yet they also suggested possible alliances with other republics in the Columbian continent, perhaps North American Columbia itself.

The passage above also reveals how Miranda continued his emphasis on print culture for ensuring the success of independence for the entire Colombian/Columbian continent, not just Venezuela. London was happy to oblige. In 1812, London printers translated and published Venezuela's declaration of independence, constitution, and other related documents.[64] Miranda then drew on his arsenal of valuable printed documents, including the Faden map of 'Colombia Prima, or, South America.' As Miranda fought on the Venezuelan front, he sent his friend and collaborator, José Cortes de Madarriaga, as a diplomat to the Reino de Santafé de Bogotá (New Granada) with a copy of the 1807 'Colombia Prima' map. Madarriaga was welcomed as a diplomat. On May 28, 1811, Jorge Tadeo Lozano and Madarriaga signed a Treaty of Alliance and Federation. By October, both states ratified the treaty. The treaty stipulated that the two formed co-states within a General Confederation, each with equal rights and representation that would be extended to any other state that joined them.⁶⁵ The gift of the map of Colombia Prima was welcomed as a show of that union. The stage was set for a growing confederation of independent states within the Colombian continent. The problem was that New Granada was not yet ready to declare independence outright. That, and the fall of Venezuela's First Republic brought this initial confederation to a standstill.

The First Republic of Venezuela was supposed to be the first of many Colombian republics. Although more successful than Miranda's Coro invasion, Miranda realized surrender was the only option after patriot forces suffered a devastating military defeat. As Miranda tried escaping back to London after signing an armistice with the Spanish, Bolívar turned on Miranda. Much like the Anglophile imagination's martyred Columbus, Miranda was now dragged off by the Spanish in chains from his beloved Colombia.

The uncertain situation of Venezuela's military and political situation, which culminated in its eventual defeat, caused several of Miranda's admirers, including Bolívar, to lose faith in the Generalissimo. Still, political events on both sides of the Atlantic allowed the dream of a continental federated Columbia/Colombia to live on. Despite Miranda's arrest, the idea of including the United States in a continental Colombia/Columbia still resonated with some friends of Miranda in Philadelphia, including the West Indian architect William Thornton. In the meantime, Simón Bolívar refashioned and downsized Miranda's Colombia. The fledgling Colombian Republic was nevertheless still grand in scale, encompassing most of the northwest corner of South America and the Isthmus of Panama. Bolívar continued to strive for a hemispheric republican unity of purpose, with Colombia leading the way. And although he may have been reticent about including the United States in this continental project, the northern republic inspired by 'Columbia' was nevertheless invited to participate.

If William Thornton (1795–1828) is remembered today at all, it is for designing the Capitol building in Washington D.C. Thornton hailed from Tortola Island (British Virgin Islands) where his family owned a sprawling plantation complex. He engaged in an impressive array of scientific, artistic, medical, and technological activities, but never received any formal education as an architect.⁶⁶ Instead, he was trained in England as a medical doctor. Despite Thornton's lack of formal training, his designs for the Capitol were chosen because, unlike those of his competitors, he forcefully developed the architectural implications of republicanism. Drawing inspiration from the Pantheon in Rome and the east front of the Louvre in Paris, the magnificent building, even while it was still under construction, caught the attention of travelers who remarked that it was the only building in Washington D.C. 'worthy to be noticed.'⁶⁷

On August 24, 1814, British troops set fire to Thornton's temple of republicanism. The effect was terrifying yet, in a way, inspiring. A flame of republican patriotism was ignited in the United States; a renewed sense of hemispheric republican unity emerged in its wake.⁶⁸ Newspapers in the

United States reported celebrations and toasts to the health of Spanish American independence leaders. These fellow Americans were fighting for the noble cause of New World republicanism against the tyranny of corrupt, Old World monarchy.[69] Thornton's 'Outlines of a Constitution for United North and South Columbia' crystalized these sentiments.

Thornton's proposed constitution circulated privately between 1800 and 1815, and the circuits of its circulation suggest a tense and shifting relationship with the original champion of a 'Colombian' hemisphere, Francisco de Miranda. The content of Thornton's continental constitution reveals remarkable parallels with Miranda's 1790s plan for a liberated continent. Consider how both plans adopted Incan nomenclature for leadership positions within the hemispheric Columbian federation. Thornton explained to his readers in 1815 how he had shared an earlier draft with a person 'in whom the worthy patriots of Caracas since confided.' The statement is a clear allusion to Miranda, but Miranda was not the only person with ties to Spanish America with whom Thornton shared the document. Late in 1810, as Miranda sailed once again for Venezuela with Simón Bolívar, Thornton had established contact with young Spanish Americans from Caracas, including Simón Bolívar's brother, Juan Vicente Bolívar, and his companion, Telésforo de Orea. The two men were received by James Monroe, and according to reports, they held several meetings with Thornton.[70] By then, Miranda had returned to Venezuela and helped mobilize the Caracas Council toward full declaration of independence. By the time Thornton published his version of a continental constitution for a united North and South Columbia, however, the First Venezuelan Republic had surrendered to the Spanish and Miranda lay dying in a prison in Cádiz.

While Thornton tried reviving Miranda's united North and South Columbia plan to audiences from Philadelphia in 1815, Simón Bolívar found himself exiled on the British island colony of Jamaica, where he sought to revive foreign support for independence. Bolívar penned a letter addressed to 'a Gentleman of this Island [Jamaica]' analyzing the status of the independence struggle. In this letter Bolívar evoked the Black Legend, anti-Hispanic narratives cultivated by French philosophes that cast Columbus as a tragic hero of tyranny and ignorance. ' "Three centuries ago," you say, "the atrocities committed by the Spaniards on this great hemisphere of Columbus began." '[71] Such French Enlightenment ideas about Colomb made their way onto printed maps as late as 1819. French mapmaker Lapie invoked 'Colombie' for North America in 1819 (Figure 3.2). Colombia had resonated globally as a term for the entire continent of America. Yet by 1819, the same year Lapie's map was printed, Colombia began to refer to a specific republic within South America, one originally envisioned by Bolívar in 1815 that encompassed a remarkably large swath of territory.

Bolívar invoked the history of Colomb/Columbus and his mistreatment at the hands of the Spanish Monarchy in part because by 1815

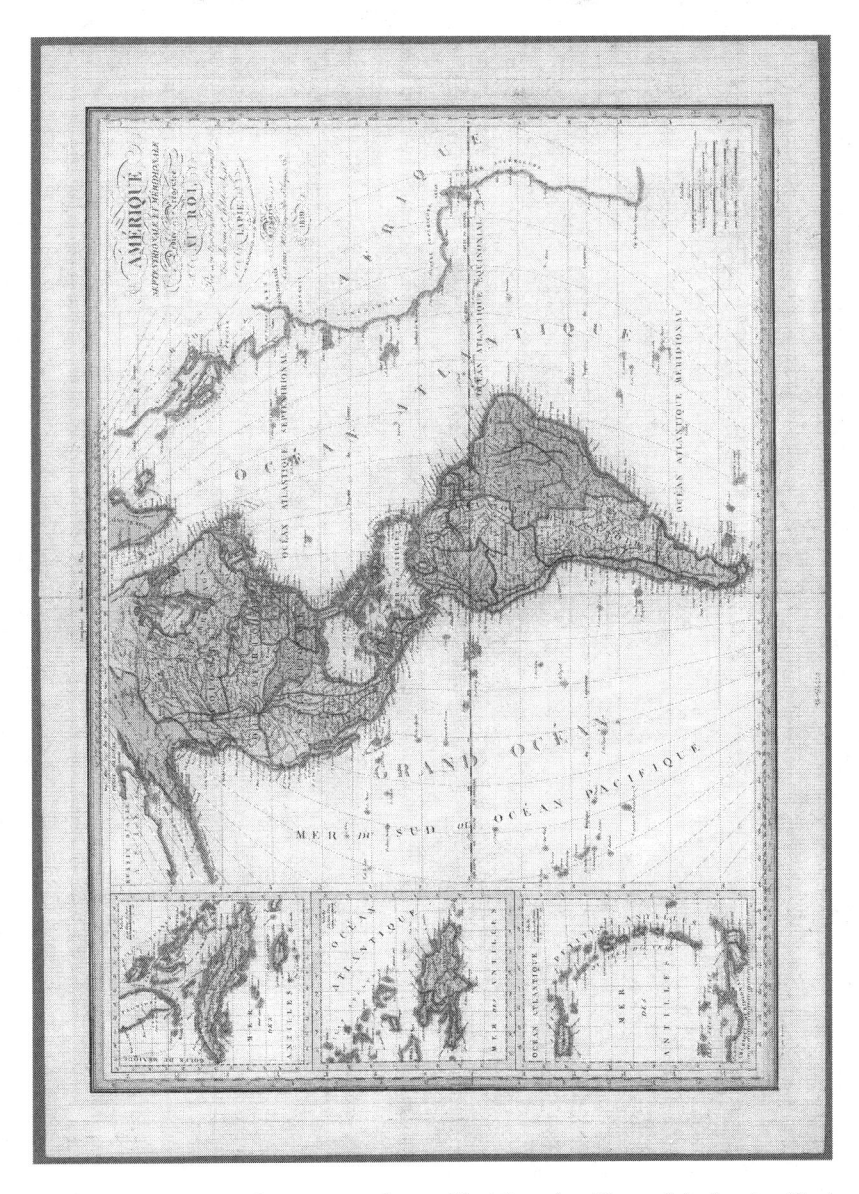

Figure 3.2 Amerique Septentrionale et Meridionale. Pierre M. Lapie (Paris, 1819).

Source: Reproduced with permission of David Rumsey Map Collection.

it was a well-worn, international trope. Unlike Miranda or Thornton, however, Bolívar argued that the entire New World could not 'at the moment, be organized as a great republic.'[72] Bolívar experienced the internal divisions that led to the failure of Venezuela's First Republic, and so understood that bringing all of America under a single government would not work. Bolívar also underscored how monarchy was anathema for the New World due to a king's constant desire to increase possessions, wealth, and authority through warfare and conquest. Bolívar reasoned that 'the Americans, being anxious for peace, science, art, commerce, and agriculture, would prefer republics to kingdoms.' He also presciently warned that any efforts by any one republic to conquer their neighbors would be 'directly contrary to the principles of justice, which characterize republican systems; and, what is more, they are in direct opposition to the interests of their citizens, because a state, too large of itself or together with its dependencies, ultimately falls into decay. Its free government becomes a tyranny.' The scale of republicanism therefore mattered. Small republics were distinctive for their permanence. Larger republics tended toward empire.

Bolívar thereby rejected Miranda and Thornton's idea that the Isthmus of Panama, the most central point of the continent, could serve as the 'parent' country for the whole continent, that is, its commanding capital. What would work, according to Bolívar, was dividing the continent up into several mutually independent republics. And yet, despite his dire warnings against large-scale republicanism, Bolívar nevertheless waxed poetic when considering a single republic for the New World. His 1815 reflections on confederating the states of the New World into a single polity bear citing at length:

> It is a grandiose idea to think of consolidating the New World into a single nation, united by pacts into a single bond. It is reasoned that, as these parts have a common origin, language, customs, and religion, they ought to have a single government to permit the newly formed states to unite in a confederation. But this is not possible. Actually, climatic differences, geographic diversity, conflicting interests, and dissimilar characteristics separate America. How beautiful it would be if the Isthmus of Panamá could be for us what the Isthmus of Corinth was for the Greeks! Would to God that some day we may have the good fortune to convene there an august assembly of representatives of republics, kingdoms, and empires to deliberate upon the high interests of peace and war with the nations of the other three-quarters of the globe. This type of organization may come to pass in some happier period of our regeneration.

To help bring that happier period into being, Bolívar proposed the creation of distinct polities, ideally all republics, that could defend against the tyranny of the Spanish. Those new polities included Colombia, a new republic that would bring together New Granada with Venezuela. Although no longer continental in scope, the Colombia Bolívar envisioned was nevertheless grand, 'a just and grateful tribute to the discoverer of our hemisphere.' Within the period of four years, Bolívar's dream for independence and republicanism in the New World, and for Colombia, began to gain ascendancy. In 1819, after a series of strategic victories by patriot forces, the Colombian Republic uniting Venezuela and New Granada was founded. The inauguration of this new republic in the world was auspiciously greeted by the rebellion of Spanish soldiers lead by General Del Riego on the Iberian Peninsula, who refused to sail to Spanish America to squelch independence movements. The rebellion culminated in the restoration of the 1812 Cádiz constitution which further worked to dissolve the foundations of sovereignty upon which Spanish monarchical rule over its kingdoms in the New World was based. Colombia's Congress happily ratified the union of Venezuela and New Granada in 1821 and worked to set the republican constitutional framework for rule. By then, Bolívar believed the stage was set to enact the hemispheric collaboration he had in mind.

Generations of historians have grappled with the extent to which the Amphictyonic Congress held in Panama was a precursor to Pan-Americanism.[73] Debates have centered on the extent to which Spanish American historical actors considered the United States a critical component to the kind of hemispheric unity that was needed in 1826. What becomes clear from these discussions is precisely how contentious US attendance and participation in the Panama Congress had become. This was as true for the historical actors in Spanish America as it was for those in the United States. The result was that, after the United States finally was invited, the invitation became so contentious within the United States that it broke the dominant political party in power into a two-party system. Delays due to debates caused the US delegates to arrive too late for substantive engagement with representatives from the region. In the meantime, the Colombian Republic, which claimed jurisdiction over the Isthmus of Panama, had already brokered significant trade deals and treaties of mutual aid with several other polities in the region that claimed their independence, even if they had not yet won it. By doing so, Colombia was gaining a level of hemispheric influence that put other world powers on edge. Perhaps that was the idea all along.

Bolívar enlisted the help of prominent leaders to lay the groundwork for a potential confederation of pro-independent states as early as 1821. They included not only people in his administration, such as Vice President Francisco de Paula Santander and Minister of Foreign Relations Pedro Gual, but also an array of diplomats. Colombia's *charge d'affaires* to the United States, Manuel Torres, was already present in Philadelphia steadily at work ensuring the United States would recognize Colombian independence. After an auspicious meeting with

Secretary of State John Quincy Adams, Torres was confident that the Colombian Republic

> will be recognized by the United States as a free and independent nation, as a sister republic. It is also hoped that, to the recognition of the independence of Colombia on the part of the United States, treaties of commerce and navigation will be added, as the most efficacious means of strengthening and increasing the relations of amity between the two republics.[74]

After the United States managed to take territorial possession of Florida upon gaining it diplomatically from Spain in 1821, it was freer to openly recognize independence of the new Hispanic American states. Colombia was the first to receive recognition from the United States on June 19, 1822.[75]

In the meantime, Torres worked with Bolívar and Gual to find ways to strategically exchange diplomats with other polities seeking independence in the region. With the help of the Mexican priest José Servando Teresa de Mier, these men decided on Miguel de Santamaría. Santamaria was born in Veracruz, Mexico, traversed the Atlantic, and there immersed himself in elite circles that linked him back to South America, where he found himself fighting on the side of Colombian independence. Santamaría helped popularize the idea of a republican overthrow of Iturbide's imperial rule. In the meantime, Bolívar deployed Joaquin Mosquera y Arboleda as a diplomat to Peru, Chile, and Buenos Aires. Much like Miranda's trusted diplomat, Cortes de Madarriaga, the primary function of these men was to ensure the formation of a 'a true American league ... that should be much stronger than that recently formed in Europe against the will of the peoples.'[76] By 1824, with the successful overthrow of Iturbide, the ideal of a continental unity of republics was at hand. By then, however, the Colombian/Columbian ideal that included the United States as a 'sister republic' had started to unravel.

The installation of the Amphictyonic Congress in 1826 was intended to generate an even deeper level of hemispheric collaboration. Peru, the United Provinces of Guatemala, and Mexico attended. Several possibilities were on the table for discussion, including the place of Haiti and slavery in the hemisphere. In the lead up to the congress, navigational charts and plans printed in Mexico City and substantial investment in naval power both by Mexico and Colombia would testify to the alliance of these two vast republics. This union had its sights on Cuba where it would deliver a deathblow to the Spanish Monarchy's efforts to retake the mainland with aid from the French.

As the Colombian Republic cajoled a post-imperial Mexico to join in on republican emancipatory efforts in Cuba, the United States and the British and French empires grew increasingly alarmed. By 1826 geopolitical forces took a sharp turn, against the Colombia they had together imagined. Colombia had grown too threatening, and not just for

Spain. Government leaders in Argentina, Brazil, and Chile began to view Colombia's military victories under Bolívar with suspicion. The United States and Britain worried about the Mexican–Colombian alliance and the unpredictable results an invasion of Cuba would likely bring. Most worrisome for the United States was the question of slavery. Would a combined Colombo–Mexican republican attack lead to the subsequent abolition of slavery in Cuba, only 90 miles from the new southern tip of the US South? Would belonging to a federation of 'sister republics' that leaned toward the abolition of slavery force the hand of the US southern states? Would instability lead to an independent Cuba's transfer to Great Britain? Great Britain, for its part, worried that an independent Cuba would fall into US hands. Transatlantic backlash quickly escalated against a Colombian-led republican hemisphere by the time of the congress in 1826. Significantly, the mere idea of attendance at the Panama Congress would also have lasting repercussions in the United States.

The 'intemperate discussion' generated by the request of President John Quincy Adams to send delegates to Panama crystalized a growing split within the country's sole major party, the Democratic Republicans, giving rise to the Second American Party System.[77] The timing of the congress may have stemmed from the military and political circumstances in Spanish America but, as Caitlin Fitz has demonstrated, its coincidence with the 50th anniversary of the signing of the Declaration of Independence brought on a soul-searching opportunity for what should be the core identity of the United States.[78] Whereas leaders of the Republican wing such as John Quincy Adams and Henry Clay, who held close confidence with Colombian *chargé d'affaires* Manuel Torres, argued that attendance would strengthen commercial relations with its republican neighbors, the southern wing of the rising Democratic Party argued that Hispanic Americans were the last people in the world with whom the United States should affiliate. Whereas Republicans championed the ideals of universalism enshrined in the Declaration of Independence, Democrats argued that what had made the United States special and superior to its southern neighbors was that it enslaved its black people rather than enfranchised them.

Conclusion

In the early decades of the American Revolutions, Columbia/Colombia named a united continental future free from the colonial tyranny of Old World monarchy. 'Columbia' was a redemptive, anglicized play on Columbus' name, coined in the eighteenth century and popularized during the American Revolutionary War. Although Columbus had never set foot on any territory that formed part of the fledgling republic of the United States, 'Columbia' became its poetic sign. Joel Barlow's poetry conjoined the cultural work of historians, songwriters, poets, cartographers, and others who saw in Columbus a martyr of New World modernity.

72 Lina del Castillo

These intellectuals had drawn on French Enlightenment imaginaries that transformed Colomb's piecemeal discovery of the Indies into the most significant feat of world history, one that, because of Spanish tyranny and ignorance, had not received proper recognition. This Franco-Anglo Colomb/Columbus thus became the founding father of a free and modern Western Hemisphere.

On the other hand, 'Colombia' was not only a hemispheric dream; it became the proper name of an actual republic of vast scale, subsequently subdivided into several new South American states. The republicanism of Colombia, officially recognized by the United States, moved to radicalize the rest of the hemisphere. The time seemed ripe to call for the continent-wide congress Bolívar had envisioned in 1815, and previously imagined by Francisco de Miranda and William Thornton. But fast-paced geopolitical shifts together with the ramping up of second slavery in the United States meant that Colombia and Columbia would take on very different meanings.

Notes

1. Benedict Anderson, *Imagined Communities: Reflections on the Origin and Spread of Nationalism* (London and New York: Verso, 2006).
2. Dane Kennedy, *Decolonization: A Very Short Introduction* (New York: Oxford University Press, 2016), 8–24.
3. Reuben Neptune, 'The Irony of Un-American Historiography: Daniel J. Boorstin and the Rediscovery of a U.S. Archive of Decolonization,' *The American Historical Review* 120:3 (June 2015), 935–950.
4. Caitlin Fitz, *Our Sister Republics: The United States in an Age of American Revolutions* (New York: W.W. Norton & Company, 2016).
5. Gordon Wood, *Empire of Liberty: A History of the Early Republic, 1789–1815*, Oxford History of the United States (New York: Oxford University Press, 2009).
6. Sam Haynes, *Unfinished Revolution: The Early American Republic in a British World* (Charlottesville: University of Virginia Press, 2010). Kariann Yokota, *Unbecoming British: How Revolutionary America Became a Postcolonial Nation* (New York: Oxford University Press, 2011).
7. Guillaume Ansart, 'From Voltaire to Raynal and Diderot's Histoire des deux Indes: The French Philosophes and Colonial America,' in Aurelian Craiutu and Jeffery C. Isaac, eds., *America Through European Eyes: British and French Reflections on the New World from the Eighteenth Century to the Present* (University Park, PA: Penn State University Press, 2009), 71–90.
8. Junia Ferreira Furtado and Nuno Gonçalo Monteiro, 'The Different Brazils in Abbé Raynal's Histoire des Deux Indes,' *Varia Historia* 32:60 (September–December 2016), 733. For the original, see Guillaume Thomas François Raynal, *Histoire philosophique des établissements et du commerce des Européens dans les deux Indes*, 6 vols. (Amsterdam: Anon, 1770). I will refer to this version as *Histoire des deux Indes*.
9. 'An obscure man, more advanced than his century in the knowledge of astronomy and navigation, seemed to watch over the enlargement of Spain. Christophe Colomb felt, as if by instinct, that there must be another continent, and that it was for him to discover it. The Antipodes, which reason itself treated of chimera, and the superstition of error and impiety was, in

the eyes of this man of genius, an incontestable truth.' Raynal, *Histoire Des Deux Indies*, t. 3, Livre Sixieme, 2.
10. Raynal, *Histoire Des Deux Indies*, t. 3, Livre Sixieme, 2. The English edition of 1788 translates the passage as: 'looked upon the scheme of discovering a new world as the offspring of a distempered brain, and treated the author of it for some time with those airs of contemptuous insolence.' Abbé Raynal, *A Philosophical and Political History of the Settlements and Trade of the Europeans in the East and West Indies, Revised, Augmented, and Published in Ten Volumes. Newly Translated from the French, by J.O. Justamond, F.R.S. in Eight Volumes* (London: Strahan and Cadell, 1788), v. 3, Book VI, 247.
11. 1788 translation reads 'added a fourth part to the earth, or rather half a world to this globe.' Raynal, *Histoire Des Deux Indies*, Book VI, 267.
12. Raynal, *Histoire Des Deux Indies*, t. 3, Livre Sixieme, 14. In 1788 translation: 'who did nothing more than follow the footsteps of a man whose name ought to stand foremost in the list of great characters.' Raynal, *Histoire Des Deux Indes*, Book VI, 267.
13. Raynal, *Histoire Des Deux Indes*, t. 3, Livre Sixieme, 14. The 1788 translation reads 'as a fatal prelude to those scenes of violence of which this unhappy country was afterwards to be the theater.' Raynal, *Histoire Des Deux Indes*, Book VI, 268.
14. Gilles Bancarel, 'La bibliographie matérielle et l'Histoire des deux Indes,' in Hans-Jürgen Lüsebrink and Anthony Strugnell, eds., *L'Histoire des deux Indes: réécriture et polygraphie* (Oxford: Voltaire Foundation, 1995), 44.
15. Jonathan Israel, *Democratic Enlightenment: Philosophy, Revolution, and Human Rights, 1750–1790* (New York: Oxford University Press, 2011), 431.
16. Roberto Ventura, 'Leituras de Raynal e a Ilustraçao na América Latina,' *Estudos Avançados* 2:3 (1988), 40.
17. William Robertson, *History of America* (Dublin: Messrs. Whitestone, 1777), v. 1, Book II, 72.
18. Ibid., 59–60.
19. Ibid., 70.
20. Ibid., 150.
21. Joel Barlow, *The Vision of Columbus; A Poem in Nine Books* (Hartford: Hudson and Goodwin, 1787).
22. Ibid. See also Joel Barlow, *The Columbiad: A Poem* (London: Richard Phillips, Bridge Street, Blackfriars, 1809).
23. Steven Blakemore, *Joel Barlow's Columbiad: A Bicentennial Reading* (Knoxville: The University of Tennessee Press), 1.
24. Barlow ignored alternative, Andean claims to American sovereignty. On the latter, see Sinclair Thomson, 'Sovereignty Disavowed: The Tupac Amaru Revolution in the Atlantic World,' *Atlantic Studies Global Currents* 13:3 (2016), 407–431.
25. James V. Walker, 'Henry S. Tanner and Cartographic Expression of American Expansionism in the 1820s,' *Oregon Historical Quarterly* 111:4 (Winter 2010), 416–443.
26. Francisco de Miranda, *The New Democracy in America: Travels of Francisco de Miranda in the United States, 1783–84*, Judson P. Wood, trans., John S. Ezell, ed. (Norman: University of Oklahoma Press, 1963), 165.
27. Elise Bartosik-Vélez, *The Legacy of Christopher Columbus in the Americas: New Nations and a Transatlantic Discourse of Empire* (Nashville: Vanderbilt University Press, 2014).
28. Miranda, *The New Democracy*, 165.
29. Columbia University, *A History of Columbia University, 1754–1904* (New York: Columbia University Press, 1904), 60–61.

30. Miranda, *The New Democracy*, 115–116.
31. Victor E. Gimmestad, 'Joel Barlow's Editing of John Trumbull's 'M' Fingal,' *American Literature* 47:1 (March 1975), 98. For copyright protections, see Will McDonald, 'Still Personal: Joel Barlow and the Publication of Poetry in the 1780s,' *The Journal of the Midwest Modern Language Association* 42:1 (Spring 2009), 89. On Trumbull's relationship with Barlow in the Hartford Wits, see Charles William Everest, ed., *The Poets of Connecticut: With Biographical Sketches*, 6th ed. (New York and Chicago: A.S. Barnes and Company, 1873), 38.
32. Everest, *The Poets of Connecticut*, 74. By December 1785, Trumbull asked John Adams to assist and encourage the publication of Barlow's *The Vision of Columbus*. See Trumbull to John Adams, December 8, 1785, in the Adams Papers, reel 366. Original held by the Massachusetts Historical Society.
33. Claudia L. Bushman, *America Discovers Columbus: How an Italian Explorer Became an American Hero* (Hanover, NH: University Press of New England, 1992), 41–51.
34. Arturo Uslar Pietri, 'Apéndice: Lista de libros en el archivo de Miranda,' in *Los Libros de Miranda* (Caracas: Comisión Nacional del Cuatricentenario de la Fundación de Caracas, 1966).
35. Bartosik-Vélez argues that even though Miranda lived in the London home of Joel Barlow, there is no evidence to suggest that Barlow's poem inspired Miranda to use the term 'Columbia' and its variants. See Bartosik-Vélez, *The Legacy of Christopher Columbus*, 109. Bartosik misses the web of connections linking Miranda to Columbian ideals from before 1788, a web that included Barlow through the Hartford Wits during Miranda's travels through the United States in 1783. For Joel Barlow's testimony in favor of Miranda during a French treason trial, see Karen Racine, *Francisco de Miranda: A Transatlantic Life in the Age of Revolution* (Wilmington: Scholarly Resources, 2003), 123–124.
36. William Spence Robertson, *The Life of Miranda* (Chapel Hill: The University of North Carolina Press, 1929). See also Miranda Mss., *The New Democracy*, v. 10.
37. Robertson, *The Life of Miranda*, v. 2, 81.
38. Ibid., 82–83.
39. Ibid., 83.
40. Ibid., 83–84.
41. Translation: 'If the favorable Horoscope that the generous heart of your Highness has wished upon the unfortunate Colombia should ever take place, I would not fail to communicate news to you.' Archivo del General Miranda, *Viajes, Cartas de Miranda: 1782 a 1801 Miscelanea 1771 a 1805 Impresos y Grabados 1771 a 1805 Tomo VII* (Caracas: Parra Leon Hermanos, Editorial Sur-America, 1930), 36.
42. Robertson, *The Life of Miranda*, v. 2, 85.
43. Richard Buel Jr., *Joel Barlow: American Citizen in a Revolutionary World* (Baltimore: The Johns Hopkins University Press, 2011), 164.
44. Thomas, 'Sovereignty Disavowed,' 421. See also Archivo General de la Nación, Mexico City, Correspondencia de Diversas Autoridades, v. 21, exp. 27, ffs. 187–191.
45. Lina Del Castillo, 'Cartography in the Production (and Silencing) of Colombian Independence History, 1807–1827,' in James R. Akerman, ed., *Decolonizing the Map: Cartography from Colony to Nation* (Chicago: The University of Chicago Press, 2017), 117. For Miranda's recollection of the cartographic interaction, see Miranda, *Tercera Sección*, 55.
46. Miranda, *Tercera Sección*, 100–103.
47. Bartosik-Vélez, *The Legacy of Christopher Columbus*, 112–113.

48. Klaus Gallo, *De la Invasión al Reconocimiento: Gran Bretaña y el Río de la Plata, 1806–1826* (Buenos Aires: A-Z Editora, 1994), 25–26.
49. Francisco de Miranda, *América espera*, (Caracas: Biblioteca Ayachucho, 1982), 286–289. Miranda drew from the *Royal Commentaries of the Incas* by Peruvian historian Inca Garcilaso de la Vega.
50. Buel Jr., *Joel Barlow*, 164.
51. Racine, *Francisco de Miranda*.
52. Del Castillo, 'Cartography in the Production,' 118.
53. Gallo, *De la Invasión*, 38–39.
54. Racine, *Francisco de Miranda*, 156.
55. Ibid., 158, citing Miranda to Jefferson (Nueva York 22 enero de 1806), in *Testigos norteamericanos de la expedición de Miranda*, Edgardo Mondolfi, ed. (Caracas: Monte Avila Editores, 1993), 181. Emphasis mine.
56. Racine, *Francisco de Miranda*, 160–161, citing the translation and reprint in John H. Sherman, *A General Account of Miranda's Expedition* (New York: McFarlane and Long, 1808), 35n–39n.
57. Cited in Racine, *Francisco de Miranda*, 161–162. See also 'Form of the Oath' (On Board the Leander, Jacquemel Harbor, March 24, 1806), in Archivo General Miranda, 18:207–208.
58. Racine, *Francisco de Miranda*, 163–165.
59. Ibid., 163–164.
60. Gallo, *De la Invasión*, 80–81. See also A. Aspinall, *The Later Correspondence of George III, 1783–1810* (New York: Cambridge University Press, 1962–70), v. IV, 469–470.
61. Pedro Grases and Caracciolo Parra Pérez, eds., *El Colombiano Francisco de Miranda y dos Documentos Americanistas* (Caracas: Coleccion serie Testimonios I, 1966).
62. Cited in Jesús María Yepes, *Del Congreso de Panamá a la Confederación de Caracas 1826–1954*, t. I-II (Caracas: Ministerio de Relaciones Exteriores, 1955), 20. See also Germán A. de la Reza, 'Panamericanismo o Hispanoamericanismo? Los antecedentes formativos del congreso anfictiónico de Panamá de 1826,' *Revista de Historia de América* (July–December 2012), n.147, 12.
63. See: Venezuela, *Interesting Official Documents Relating to the United Provinces of Venezuela viz. Preliminary Remarks, the Act of Independence, Proclamation, Manifesto to the World of the Causes Which Have Impelled the Said Provinces to Separate from the Mother Country; Together with the Constitution Framed for the Administration of Their Government in Spanish and English* (London: Longman and Company, 1812), 238.
64. Ibid.
65. The original in Luis López de Mesa, *Breve comentario inicial a la historia de la Cancillería de San Carlos* (Bogotá: Imprenta del Estado Mayor Genera, 1942), 20–21.
66. George W. Paulson, *Thomas Jefferson's Favorite Architect William Thornton: Washington Capital* (Dallas, TX: Monticello West, 2007).
67. Carole L. Herrick, *August 24, 1814: Washington in Flames* (Falls Church: Higher Education Publishing, 2005), 92.
68. On the War of 1812, see J. C. A. Stagg, *Mr. Madison's War: Politics, Diplomacy, and Warfare in the Early American Republic, 1783–1830* (Princeton: Princeton University Press, 1983); J. C. A. Stagg, *The War of 1812: Conflict for a Continent* (New York: Cambridge University Press, 2012); Paul A. Gilje, *Free Trade and Sailors' Rights in the War of 1812* (New York: Cambridge University Press, 2013). Fitz, *Our Sister Republics*.
69. Caitlin Fitz, *Journal of American History* (forthcoming) recent article on toasts post War of 1812. See also: Bruce B. Solnick, 'New York Celebrates

Spanish-American Independence,' *New York History* 64:4 (October 1983), 408–424.
70. Gordon Brown, *Latin American Rebels and the United States, 1806–1822* (North Carolina: McFarland and Company, 2015), 43. See also Angel del Rio, *La Misión de Don Luís de Onis en los Estados Unidos, 1809–1819* (New York, 1981), 71.
71. Simón Bolívar, 'Letter from Jamaica,' Kingston, September 6, 1815.
72. Ibid.
73. Germán de la Reza, 'Panamericanismo o Hispanoamericanismo?' argues that Bolívar explicitly did not see the Panama Congress as one that should include the United States. Rather, it was an opportunity for strategic, deeper integration among a select group of emerging, pro-independence polities formally under Spanish rule. Other scholars have argued a different point, minimizing Bolívar's opposition to highlight how the diplomatic endeavor, at least from the point of view of Santander and other diplomats from Colombia, was one that included the United States. See: Joseph Byrne Lockey, *Orígenes del panamericanismo* (Caracas: Editorial El Cojo, 1927); Daniel Íñiguez Guerra, *Bolívar, creador del panamericanismo actual* (Caracas: Imprenta nacional, 1946); Arthur Whitaker, *The Western Hemisphere Idea: Its Rise and Decline* (Ithaca: Cornell University Press, 1954); José Caicedo Castilla, *El Panamericanismo* (Buenos Aires: Roque Depalma, 1961); Henry Bernstein, *Formación de una conciencia interamericana* (México: Limusa-Wiley, 1961); Antonio Castillo Martinez, *El Congreso de Panamá de 1826 convocado por el Libertador, iniciación del panamericanismo* (Bogotá: Universidad de Bogotá Jorge Tadeo Lozano, 1972); Hiram Bingham, *The Monroe Doctrine: An Obsolete Shibboleth* (New Haven: Yale University Press, 1976). As De La Reza explains, the Ministry of Exterior Relations held an essay contest explicitly seeking to find connections between Pan-Americanism and the Congress of 1826. Several publications on the 1826 Congress that emerged in 1954 did exactly that. See Yepes, *Del Congreso de Panamá a la Conferencia de Caracas 1826–1954*, t. I-II; Francisco Cuevas Cancino, *Del Congreso de Panamá a la Conferencia de Caracas 1826–1954. El genio de Bolívar a través de la historia de las relaciones interamericanas*, tomos I-II (Caracas: Gobierno de Venezuela, 1955); Ulpiano López, *Del Congreso de Panamá a la Conferencia de Caracas 1826–1954, El genio de Bolívar a través de la historia de las relaciones interamericanas* (Quito: Imprenta del Ministerio de Educación), 1955.
74. Torres to Adams, February 20, 1821, William R. Manning, ed., *Diplomatic Correspondence of the United States concerning the Independence of the Lain American Nations*, 3 vols. (New York: Oxford University Press, 1925), v. I, 1208–1209.
75. Charles Bowman, Jr. 'Manuel Torres in Philadelphia and the Recognition of Colombian Independence, 1821–1822,' *Records of the American Catholic Historical Society of Philadelphia* 80:1 (March 1969), 17–38.
76. Instrucciones, Cúcuta, 11 of October 1821, See Lockey, *Origenes*, 1927, 291–292 and De La Reza, 'Panamericanismo,' 19.
77. Andrew R. L. Clayton, 'The Debate Over the Panama Congress and the Origins of the Second American Party System,' *The Historian* 47:2 (February 1985), 219–238.
78. Fitz, *Our Sister Republics*, 194–207.

4 Race and Revolution in Colombia, Haiti, and the United States

Marixa Lasso

During the Hispanic American 'revolutions of independence,' one patriot movement after another declared the equality of humankind regardless of race. Indeed, it was in the heat of these prolonged wars of the Age of Revolution that the world first confronted a burning question: How to construct raceless political communities of equals in a world riddled with racial and imperial hierarchies? Contrary to a common prejudice, Creole elites did not decide this issue alone. Mixed-race lower classes, indigenous peoples, and enslaved and free peoples of African descent all played crucial roles in the making of the ex-colonial republics of Hispanic America.[1] To ignore this history is to erase these peoples from the global story of political modernity, obscuring what may be Latin America's most original contribution to the history of revolution and decolonization at large.

As we shall see in this chapter, race did not play out the same everywhere in the revolutionary, decolonizing Americas of the late eighteenth and early nineteenth centuries. Although the first historians of comparative race relations in the Americas tended to emphasize colonial differences, more recent histories argue that variations reflect not differences between British and Iberian empires but instead regional modalities that cut across those empires. These historians have also argued that the emphasis on historical differences between Iberian and Anglo slavery was the product of nineteenth-century nationalisms. Studies of race relations in the United States have demonstrated that characteristics previously thought to be exclusively Latin American were also present in the north.[2]

The British, Hispanic, and Portuguese empires all supported urban multiracial lower classes that lived, worked, rioted, and made politics together. African-American artisans were an important part of the colonial workforce and free people of African descent a common component of urban societies across the Americas. Moreover, race was but one level of difference in colonial societies characterized by multiple layers of social rank. Historians of the anglophone United States have noted that race relations became worse, prejudice against people of colour stronger, and white identity more important after independence.[3] As we shall see, the opposite occurred in Hispanic or Latin America. Meanwhile, in the francophone Caribbean blackness and mulatto ascendency were emphasized.

Although much more research needs to be done on the impact of the Age of Revolution's wars of independence on modern race relations, some common threads are visible. In the late eighteenth century, Creoles across the Americas sought to assert their identity against a wave of European disdain and colonial subordination. Northern European philosophes such as Cornelius de Pauw and George Louis Leclerc Comte de Buffon had popularized the notion of America's inferiority, arguing that its clime had degenerative effects on animals, plants, and men. This degeneration touched Creoles of European descent who suffered the enfeebling effects of the humid, American environment. Creole intellectuals such as Thomas Jefferson and Antonio Clavigero responded by defending the American continent's nature and civilization. Creoles also confronted accusations of degenerative racial mixing that questioned their equality with European-born whites.[4] In addition, in the last quarter of the eighteenth century, Creoles saw their racial and social prominence challenged by demographic changes and imperial policies. In Colombia, Venezuela, and Saint Domingue they responded with anger to colonial reforms that, in efforts to encourage participation in militias, recognized the demographic and economic importance of free people of African descent.[5] Threatened by such changes, some Creoles asserted European descent, thereby distinguishing themselves from blacks and mulattos. In 1795, the Caracas town council wrote to the Crown about the necessity to 'keep *Pardos* in their present subordination, without any laws that confuses them with whites, who abhor and detest this union.'[6] In the United States, James Otis similarly insisted that the Northern Colonies 'are well settled, not as the common people of England foolishly imagine, with a compound of mongrel mixture of English, Indian and Negro, but with freeborn British white.'[7] In Haiti, the white colonial intellectual Emilien Petit, proposed strict racial segregation as a way to strengthen French identity and loyalty among white colonials.[8]

In the late eighteenth century, many Creoles across the Americas hoped to construct a national or imperial identity based on white-only membership. Yet only the United States followed this path. By the 1820s, Colombians had developed a national ideology that proclaimed the equality and harmony of peoples of European, African, and indigenous descent. This transformation echoed similar changes in the other Hispanic American republics and foreshadowed the position of Cuban patriots in the late nineteenth century. In contrast, Haiti constructed a national identity that excluded whites. Only the United States constructed its national identity as a white country, excluding non-whites from the nation's imagined community.

What produced these divergent paths? The evidence strongly suggests that the nature of the anti-colonial wars of the Age of Revolution were themselves largely responsible for these outcomes. During these wars, the new American nations developed new national identities, struggling over who to include and exclude from national polities that otherwise openly declared the liberty and equality of mankind.

The combination of wars of independence with anti-monarchical, republican cultural politics is critical for understanding concepts of race and equality in Hispanic America during this period. Black Colombian patriots understood equality among the races to be the opposite of the aristocratic, colonial divisions of the old Spanish regime. For them, racial equality was a sign of new times. To be free was to be republican.

Granting the anti-colonial, republican history of nineteenth-century anti-racism in Hispanic America its due in the grand narratives of the Age of Revolution requires both building upon pioneering work in the Latin American historical field and overcoming some enduring misconceptions about the period. Since the works of François-Xavier Guerra and Antonio Annino were published in the early 1990s, the historiography of the Hispanic American wars of independence has benefitted from an approach that took ideological changes seriously and showed the importance of the revolution in shaping moderns forms of political participation and citizenship.[9] This work was enriched by a new generation of historians who shifted the focus of political analysis from the elite to the lower classes.[10] Despite the richness and rigour of this new historiography, Guerra's dictum that what singles out the Spanish American revolutions was 'the absence of modern popular mobilization' unfortunately continues to orient many general accounts of Latin American history.[11] The persistence of this notion derives in part from a historical teleology that reads this period through the retrospective lens of a future failure. This teleological structure hinders our ability to appreciate the novelty of social and political changes during this period.[12] The wars of independence not only inaugurated a new political system organized around legal racial equality; they also opened avenues for social mobility and political participation. This is not to say that the broad patterns of economic inequality that kept people of African descent at the bottom of society ended, but rather that the terms of unequal social relations had shifted dramatically.[13] This shift was seized upon by the subaltern classes.

Gran Colombia

From the start of the wars, the equality and citizenship of free people of African descent became a major issue in the struggle against Spanish rule. It soon became clear that the support of people of African descent was critical for securing military victories. Many blacks had good reason to support the royalists. Some received favours and special privileges from the King as members of the black militias. Others joined the royalist forces because they offered the opportunity to fight landowners and slave owners under the legitimacy of the King's banner. To counter this sentiment, the first revolutionary juntas of Caracas and Cartagena courted the support of blacks and mulattos with new promises of equality. In Cartagena, the Creole elite sought the support of Pardo (free black or coloured) artisans before deposing the Spanish governor in May 1810. By December of the same year, the electoral instructions for the Supreme Junta of the province of Cartagena included all races: 'All parishioners, whites, Indians, mestizos, mulattos, zambos and blacks, as long as they were household heads and lived from their own work, were to be summoned for elections.' Only 'vagrants, criminals, those who were in servile salaried status, and slaves are excluded.'[14] Similarly, some of the first measures of the Caracas *Junta Suprema* sought to include Pardos. The Caracas Junta Suprema named a white representative of the Pardo guild, increased the stipends of Pardo militia officers, and promoted Pardos to ranks beyond the previous colonial limit of captain, to the rank of coronel. The Junta Suprema of Caracas also awarded Pardo officers with medals for their 'courageous and enthusiastic patriotism,' and their 'virtue and patriotism.'[15] As in Cartagena, the Caracas Junta's electoral laws for the General Congress of Venezuela, published in June 1810, included all free men without distinction of colour as long as they were not salaried or dependent, thereby including independent artisans.[16] These tactics bore fruit. Members of the Pardo guild began to make monetary contributions to the Junta and their donations were duly published by the Gaceta de Caracas, further fostering a sense of unity between Pardo and Creole patriots.[17]

Free men of African descent soon began to actively participate in the radical groups pressuring for independence. One of these groups was Caracas' *Sociedad Patriótica*, which counted among its members the Bolívar brothers, the Montillas, and Francisco Miranda, who in 1806 had proposed granting citizenship to natives, free blacks, and mulattoes. The Sociedad Patriótica drew inspiration from the French Jacobin Clubs and admitted people of all types and conditions. When Miranda became its president, one of his first steps was to invite four free black and mulattos to become members. According to contemporary witnesses, the support of men of colour of the Sociedad Patriótica was due to the 'warmth and enthusiasm with which the liberty and equality of mankind was discussed.'[18] This embracing inclusiveness contrasted with the lukewarm overtures of royalists and moderate independentists, who included only a few Pardos of great distinction (*Pardos beneméritos*). In 1811, the foreign observer Gregor McGregor stated that the Sociedad Patriótica had given Pardos confidence in their rights to equality with Creoles. In Cartagena, patriot politics were similarly divided between a radical group called *piñeristas* and a moderate group known as *toledistas*. Although both groups courted Pardos, the toledistas tried to control the extent of their participation to a few members of the Pardo elite. In contrast, the piñeristas actively encouraged the political participation of black and mulatto artisans in the streets while emphasizing a radical rhetoric of equality. According to their leader, Gabriel Gutierrez de Piñeres: 'In a popular government no man should be superior to another; if José María Toledo [the Junta's President] enjoyed too much recognition and esteem, it was necessary to level him.'[19] In both cities the links between Creole radicals and the lower and darker classes was subject to criticism. Opponents labelled these radical groups as demagogues, Jacobins, or Sans Culottes and Sin Camisas.

In Caracas and Cartagena, the radical groups that enjoyed Pardo support were also strong supporters of independence. In Cartagena, the Pardo militias played a crucial role in pressuring the undecided Creole Junta to declare independence on November 11, 1811. In Caracas, the Sociedad Patriótica joined with people of African descent in the streets to celebrate the July 5 declaration of independence. Pardos also took the initiative of defending Cartagena's Junta against the insurrection of the Spanish Fijo Battalion in February of 1811. Similarly, the *teniente coronel* of the Pardo militias, Manuel Caballero, led the patriot defence against a group of Spanish men from the Canary Islands who challenged Caracas' declaration of independence.[20] In Caracas, the same Junta session that voted in favour of independence received a proposal to debate 'the destiny and circumstance of Pardos [la suerte y condición de los Pardos].' Although this discussion was postponed, it was so only on the condition that it be 'the first thing to be addressed after independence.'[21] When the first constitution of Venezuela was sanctioned in December of the same year, it contained a decree that granted free people of African descent the same rights and privileges as whites.[22] Similarly, the new republic of Cartagena granted equality to free blacks and whites. When it published its first constitution in 1812, two Pardo deputies signed it.[23] Although some Afro-Colombians remained royalists to the end of the war, it was the alliance forged by black and white republican patriots that would create the legislation and language that oriented modern race relations in Gran Colombia.

During the same months that patriots in Caracas and Cartagena agitated for independence, representatives from the various parts of the Spanish monarchy discussed whether people of African descent should have the same rights of representation and citizenship as whites. The proportion and indeed possible majority of the American representatives depended upon the answer to this question. Spanish and American delegates soon parted over this issue, with American or Overseas delegates favouring African-American citizenship and Peninsular delegates opposing it. The constitutional debates helped foster alliances between Creole and Pardo patriots in two major and unintended ways. First, they forced American delegates to develop a series of arguments, widely disseminated throughout the Americas, in defence of black equality. Second, it allowed patriots to link the issue of racial equality to their cause. Patriot speeches could now promote a nationalist rhetoric that linked racist laws with Spanish tyranny.[24]

The speech of Venezuelan José Francisco Bermudez in the city of Cartagena in 1815 reflected this rhetoric and sentiment. He addressed his compatriots thus:

> Remember above all, you men of colour, how this conflict began . . . In forming its government, Spain excluded America from its rightful share of representation; American government opposed this arbitrary measure by force. Spain modified it by granting whites their right, denying them completely to men of colour; and the whites then cried out that they would defend with weapons in hand the rights that belong to you. Could you fail to respond to such a generous resolution?[25]

In 1817, Bolivar contrasted republican racial equality with Spanish despotism under which '*Pardos* were degraded by the worst humiliation, being deprived of everything.'[26] By 1821, years of war and propaganda had taught patriots to associate independence with racial equality. This link became apparent to a Spanish envoy who upon visiting Paez's camp in 1820 noted that 'the Spanish constitution does not suit them because it denies citizenship to those of African descent.'[27]

The discourse of equality among the races developed during the wars maintained its prominence during the first years of independent, republican rule. It influenced the rhetoric on slavery and abolition and the ways in which whites and blacks addressed racial tensions in the post-colonial period. When Gran Colombia's Constitutional Convention gathered in 1821, legal racial equality between free men was no longer a subject of debate. In contrast, abolition remained a looming issue. The slave trade had been abolished during the early years of the war, and many slaves had joined the Spanish and patriot armies in exchange for their freedom. The question was whether Gran Colombia would be a slave republic or not.[28] The answer was a compromise. The 1821 Constitution instituted a free womb law similar to Pennsylvania's. The enormous difference between Gran Colombia and the northern US states was the status of manumitted slaves. While in the US North, free blacks faced increasing segregation and political disenfranchisement, in Colombia free blacks enjoyed the same legal rights as white citizens. Colombian whites did not deny blacks from belonging to the Colombian nation nor did they oppose their right to be full citizens. Instead, tensions between whites and blacks centred on the nature of Afro-Colombian participation in the independence wars, upon who best embodied revolutionary values, and whether real racial equality had already been achieved.

In the early years of the republic, the transformation of slave into citizen was magnificently represented during the manumission ceremonies of

Independence Day celebrations. These celebrations were didactic spaces that invited Colombians to rejoice at seeing the rebirth of manumitted slaves as fellow citizens and presented an official patriot history that linked slavery to Spanish tyranny and abolitionism to republican virtue. An 1823 speech from Mompox, Cartagena, denounced that, 'after depopulating our country with fire and sword [the Spaniards] were compelled to commit the equally horrible crime of repopulating it with slaves.'[29] Cruel Spaniards had decimated native populations and imported slaves to replace them. Racial antagonism as it existed among Colombians was the product of Spanish cruelty and indifference. In sharp contrast, Colombians loved their fellow citizens regardless of colour. They opposed and despised racial discrimination and slavery as the traces of an old despotic regime. Under the Republic enlightenment, harmony, and unity would prevail.

As we have seen, in Gran Colombia blacks actively participated in the independence wars and were instrumental to the establishment of the state's official commitment to legal racial equality. During the wars, some Pardos reached positions of political and military authority. Some became governors, generals, senators, or congressmen. Pardo political participation, however, was not so easily controlled. Pardos tended to press for notions of justice and equality that went beyond the Creole elite's original intentions. Afro-Colombians and Creole elites disagreed over the reality of race relations. Far from being deluded by Colombia's nationalist ideology of racial harmony and equality, Afro-Colombians of the post-independence period were quick to point out instances of race discrimination in their towns. They spoke out when they were not allowed to sit in cafes; Pardo officials protested about not receiving the same respect and polite treatment as white counterparts; they spoke out against the discrimination suffered at the hands of criminal authorities. Eventually, however, such denunciations were increasingly criminalized as seditious attempts to promote 'race war.' Pardos accused of promoting race wars suffered imprisonment, trial, banishment, and sometimes even execution.

The rhetorical ghost of race war played an important role in setting limits to the ideal of racial equality and harmony enshrined during the revolutionary period. Race-war rumours tended to surface when Pardo political pressure seemed most threatening; that is, rumours peaked when Pardos rose to political positions of power over Creole elites. Pardos with political authority were symbolically charged figures that embodied revolutionary change. For example, the appointment of Remigio Marquez as governor of the important city of Mompox in 1822 led to charges that he had broken 'the fraternal union' between Pardos and Creoles. Ten years later, he would face similar accusations. When the government sought to appoint him military commander of the city of Santa Marta, the governor of Cartagena warned that Marquez was 'proud and domineering, particularly over the good families, all of which, along with some aspirations among people of colour, leads me to conclude that Marquez could cause great prejudice.'[30] At other times, race-war rumours arose at foundational political acts, such as the summoning of juntas or constitutional conventions. The armed insurrections or threats thereof that often accompanied these political conjunctures also played a role. Rumours of race war and threats of insurrection may thus have reflected both Creole fear and *Pardo* hope that the inability to fulfil Pardo expectations of equality might lead to violent conflict.

The concept of 'race war' exercised a profound effect on Colombian racial constructs. It was key to consolidating the nationalist discourse of racial harmony. At the same time, it set boundaries to the legitimate ways and means to address racial inequality. Colombian policymakers used the threat of race war to convince recalcitrant elites that anything short of full legal equality and official commitment to manumission could transform the Wars of Independence into a racial conflict à la Haiti. Accusations of racial enmity could also reflect Creole fear that Pardos might successfully challenge their control; in this register, the race-war spectre could serve to deprive Pardo grievances of political legitimacy. Pardos who denounced racial discrimination could face similar charges. Accusations of racial enmity levelled against such Pardos often ended in banishment or execution. In short, it was dangerous and unpatriotic to seek public redress for racial inequality. Republican discourse rendered expressions of racial grievance synonymous with declarations of racial war and therefore seditious and unpatriotic. Still, each time Creole elites accused Pardos of racial enmity they were obliged to reiterate their commitment to racial harmony and equality. To give legitimacy to their accusations of race war, local elites had to claim that racial harmony reigned in their towns and that social disruption resulted only from the actions of a few seditious Pardos.

Despite these issues, Afro-Colombians did not question the glory and legacy of the revolution of independence as, as we shall see, blacks in the United States would. Rather, they presented themselves as the revolution's rightful heirs and protagonists. In this way, Colombian veterans sought to vindicate their role in the independence wars. When disputes over black participation arose, Afro-Colombians were quick to point out that they had been the true defenders of the revolution; that they embodied the ideals of democracy and equality of humankind.

Few figures embodied this conflict more than the Afro-Colombian General José Prudencio Padilla. As an Afro-Colombian of prestige and power, Padilla was subjected to frequent attacks by the Creole elite. In 1824, General Padilla publicly denounced some of these attacks. Such attacks failed to comply with the republican virtue of equality; they degraded the Pardo class and restored the aristocratic dominion of the old families. Padilla turned colonial notions of honour upside down by publicly denouncing that the old families should be ashamed, not proud, of being descendants of 'ferocious Spaniards' who 'accumulated riches through their atrocities against unfortunate Indians.' Unlike them, Padilla had earned his prestige and position defending the Fatherland. Creole attachment to traditional honour and hierarchy was fundamentally anti-republican.[31] He accused his enemies of wanting to 'undermine the holy edifice of the people's freedom and equality.' They would 'replace republican ways with old privileges and the exclusive domination of a small and miserable portion of [the nation's] families over the great majority of the people.'[32]

Padilla soon became a symbol of revolutionary hopes and fears. Bolívar and his supporters feared Padilla's popularity among blacks and mulattos; this fear would eventually lead to an accusation, trial, and execution for sedition in 1828. When a new liberal government took control of Colombia in 1832, Padilla became again an important political symbol. His memory was vindicated, and the city of Cartagena organized celebrations in his honour. Afro-Colombian veterans took an important role in these events. As members of the *Sociedad de Veteranos Amigos de la Libertad*, they offered public condolences to Padilla's family and attended the public ceremonies dressed in black with a liberal red ribbon. Despite Afro-Colombian efforts to highlight their contribution to Colombian independence, official stories of the revolution soon began to erase and depoliticize them. The most influential account was José Manuel Restrepo's history of the revolution, published in 1858. Restrepo's canonical history depicted Afro-Colombian participation in the independence wars as the product of cash and booze.[33]

Haiti

In Haiti, the relationship between anti-colonialism, republicanism, and racial equality followed a different path. The violent military, political, and ideological conflicts of the Haitian revolution were not between colonials and colonizers but between those for or against the Republic. Unlike in Spanish America, racial equality did not become a source of conflict between metropolitan Frenchmen and Haitians but between two groups of colonial subjects: white colonials and free coloured. When news of the French Revolution arrived in Haiti, free coloured claimed that the Rights of Man meant racial equality between free blacks and whites. Even if free coloured, many of whom were planters and slave owners themselves, were not asking for abolition, white colonials considered racial equality as the first step toward the end of slavery. They reacted with hostility and violence. Rising tensions between white colonials and free coloured over racial equality escalated into open armed conflict when a group of wealthy free coloured arrived from France to impart military guidance and leadership. Unwilling to arm slaves and outnumbered by white colonials, the free coloured were defeated. Twenty were executed and two of their leaders suffered torture at the wheel. Consequently, racial equality for free men of African descent was declared first in Paris, not Haiti. Under pressure from the Société des Amis des Noirs and free coloured in France, the French National Assembly gave free coloured born of free parents, equal political rights in May 15, 1791. Abolition and racial equality would be obtained through the alliance of white French republican soldiers, black slaves, and free coloured, who had fought together against white colonials.[34]

When the republicans triumphed, white colonial planters, not the French, were excluded from the republican patriot imaginary. In the 1790s, Bastille Day and Emancipation Day were celebrated together and both the French general Santhonax and the black general Touissant L'Overture were revered as founding fathers. In the republican imaginary, colonial planters were 'attached to slavery as nobles were to their vassals.'[35] It was not until Napoleon sought to reinstate slavery in 1802 that a distinction between liberty-loving Haiti and a tyrannical France was established. By then, white colonials had been erased from the national imaginary. The national pantheon of founding fathers now only included men of African descent such as Ogé, Chavanne, and L'Overture. White men included in nationalist representations were European abolitionists, not white Haitians.[36] When national images and ceremonies proclaimed racial harmony, it was between blacks and mulattos, not whites and blacks. Haiti had become a black and mulatto nation.[37]

The United States

The revolutionary wars in the United States followed another path. Abolition and racial equality did not become a republican or a patriot slogan in the United States. There was no clear-cut distinction between the royalists and the patriots on issues of abolition and racial equality. If anything, patriot propaganda tended to portray Britain as the champion of black rights.[38] Unlike Haiti and Spanish America, the ideology of racial equality did not become a source of national unity and pride in the fight against the Old Regime. As David Roediger points out, when the revolution began, blackness was not exclusively associated with servitude, and whiteness was not chained to freedom and independence. This situation would change during the revolutionary period when the Republic failed to address the issue of black oppression. Slavery increased in the South, while white indentured servitude generally decreased. In the United States, manumitted slaves did not automatically become citizens with equal legal rights, as in Colombia. Free blacks were increasingly disenfranchised while the white lower classes were incorporated into the electoral system. Most states—including northern abolitionist ones—instituted segregationist laws that disenfranchised free blacks, denied them access to white public education, outlawed interracial marriage, forbade free blacks from the right to bear arms, and excluded them from the right to equal protection under the law.[39]

Far from being a mere holdover of colonial slavery, these exclusionary laws reflected how the Republic defined new citizenship rights. Colombian and American laws mirrored each other in that both considered access to public education, equal rights before the law, enfranchisement, and the right to marry across race and class inherent citizenship rights. The key difference was that the Colombian government used these laws to grant new rights to people of African descent, ease tensions between blacks and whites, and foster a new sense of national unity. The United States used them to define its identity as a white nation.[40] Therefore, when in the 1820s lower-class whites pushed for inclusive suffrage laws that recognized the equality among all men, they referred to white men only.[41] In 1857, the famous *Dred Scott* Supreme Court decision stated that free blacks were not US citizens and were, therefore, not able to sue in federal court. The Court justified its ruling by arguing that free blacks were not citizens when the Constitution was ratified. They were yet again excluded from the nation's foundation. And even when individual states opposed this decision and gave free blacks legal rights in state law, they did not enjoy the same rights of white citizens.[42] By the time slavery was completely abolished in the United States, the disenfranchisement of free blacks could build on a long tradition that went back to the revolutionary era and the early nineteenth century.

The profound disconnection between nationalism, patriotism, and racial equality in the United States was apparent on many levels. As in Colombia and Haiti, in the United States the issue of national unity was intimately linked to race relations. However, the problem that race posed to national unity took on a very different connotation in the United States. Racial inequality did not pose a challenge to national unity. What was deemed unpatriotic in the United States was to foster divisions and conflicts between the North and the South by mentioning the contradiction between slavery and republicanism.[43] Thus, racial equality was not only excluded from nationalist rhetoric; instead, it was in direct opposition to the rhetoric of national unity and patriotism.

Few things reflected the deep disconnect between patriot nationalism and racial equality than the Independence Day celebrations of the 1810s–1830s, when free blacks were harassed and expelled from the celebrations by rowdy mobs that claimed that the Fourth of July 'belongs exclusively to the white population.'[44] Even at a symbolic level, the American Revolution failed to inaugurate a new era in race relations. The struggle for racial equality in the United States would become linked to bloody regional conflicts, not to a unified front against a common enemy.

Confronted with their exclusion from the political process and the national body, blacks in the United States challenged the very legacy of the American Revolution. In contrast to Afro-Colombians' denunciations,

African-American criticism of slavery and racial discrimination was not and could not be framed as betrayal to a revolutionary legacy to which both blacks and whites belonged. Therefore, they developed an outsider counternarrative of the American Revolution that questioned its central claim to have inaugurated an era of freedom and equality.[45]

African Americans used the tropes of the enlightenment, including reason, liberty, natural rights and equality, turning them against the dominant language of the American Revolution. They deployed arguments very similar to those used in Colombia in favour of racial equality, albeit with crucial variations that reveal their different stations within (or without) the national imaginary. While Afro-Colombians questioned whites' commitment to implement the revolutionary legacy of legal racial equality, African Americans would challenge a notion of equality that did not include blacks. From the early years of the revolution, they petitioned for abolition and equal citizenship rights. Unlike northern abolitionists, they asked for immediate—not gradual—emancipation.[46] They challenged a discourse of freedom that did not address black bondage and a discourse of equality that did not take into account that 'Reason and Revelation join to declare that we are the creatures of that God, who made of one Blood and Kindred all the Nations of the Earth.' From this perspective, a nation that prided itself on its liberty could not support racism and racial inequality. They also had to challenge the premises of white racism. In 1813, the black intellectual George Lawrence stated, 'vacuous must the reasons of that man be . . . who dared to assert that genius is confined to complexion, or that nature knows difference in the immortal soul of man.'[47] In 1811, during the fourth anniversary of the abolition of the slave trade another African-American critic denounced that people who defended racism and racial difference showed a 'depravity of mind or profligacy of morals inferior to that imputed to us.'

The different place and status of Afro-Colombians and African Americans had further implications. African Americans could not claim to embody the revolutionary legacy of the founding fathers. Unlike Simón Bolívar, who confined his racial fears to his private correspondence while emphasizing racial equality in his public speeches and writings, Thomas Jefferson was not afraid to publicly express his racial views on blacks. In his *Notes on the State of Virginia*, Jefferson concluded that the reasoning abilities of blacks was inferior to that of whites. Free blacks had no place in his vision of the new American Republic. He contrasted emancipation in Rome with emancipation in the United States. In his view, 'Rome could relatively easily free its slaves' since a freed slave mixed into the general population 'without staining the blood of his master.' In America, emancipation must be followed immediately by removal 'beyond the reach of mixture.'[48] This view contrasted notably with the vision taken by most Colombians that mixture would be the solution to racial conflict. Clearly, this American founding father would not be an inspiration for black national inclusion and racial equality. The black mathematician Benjamin Banneker pointed out in a 1792 letter to Jefferson how deplorable it was that the man who wrote the Declaration of Independence held, 'by fraud and violence, so numerous part of my brethren, under groaning captivity, and cruel oppression.'[49] Notably, some African Americans looked abroad for a founding father. They found him in Bolívar, and some even named their children after him.[50]

Denunciations of the origins of slavery also reflected regional differences that may be attributed to contrasts in the ways in which race and nationalism were configured in the revolutionary and post-revolutionary periods. In the 1820s, both the United States and Colombia developed a similar narrative about the evil origins of slavery. According to an 1820s public speech by Maria W. Steward, an African-American woman, the 'unfriendly whites first drove the native American from his much-loved home. Then they stole our fathers from their peaceful and quiet dwellings, and brought them hither, and made bond-men and bond-women of them and their little ones.'[51] This denunciation reflects almost verbatim the speeches delivered in Colombia during manumission ceremonies of the 1820s and are revealing of similar discourses of racial equality that circulated at the time. The enormous difference is the context. While in Colombia these statements were argued during official Independence Day celebrations in which both black and whites participated, in the United States they were confined to segregated black churches and addressed to a black audience. In the United States, they did not belong in official national celebrations.[52] Moreover, in Colombia these speeches were often delivered by white Colombians and they blamed Spaniards not whites for slavery. In contrast, in the above speech, 'unfriendly whites,' not just the British, carried the blame. With no end to slavery or racial discrimination in sight, African Americans had no reason to exculpate white Americans from the sin of slavery and to attribute it only to the British. In the 1820s, the United States provided no space where whites and blacks could rejoice together in the steps taken by the Republic to abolish slavery and end racial inequality.

Unable to participate in national spaces, in the United States African Americans had fewer opportunities to address a multiracial community. While Afro-Colombians tended to address their speeches to all Colombians, African Americans were more likely to address theirs to fellow African Americans. This is clear in David Walker's famous 1829 *Appeal* denouncing the emptiness of the Declaration of Independence and comparing whites' paltry 'suffering under Great Britain' with the 'cruelties and murders' inflicted on black people. The title of Walker's work, *Appeal, in Four Articles, Together with a Preamble, to the Coloured Citizens of the World, But in Particular, and Very Expressly, to those of the United States of America*, explicitly targets people of colour as its intended audience. The American Revolution had clearly not produced a political rhetoric of common suffering under colonialism nor of common liberation under the Republic.

Divergent Paths

The divergent associations between patriotism and race developed during the wars of independence exercised an enormous influence on national identities. Racial equality could become a core element of the national ideology, as in Spanish America, or it could hover as a precarious concept constantly subject to challenge, as in the United States. In Colombia, the revolution transformed racial equality from one political position among many to an unchallengeable principle. And so, despite the numerous civil wars and constitutional changes, the principle of legal racial equality was never questioned in Colombia. The power and endurance of this notion became apparent during the height of scientific racism in the late nineteenth century, when many Latin American intellectuals refrained from wholeheartedly embracing European racism. They tended to reject the European condemnation of miscegenation. Instead, they hoped that their nations would progressively whiten through racial mixing. More to the point, the moderate racial discourse of whitening continued to emphasize racial unity and equality.[53]

Subsequent struggles to end formal and informal racial inequality would have to confront the diverse legacies of the Age of Revolution. In the United States, blacks would be excluded from the national imaginary and denied equal legal rights. Yet they would form powerful and lasting political organizations to fight against formal and informal discrimination and prejudice. In Colombia, blacks would enjoy legal equality. At the same time, they would face great difficulty in fighting prejudice and informal discrimination in an environment that had made the denunciation of racism taboo.

Paradoxically, Colombian nationalist ideology of racial harmony and equality was further consolidated by the discrimination practiced against blacks in the United States. When the United States replaced Spain as the new imperial power in the region, it assumed Spain's former place in the nationalist rhetoric that distinguished between Colombian racial tolerance and imperial discrimination. In the wake of United States expansionism, Colombian intellectuals highlighted the differences between United States racism and the liberties that *gente de colour* enjoyed in Colombia.[54] Over time, Spain ceased to be blamed as the source of slavery and racism. Instead, old Spain now began to be recognized as the cultural foundation of Colombian racial tolerance. This new national ideology would now distinguish between Anglo-Saxon racism and Hispanic tolerance. Already in 1869, Sergio Arboleda attributed to Spanish Catholicism a special degree of racial tolerance. Due to the influence of 'Catholic fraternity the Spanish slave was not, like the English, a beast of labour, but . . . the labour partner of his master and almost a family member. Of all the slaves in the American colonies, the Spanish were the least miserable.' Because of Spanish laws, he continued, 'Blacks multiplied and were incorporated in the new society, without the diversity of their colour or origin being an obstacle: they were Christian, and baptism made them equal to the other members of the Church.' Thus, 'of all the nations that colonized these countries, Spain was the only capable of creating this society of heterogeneous elements.'[55]

Racial equality had ceased to be a republican novelty. It had now become an Iberian and Catholic cultural heritage that distinguished Latin America from the Anglo-Saxon United States. The process of forgetting the foundational significance of the age of republican revolutions for the ideology of racial equality had begun. With it, Colombia's contributions to the history of decolonization were likewise erased. Its vanguard role in decolonizing race and forging political modernity would be overshadowed by narratives that assigned those roles to Europe and the United States.

Notes

1. For an earlier version of this argument, see Marixa Lasso, 'Race War and Nation in Caribbean Gran Colombia, Cartagena, 1810–1832,' *American Historical Review* 111:2 (2006), 336–340. On the participation of people of African descent in the Wars of Independence, see George Reid Andrews, *The Afro-Argentines of Buenos Aires, 1800–1900* (Madison: University of Wisconsin Press, 1980); Peter Guardino, *Peasants, Politics, and the Formation of Mexico's National State* (Stanford: Stanford University Press, 1996); Alfonso Múnera, *El fracaso de la nación: Región, clase y raza en el Caribe colombiano, 1717–1821* (Bogotá: Ancora Editores, 1998); Aline Helg, *Liberty & Equality in Caribbean Colombia: 1770–1835* (Chapel Hill: University of North Carolina Press, 2004); Seth Meisel, 'From Slave to Citizen-Soldier in Early Independence Argentina,' *Historical Reflections*, 29:1 (2003), 65–82; Marixa Lasso, *Myths of Harmony: Race and Republicanism During the Age of Revolution, Colombia 1795–1831* (Pittsburgh: University of Pittsburgh Press, 2007); Alejandro E. Gómez, 'La revolución de Caracas desde abajo,' *Nuevo Mundo Mundos Nuevos* (17 May 2008), http://journals.openedition.org/nuevomundo/32982; Alejandro E. Gómez, 'Del *affaire* de los mulatos al asunto de los Pardos,' in María Teresa Calderón y Clément Thibaud, eds., *Las Revoluciones del Mundo Atlántico* (Bogotá: Taurus, 2006), 301–321; Peter Blanchard, *Under the Flags of Freedom: Slave Soldiers & the Wars of Independence in Spanish South America* (Pittsburgh: University of Pittsburgh Press, 2008); Hendrik Kraay, *Race, State, and Armed Forces in Independence-Era Brazil: Bahia, 1790s-1840s* (Stanford: Stanford University Press, 2001); Marcela Echeverri, *Indian and Slave Royalists in the Age of Revolution: Reform, Revolution, and Royalism in the Northern Andes, 1780–1825* (New York: Cambridge University Press, 2016).
2. See David Brion Davis, *The Problem of Slavery in Western Culture* (Ithaca: Oxford University Press, 1966), 229 and Anthony Marx, *Making Race and Nation: A Comparison of South Africa, the United States, and Brazil* (New York: Cambridge University Press, 1998), 10.

3. Alexander Saxton, *The Rise and Fall of the White Republic: Class Politics and Mass Culture in Nineteenth-Century America* (New York and London: Verso, 2003); David R. Roediger, *The Wages of Whiteness: Race and the Making of the American Working Class* (New York and London: Verso, 2007); Douglas Bradburn, *The Citizenship Revolution: Politics and the Creation of the American Union* (Charlottesville: University of Virginia Press, 2009).
4. Antonello Gerbi, *The Dispute of the New World: The History of a Polemic, 1750–1900* (Pittsburgh: University of Pittsburgh Press, 1973), 3–79, 195–208, 252–268.
5. For Saint Domingue, see John D. Garrigus, *Before Haiti: Race and Citizenship in French Saint-Domingue* (New York: Palgrave Macmillan, 2006), 123.
6. 'Informe que el Ayuntamiento de Caracas hace al Rey de España referente a la Real Cédula de 10 de febrero de 1795,' in José Félix Blanco, ed., *Documentos para la Historia de la vida pública del Libertador* (Caracas: Ediciones de la Presidencia de la República, 1878), 293.
7. James Otis, *The Rights of the British Colonies Asserted and Proved* (Boston, reprinted for J. Almon: London, 1764), 36.
8. Garrigus, *Before Haiti*, 111–114.
9. François-Xavier Guerra, *Modernidad e Independencias: Ensayos sobre las revoluciones hispánicas* (México: Fondo de Cultura Económica, 1993); François-Xavier Guerra, Antonio Annino and Luis Castro Leiva, eds., *De los imperios a las naciones: Iberoamérica* (Zaragoza, Spain: Ibercaja, 1994).
10. See Gabriel Di Meglio, *¡Viva el bajo pueblo! La plebe urbana de Buenos Aires y la Política entre la Revolución de Mayo y el Rosismo* (Buenos Aires: Prometeo Libros, 2007); Laurent Dubois, *A Colony of Citizens: Revolution and Slave Emancipation in the French Caribbean, 1787–1804* (Chapel Hill: University of North Carolina Press, 2004); Guardino, *Peasants, Politics*; Peter Guardino, *The Time of Liberty: Popular Political Culture in Oaxaca* (Durham: Duke University Press, 2005); Marixa Lasso, *Myths of Harmony*; Daniel Gutiérrez Ardila, *La Restauración en la Nueva Granada (1815–1819)* (Bogotá: Universidad Externado de Colombia, 2016); Jairo Gutiérrez Ramos, *Los indios de Pasto contra la República, (1809–1824)* (Bogotá: ICANH, 2007); Florencia Mallon, *Peasant and Nation: The Making of Postcolonial Mexico and Peru* (Berkeley: University of California Press, 1995); Cecilia Mendez, *The Plebeian Republic: The Huanta Rebellion and the Making of the Peruvian State, 1820–1850* (Durham: Duke University Press, 2005); James Sanders, *Contentious Republicans: Popular Politics, Race, and Class in Nineteenth-Century Colombia* (Durham: Duke University Press, 2004); Alfonso Múnera, *El fracaso*; Ricardo Salvatore, *Wandering Paysanos: State Order and Subaltern Experience in Buenos Aires During the Rosas Era* (Durham: Duke University Press, 2003); Sinclair Thomson, *We Alone Will Rule: Native Andean Politics in the Age of Insurgency* (Madison: University of Wisconsin Press, 2002); Mark Thurner, *From Two Republics to One Divided: Contradictions of Postcolonial Nationmaking in Andean Peru* (Durham: Duke University Press, 1997); Michel-Rolph Trouillot, *Silencing the Past: Power and the Production of History* (Boston: Beacon, 1996).
11. Guerra, *Modernidad e Independencias*, 36.
12. See Elias Palti, 'Beyond Revisionism: The Bicentennial of Independence, the Early Republican Experience, and Intellectual History in Latin America,' *Journal of the History of Ideas* 70:4 (October 2009), 593–614.
13. Some of these arguments appeared in Marixa Lasso, 'Los grupos afrodescendientes y la independencia: ¿un nuevo paradigma historiográfico?' in Alejandro Gómez, Clément Thibaud, Gabriel Entín y Federica Morelli, eds., *L'Atlantique révolutionnaire: Une perspective ibéro-américaine* (Perséides, 2013), 359–378.

14. 'Instrucciones que deberá observarse en las elecciones parroquiales, en las de partido y en las capitulares, para el nombramiento de diputados en la Suprema Junta de la provincia de Cartagena,' 11 December 1810, in Manuel Ezequiel Corrales, ed., *Efemérides y anales del Estado de Bolívar* (Bogotá: Editorial de J. Peréz, 1889), 2:48.
15. Gómez, 'La revolución de Caracas,' 12.
16. Ibid., 13.
17. Ibid., 12.
18. Ibid., 15–16.
19. Lasso, *Myths of Harmony*, 79.
20. Gómez, 'La revolución de Caracas,' 20.
21. Ibid., 18.
22. Ramón Díaz Sánchez, *Libro de Actas del Supremo Congreso de Venezuela, 11811–1812* (Caracas: Academia Nacional de la Historia MCMLIX, 1959), 254–262; Manuel Alfredo Rodriquez, 'Los Pardos libres en la colonia y la independencia,' *Boletín de la Academia Nacional de la Historia* 75:299 (1992), 52.
23. Lasso, *Myths of Harmony*, 47.
24. I develop these arguments further in 'Race War and Nation in Caribbean Gran Colombia,' 341–347, and *Myths of Harmony*, 34–57.
25. Lasso, *Myths of Harmony*, 55.
26. Simón Bolívar, 'A los pueblos de Venezuela,' Guyana, August 5, 1817, in *Obras Completas* (Madrid: Ediciones Alonso, 1960), 647.
27. Ibid.
28. Jaime Jaramillo Uribe, 'La controversia jurídica y filosófica, librada en la Nueva Granada en torno a la liberación de los esclavos y la importancia económica y social de la esclavitud en el siglo XIX,' *Anuario de Historia Social y de la Cultura* (1969), 4, 63–86; Margarita González, 'El proceso de manumisión en Colombia,' 150–240; Harold A. Bierck, Jr., 'The Struggle for Abolition in Gran Colombia,' *HAHR* 33:3 (1953), 365–386; Marcela Echeverry, *Indian and Slave*, 157–190.
29. This speech took place in Mompox on Independence Day celebrations in 1823 and was printed in *Gaceta de Cartagena de Colombia*, January 17, 1824.
30. For a detailed analysis of the case, see Lasso, *Myths of Harmony*, 108–115.
31. For a more detailed analysis, see Lasso, *Myths of Hamony*, 115–128, 144–148. For a different perspective, see Aline Helg, *Liberty and Equality*.
32. General José Padilla, 'Al respetable público de Cartagena' (November 15, 1824), AGN-Colombia, Restrepo, Fondo 11, caja 88. Translation in Helg, *Liberty and Equality*, 195.
33. José Manuel Restrepo, *Historia de la Revolución de la República de Colombia* (1858 Reprint Medellín: Editorial Bedout, 1974), v. 1, 189–190.
34. David Geggus, 'Racial Equality, Slavery, and Colonial Secession During the Constituent Assembly,' *American Historical Review* 94 (1989), 5, 1290–1308, and David Geggus, *Haitian Revolutionary Studies* (Bloomington: Indiana University Press, 2002), 8–11.
35. Quote in Laurent Dubois, *Avengers of the New World: The Story of the Haitian Revolution* (Cambridge: Harvard University Press, 2004), 195.
36. Carlo Célius, 'Neoclassicism and the Haitian Revolution,' in David Geggus and Norman Fiering, eds., *The World of the Haitian Revolution* (Bloomington: Indiana University Press, 2008), 352–392.
37. David Nicholls, *From Dessalines to Duvalier: Race, Colour and National Independence in Haiti* (New Brunswick: Rutgers University Press, 1996 [1979]), 55–57, 71–73.
38. I am summarizing Woody Holton, *Forced Founders: Indians, Debtors, Slaves, and the Making of the American Revolution in Virginia* (Chapel Hill:

University of North Carolina Press, 1999), 133–163; John Wood Sweets, *Bodies Politic: Negotiating Race in the American North, 1730–1830* (Baltimore: Johns Hopkins University Press, 2003), 189–191.
39. Bradburn, *The Citizenship Revolution*, 235–271.
40. Ibid., 256–262, Lasso, *Myths of Harmony*, 60–67.
41. Roediger, *The Wages of Whiteness*, 27.
42. Martha S. Jones, 'Hugues V Jackson: Race and Rights Beyond Dred Scott,' *North Carolina Law Review* 91 (2013), 1757–1783.
43. Roediger, *The Wages of Whiteness*, 24.
44. Leonard I. Sweet, 'The Fourth of July and Black Americans in the Nineteenth Century: Northern Leadership Opinion Within the Context of Black Experience,' *Journal of Negro History* 61:3 (1976), 258–259; Shane White, '"It was a Proud Day": African Americans, Festivals, and Parades in the North, 1741–1834,' *The Journal of American History* 81 (1994), 38–41; Gary Nash, *The Forgotten Fifth: African Americans in the Age of Revolution* (Cambridge: Harvard University Press, 2006), 121–168.
45. Manisha Sinha, 'To "cast just obliquy" on Oppressors: Black Radicalism in the Age of Revolution,' *William and Mary Quarterly*, 3d series, 64:1 (2007), 149–160.
46. Ibid., 151.
47. Ibid., 156.
48. Saxton, *The Rise and Fall of the White Republic*, 31.
49. Sinha, 'To "cast just obliquy" on Oppressors,' 153.
50. Caitlin Fitz, *Our Sister Republics: The United States in an Age of American Revolutions* (New York: Liveright Publishing Corporation, 2016), 80–155, 194–239.
51. My emphasis. Quoted in Sinha, 'To "cast just obliquy" on Oppressors,' 158.
52. Ibid., 152.
53. For Latin American ideas on race, see Richard Graham ed., *The Idea of Race in Latin America, 1870–1940* (Austin: University of Texas Press, 1990). For a careful analysis of the relationship between racial discourse and Afro-Cuban political participation in the twentieth century, see Alejandro de La Fuente, *A Nation for All: Race, Inequality, and Politics in Twentieth-Century Cuba* (Chapel Hill: University of North Carolina Press, 2001).
54. I am building on Aims McGuiness, 'Searching for "Latin America": Race and Sovereignty in the Americas in the 1850s,' in Nancy P. Appelbaum, Anne S. Macpherson, and Karin Alejandra Rosemblatt, eds., *Race and Nation in Modern Latin America* (Chapel Hill: University of North Carolina Press, 2003), 97.
55. G. de Soroa, *La República en la América Española* (Bogotá: Imprenta Foción Mantilla, 1869), 34. 'G de Soroa' was Sergio Arboleda's pseudonym.

5 Decolonizing Europe

James Sanders

By the middle decades of the nineteenth century, many Colombians and Mexicans were confident that their societies were well on the way to overcoming the legacies of colonialism. Freed of the shackles of the past, their young nations were actively engaged in the collective creation of a new civilization based on equality among men.[1] Were they all simply deluded? Were journalists, lawyers, peasants, Indians, and ex-slaves all trapped in a 'colonialist mentality' that prohibited them from even imagining 'decolonization,' as decolonial theorist Walter Mignolo imagines?[2] Today's critics of modernity applaud themselves for dismantling the totalizing claims of European modernity. But nineteenth-century Latin Americans beat them to it. They dismantled Europe's claims to modernity and civilization,[3] thereby 'provincializing Europe' long before postcolonial and decolonial theorists said they could not.[4]

From the 1850s to the 1880s many Mexicans and Colombians firmly believed it was not Latin America that must be decolonized but Europe. Mexicans and Colombians were busy creating new nations with a vibrant new citizenry that would enjoy and export the fruits of liberty, equality, and fraternity. Meanwhile, the European landscape was characterized by monarchy, aristocracy, feudalism, ultramontane religion, and the 'internal colonization' of the Irish, Italians, Hungarians, and Poles. Europe was lorded over by inbred tyrants and a corrupt and decadent aristocracy, while most of its subjects—not citizens, as in the Americas—were so oppressed that they 'almost do not feel their chains.'[5] There was hope, however. 'The eagles of American democracy' would cross the Atlantic and transmogrify Europe, inspire internal rebellions, and regenerate European society. In short, the Americas would decolonize Europe.[6]

In this chapter, I outline Mexican and Colombian views of colonialism and Europe during the key, mid-century decades of civil war and republican reformism in the Americas. I briefly explore how subaltern Mexicans and Colombians expressed great faith in the potential of their new nations to free them from the shackles of colonialism, and I compare these period attitudes with more current conceptions of the Latin American nation. I then outline how Hispanic American ideas about European backwardness crossed the Atlantic via the Garibaldinos in Uruguay and the debate over Maximilian's execution by a Mexican firing squad. Finally, I consider how this Hispanic American history of republican decolonization urges us to rethink Europe's role in the history and theory of decolonization.

Europe: 'Land of Tyranny and Human Degradation'

As French troops invaded Mexico in 1862 and civil war wracked the failing and divided United States, a Guadalajara newspaper exclaimed that Mexico 'represents the interests of the New World, land of democracy, combating the interests of the Old World, land of tyranny and human degradation.'[7] In Mexico and Colombia from the late 1840s until the 1870s, such proclamations of the vanguard role in the world of the Hispanic American republics were not at all uncommon. Mexicans and Colombians—writing in newspapers and orating at public gatherings— regularly contrasted American progress with European backwardness.

By the 1860s a broad consensus had emerged in both Colombia and Mexico that the future of the world lay in their own hands. While many still saw Europe as cultured and powerful, republican politics and discourse in the Americas had shifted the center of civilization. A Mexican provincial newspaper was typical: by instilling 'democracy' at home Mexico had not only reached the same level of civilization as Europe; it would now 'resuscitate the republican genius of France, awakening her subjects and slaves.'[8] A Colombian newspaperman put it more succinctly in 1864: 'Europe is the past, America the future.'[9] Civilization, once defined by Europe, had now passed to the Americas, and the flow of modernity, once imagined as emanating from Europe to the Americas had been reversed, following the Gulf Stream from the New World to the Old.[10] In my recent book I call this alternative vision of civilization that ruled the mid-century public sphere 'American republican modernity.' In this mentalité and discourse, modernity was not defined by European culture or economic advancement but by republican political culture, enacted by citizens, and whose locus was the Americas, not Europe.

This discourse was by no means limited to Mexico and Colombia. In 1860, *El Ferrocarril* of Chile complained of Europeans' continued assertions of dominance and superiority in civilization, demanding: 'Where is our inferiority?' The paper argued that Europe was built both upon an 'ancient lie—the divine right of kings—and now upon a brand-new sophism—constitutional monarchy.' The Americas therefore enjoyed a 'decisive superiority' over Europe, due to its republicanism. The New World had already progressed further down the road of modernity and civilization than had Europe: 'America, *throwing off the iron collar of colonialism*, already has completed the great revolution, the great transformation, the grand execution of the past' while Europe still suffered monarchs and caudillos. Finally, the essayist asserted that the influence of America would spread to Europe, as 'democracy will destroy current European society.'[11] Colonialism—associated with monarchy—was European, and Europeans still suffered under it; Americans had embraced democracy, conquering their colonial past via revolution.

The Americas would spread their democracy to Europe—they would decolonize and repair Europe's backwardness. In the dusty provincial town of Chihuahua in 1868, a crowd gathering to celebrate Mexico's independence listened as an unremarkable orator (Manuel Merino) made a very remarkable but not uncommon assertion about the origin and spread of modernity in the nineteenth-century Atlantic world: 'the Eagles of American democracy, crossing the Atlantic, will import into the Old World the modern doctrines of political association, thereby emancipating those peoples.'[12] The speech, made in the context of Mexico's victory over Maximilian and his French Army, celebrated the restoration of the republic in Mexico.

America had broken colonialism's chains, but the spirit of imperialism still lived on in Europe, and Americans must be ready to resist Europe's attempts to crush their progress. Gabino Ortiz, speaking to the Morelia National Guard in 1862, mocked:

> The decrepit nations of Europe, the rotten thrones of their sickly dynasties, the rancid and strange institutions that rule them, all feel the convulsions of their final agony. In order to distract themselves from the frightening spectacle of a past from which they flee, from a present that escapes them, and from an inevitable future, they turn their sights on young America, object of their envy, hatred, and insatiable greed.[13]

Ortiz, addressing perhaps four thousand men, now equated modernity with 'young America,' a discourse powerfully resonant in the public sphere.[14] Instead of bringing civilization, Juan Cervin de la Mora claimed in a speech to artisans, the European invasion of Mexico would only 'regress us back to the times of horror and barbarism'—in other words, to colonialism.[15] American republicanism associated feudalism and the Inquisition with Europe, the origin of that putrid 'fanaticism' that New World societies struggled to destroy.[16] Ortiz mocked the Spanish pretension to bring 'the inquisition, the cowl, and stocks' back to Mexico; such Old World 'fanaticism,' its colonial spirit, was inappropriate in the Century of Enlightenment.[17]

In Peru, Federico Flores described the race to civilization, and the divide between Europe and America, in historical terms, a conception that challenges our own notions of the history of decolonization. America began to gain in the race of civilization upon the independence of the United States, followed by the nations of Spanish America, where 'democracy triumphed.' Since then, America had taken the lead: 'The Old World has sunk and will sink further into decadence, it continues converting its proverbial culture and progress into nothing but ruins; this has come to pass because those states do not have Republican Governments.' Meanwhile, American republics, following the law and 'the will of the people' were 'every day moving closer to the apex of civilization.' Perhaps Europe once held a claim on modernity, but no longer. And unlike Europe, America would not retrogress as France had after her revolution, degenerating from republic to monarchy.[18] Europe had tried to achieve modernity—with the French Revolution—but the forces of retrogression had triumphed. The River Plate–born Héctor Varela had a similar, if chronologically deeper historical understanding. Writing from Paris, he founded *El Americano* to introduce Europe to the true progress of 'Latin America.' He argued that the New World marked the end of the 'Middle Ages' in which Europe and Christianity were champions of civilization. Now, however, the Americas had progressed beyond Europe in their adoption of 'the democratic doctrine,' liberty, rights, and state institutions, but most especially, 'the Republic,' which was 'the definitive form of our spirit.' Varela asserted, 'Taking this point of view, one can say that the New World is the most potent incarnation of the modern spirit.' The New World was modern, and if Europe would listen it could learn valuable lessons to help bring about 'universal democracy.'[19]

If Europe were to advance, its own peoples must engage in the republican revolutions that had already succeeded in the Americas. Europeans would have to decolonize themselves, breaking up their old monarchies and empires. 'Decrepit Europe retrogresses in all parts,' Jesús Escobar y Armendáriz argued, adding, 'We are heading toward a universal Republic' that had already been achieved in Mexico and much of Spanish America, even if in Europe Hungary, Poland, and Italy were still struggling against despotism.[20] Mexico's *El Republicano* warned that 'the thrones that exist there do not want to see even one flourishing republic in the world,' since this might serve as a lesson for their own people to rebel and establish republics.[21] In short, the New World was now civilization's best hope.

Dipesh Chakrabarty argues that outside of Europe, modernity is always imagined as something that happens elsewhere, an argument echoed by some Latin Americanists, one of whom declares that nineteenth-century Hispanic Americans always felt that modernity flowered 'somewhere else.'[22] In this period in Mexico or Colombia such a sentiment would have been expressed only by the most reactionary Europhiles. In contrast, the Chilean progressive Francisco Bilbao understood that civilization was not a fixed concept or station; he proposed that there was a vast struggle underway of 'American civilization against European civilization.'[23] Bilbao proclaimed that Europe had declined due to its monarchies and imperialism, that it was lacking in true liberty and justice; it would have to wait for American influence to incite republican revolutions if it hoped to progress once again.[24]

The challenge to Europe found its most forceful enunciation in Mexican society during and after the French Intervention (1862–1867). In this era, Mexican Liberals not only asserted that the Americas were more modern and that her modernity would come to influence change in Europe, but that American republicanism was a direct threat to the backward European status quo. As the French invaded in 1862, *El Voto del Pueblo* claimed: 'Luis Napoleon has made war on us because he fears America, because he hates republics, and because he sees in Mexico democracy and the Reform made real.' If Mexico 'had stayed in a state of barbarism and fanaticism' and had not 'transformed itself through La Reforma and launched itself towards a future of progress and liberty; if [Mexico] had not adopted as dogma the sovereignty of the pueblo and exposed as a lie and sarcasm the divine right of kings,' then Napoleon III would not have needed to invade.[25] Here, barbarism is explicitly linked with colonialism and monarchy. Mexico was not waiting blindly to receive and imitate modernity from Europe; rather, with victory, Mexico would bring modernity to Europe, who would follow the lead of the Americas.[26] In 1871, *El Aguijón* mocked France for still being ruled by a monarch as laughable as Napoleon III, calling him 'the Jester of the Tuileries.'[27] Mexico's newspapers predicted the French people would soon awaken from its slumber and, inspired by 'our 57'—la Reforma, in other words—execute another monarch and thus initiate a new future.[28]

While most of this American discourse held that republicanism in general was a threat to the ancien régime, Juan González Urueña, writing from Morelia, explicitly focused on liberty and equality. He argued that European monarchs feared 'the spread of, as much in the Old World as the New, the ideas of republican equality and political and religious liberty, all of which are undermining slowly but surely their thrones' support.'[29] If allowed to spread, such ideas would eventually destroy Old World monarchies. The Atlantic world was a vast arena in which the forces of equality, enlightenment and republicanism confronted aristocracy, superstition, and monarchy. Yet by staking the justification for American defense on equality, Mexico's elite republicans reified in the public sphere a notion that subalterns could easily seize and exploit. Equality was a threat to European thrones, but also to the Hispanic American ruling class and the incipient capitalist development that it hoped to foment.

As this discourse reveals, many Hispanic Americans thought European societies must be transformed if they were to progress, to become modern. Although they did not use the French term 'decolonization' they did use the verb 'decolonize' and the concept of 'colonial system,' as Mark Thurner demonstrates for Peru in this volume. By mid-century, for Liberals, colonialism's meaning had hardened, equated with monarchy, aristocracy, feudalism, backwardness, racism (the caste system), obscurantism, and the lack of national independence—and it is these elements that still defined Europe in Hispanic American eyes. Hispanic Americans thus thought Europe was still internally colonized, in two senses. First, Europe still suffered actual internal colonies—Ireland (which should 'imitate one day Mexican heroism' and rebel against England[30]), Poland, and Hungary—and it also harbored peoples lacking a national state and divided among feudal states—most notably, Italy. As Italy struggled for nationhood, a Cali newspaper swooned: 'When we speak of the Old World, we do not speak of you, young Italy! You are the America of Europe.'[31] Second, Europe's 'decolonization' would mean that internal revolutions were required to establish democratic republics of citizens, 'emancipating those peoples from the backward and humiliating servitude by which their Lords have them enchained . . . in order to establish popular sovereignty.'[32] In short, republicanism or 'republicanization' would have far-reaching, decolonizing effects on politics and society.

If, in this vision, Europe appeared to need decolonizing more than its former colonies, this did not mean that destroying colonialism's legacies was not a domestic concern in Colombia and Mexico. Decolonization (and modernity) had begun with independence, when the Americas broke from a barbarous Spain, and 'exchanged liberty for slavery, justice for arbitrary despotism, enlightenment for ignorance and fanaticism, civilization for heinous customs of barbarism, and finally, our new institutions for those stale ones of subjecthood.'[33] The colonial epoch was shorthand for backwardness: domination by an ultramontane clergy, indigenous communal landholding, the caste system, and economic stagnation.[34] Spain had enriched itself, leaving nothing of value behind; only brutalizing, physically and intellectually, its colonies' inhabitants.[35] The broader public sphere's vision of Spain under mid-century American republicanism contrasts sharply with the lettered elite's growing embrace of the Iberian heritage, detailed by Rebecca Earle, later in the century.[36]

Independence from Spain, however, was only the first step. The mid-century triumphs and reforms of liberal republicans were more important. The new nations' problems could be blamed on Spanish colonialism and lingering European influence. In 1855, Ramón Mercado argued that Independence had not really changed the colonial system, as 'the war against Spain was not a revolution'; it had not ended slavery, the power of the Church, or the aristocracy, and most people were still excluded from a role in governance.[37] All of these hallmarks of colonialism—save slavery—were still powerfully associated with Europe. It would take the 'social revolution' of liberal reforms to truly remake society, a revolution carried out by the poor and dispossessed who 'contributed to the triumph of Democracy.'[38] By 1852, Colombian President José Hilario López declared in a speech that 'a social revolution' had occurred as 'the reign of democracy and liberty had arrived' to destroy the 'feudalism of the Middle Ages' which still oppressed society, specifically referring to slavery.[39] In Mexico, the failures of the pre-Reform era were simplified as the aristocracy's success in maintaining their colonial prerogatives against reformers' efforts. Santa Anna's complex political career, during which time he won support from and supported federalists and centralists, could now be summed up as his attempt to organize an 'aristocratic government.'[40] Opposing reform, of course, were Conservatives, who Liberals believed wanted to return Mexico to the 'colonial regime.'[41] Leading liberal historian Justo Sierra defined the conservatives as those who 'wished to maintain Mexico indefinitely in a colonial state.'[42] After the consolidation of La Reforma many Mexicans expressed great confidence in a future free of the shackles of colonialism. In Colombia by the 1860s many came to echo President López's similar optimism.

This republican confidence in a decolonized future belies Walter Mignolo's assertion that Latin America was trapped by the remnants of colonialism and an unsuitable and foreign Atlantic republican tradition, and that as a result 'decolonization' was not an option in the nineteenth century.[43] On the contrary, many Colombians and Mexicans did not think themselves doomed or trapped by the European 'colonial system.' Indeed, they saw their societies leading the way in the creation of a new civilization that would root out any remnants of European colonialism. If the goal of postcolonial critique is 'the pursuit of liberation after the achievement of political independence,' then mid-nineteenth century Colombians and Mexicans thought they were further along this path of liberation than Europe itself.[44]

If European colonialism was still a threat to republican Mexico, it was so less in the form of lingering internal colonial legacies and more in the external threat posed by renewed European imperial adventures. While Europe was embarking on its second great wave of imperial conquest abroad, creating a new colonialism that would define 'colonialism' and 'modernity' to this day, Mexicans proposed a counter-modernity that rejected the equation of civilization with Europe. Thus, Jesús Escobar y Armendáriz blamed the current state of Asia and Africa on ancient European colonial incursions by 'the barbarians of the North,' from Alexander the Great to the Crusades; now Napoleon III invaded Mexico, where 'he tried to civilize with 50,000 bayonets.'[45] Europe was not only lacking civilization in this view but was responsible for exporting barbarism.[46]

The mid-century American critique of Europe prefigured that of today's postcolonial and decolonial critics, who point out that the violent cost of European modernity was borne by colonial peoples.[47] Yet, more than a century before the emergence of postcolonial and then decolonial theory, many Hispanic Americans had widely mocked European pretensions to civilization, equating Europe with backwardness and colonial conditions.[48] Francisco Bilbao also denounced the French (and, indirectly, Hegel) for claiming that civilization was a 'Spirit' that created the 'modern world,' thereby justifying their imperialist adventures in Algeria, China, and Mexico.[49]

After the defeat of the French Intervention in Mexico and the liberal victory in the 1860–1863 civil war in Colombia, liberals of all social and ethnic groups in both nations grew increasingly confident in their futures. Yes, they knew they had not achieved the economic progress of Europe and the United States, but many argued that the most important step—the political and social revolution—had been achieved. Europe's 'dazzling and corrupt materialism' was not nearly as important as the American success in securing rights and liberty.[50] Further, they were confident that the political modernity they created—the triumph over colonialism—would soon produce economic progress as well. Finally, they waited for the inevitable revolutions that would sweep and transform Europe—revolutions that they had inspired.

America: 'A Republican and Democratic Government . . . will not allow such Monstrosities'

The mid-century Hispanic-American discourse of European backwardness emanated from a public sphere produced primarily by elite and middling actors but frequently shared by popular sectors as well, mainly as criers, listeners, and readers. What did popular groups have to say about republican decolonization? Subalterns did not, in most cases, much concern themselves with Europe, but many studies have demonstrated that they did engage with one of the key vehicles of Hispanic American decolonization: the ex-colonial republican nation.[51]

The decolonization literature has, to put it mildly, looked with great suspicion on the postcolonial or ex-colonial 'liberal' nation as a vehicle for subaltern agency and inclusion.[52] That the twentieth-century nation was a 'failure' seems hardly open to debate anymore. But what about the nineteenth-century nation? For many if not most postcolonial, decolonial, and Subaltern Studies scholars, the Third World or postcolonial nation was always a failure.[53] This sense of national failure founded, for example, the project of South Asian Subaltern Studies. As Ranajit Guha noted, 'it is the study of this failure which constitutes the central problematic of the historiography of colonial India.'[54] Such a hopeless and teleological notion of national failure was foreign to most subalterns in nineteenth-century Mexico and Colombia, however, when the ex-colonial republican nation promised meaningful citizenship and the tools to shape the future of the national community. After independence, Mexican and Colombian popular actors, be they freed people of color, Indians, or peasants, eagerly claimed citizenship rights. A traditional view of the post-independence nation suggests its subaltern inhabitants were merely concerned with the *patria chica* or parish pump of their immediate surroundings. In this view, the state barely existed and the nation not at all, except as a glimmer in the minds of bureaucrats and intellectuals (the infamous *letrados*) in Bogotá or Mexico City. Subalterns should have been unaware, unconcerned or actively hostile to the very idea of these inscrutable new nations, which in any case were illegitimate. But such was not the case.[55] Indians, long presented as being the most indifferent and hostile to national projects, often passionately asserted their identity as citizens.[56] A common opening to petitions in Colombia was some variation of 'using the right to petition that the constitution conceded to every Granadan.'[57] The governor of an indigenous hamlet testified in a court case on voter fraud that Indians from his village, in spite of 'being citizens, were not able to deposit their votes in the ballot box.'[58] In another case, Indians from three villages wrote 'you are the father of us unfortunate citizens,' to the new governor, hoping for a more sympathetic treatment of their case.[59] Indians from yet another village in the Cauca state claimed, 'We are free citizens, like any other civilized Caucano.'[60]

Poor whites and mestizos likewise demanded the title and privileges of citizenship, simply by opening a petition as 'citizens of the Republic of New Granada,' or, in more complex form, by claiming to be critical components of the nation.[61] The residents of a frontier settlement in Colombia, after noting how they and their families had sacrificed to create a village, and had even built a church, out of a 'miserable wilderness,' asserted that before their arrival the land did not give 'any benefit to the nation' but that they would now 'give to the nation the benefit of a civilized and religious village.'[62] A petition from another frontier village reveals the petitioners' determination to take a place at the table of the nation. They wrote to get their elected head of district demanding 'the dispatch of a legislative act that assures the complete exercise of the sovereignty that the constitution delegates to citizens.' They closed their petition by reminding the legislators that 'liberty and independence are found in the cabin of the peasant, too.'[63]

Afro-Colombians also embraced citizenship, perhaps even more fervently since their colonial identity was associated so powerfully with slavery. From the coastal village of San Juan, ex-slaves wrote to the National Congress in these terms: 'We enjoy the precious possession of liberty, so long usurped, and with it all the other rights and prerogatives of citizens.'[64] Boatmen who ferried goods from the coast into the interior also protested in similar terms: 'We should be treated like citizens of a republic and not like the slaves of a sultan.'[65] Freedmen petitioning for land identified themselves as 'inhabitants of the San Julián Hacienda to which once we belonged as slaves,' but now presenting themselves 'before you, in the use of our rights as citizens.'[66] Although middling lawyers or scribes penned many of the petitions, it is clear that subalterns not only recognized the republican nation as new and distinct from the colonial regime, but that they also identified with the nation through the practice of citizenship.[67] Citizenship was the magnet that attracted subalterns. As Eric Hobsbawm noted for the European case, 'whatever else a nation was, the element of citizenship and mass participation or choice was never absent from it.'[68] Citizenship was perhaps even more attractive in the Americas, I would argue, for the radical-democratic conception of the nation that emerged across Latin America in the postcolonial era was in many ways more promising than its European counterpart. Thus, while Hobsbawm argues that what mattered to self-declared subaltern 'citizens' in Europe was an awareness of belonging to a historically 'lasting political entity,' in ex-colonial Hispanic America an awareness of belonging to a bold new political community made citizenship more appealing.[69] Historically, subalterns had known their position as subjects and had worked out fairly impressive ways of exploiting their relationship as such with the royal bureaucracy and Church, and Indians had been especially adept at this. I do not wish to suggest here that all subalterns embraced the nation—some sought their own independence outside the nation, others imagined new forms and vessels of politics, others held onto colonial identities to protect their life-ways.[70] My point is that for many lower-class people in Mexico and Colombia, citizenship presented an opportunity to carve out a more advantageous and egalitarian position.

Subalterns not only claimed citizenship in the new nations, they expected citizenship to matter. They quickly grasped that they now inhabited a new political and social space, and they seized the opportunities that the nation and republicanism presented. In a land dispute with merchants who wanted to limit the extraction of forest products, the residents of Tumaco, Colombia, derided their designs as a veiled attempt to reestablish 'a wretched feudalism,' while demanding that the national government protect their 'equality of rights.'[71] Subalterns often compared the denial of their access to land as a backward 'feudalism' opposed to the republican system.[72] Indians assumed in their petitions that a 'democratic' government would accede to their demands and let them keep their communal lands.[73] The largely Afro-Colombian members of one of the new Democratic Societies (political clubs) argued that without land of their own they would be reduced to becoming 'the peons and tributaries of an individual and ceasing to be citizens of a free people.'[74] In 1871 Indians from the Aldea of Cajamarca in Colombia wrote to the Cauca State president to insist that their *resguardos* not be subdivided. They noted how, under colonialism, they had been 'beaten down by Spanish greed into the most degrading state of slavery and misery.' But now that an 'enlightened republican government' was in power that 'proclaims equality and works to improve the unhappy situation of the noble aboriginal race,' their rights as citizens should be upheld and respected.[75]

Citizen petitioners did not hesitate to hold officials' feet to the republican fire. One petition from over forty residents of Paso del Bobo,

Veracruz, who lived 'by the sweat of the pueblo,' and most of whom could not sign their names, demanded that they be allowed to continue renting lands from the state at the same rate (the lands in question had been seized from the estate of General Santa Anna), as before their illegitimate eviction. The citizens continued, 'We expect that neither your Excellency nor the law will permit that the pueblo lives under oppression . . . as if the fight to enjoy Liberty in which our poor Patria is now engaged had been lost.'[76] These illiterate citizens thus made a direct connection between revolutions for liberty and their need for land.

Similarly, in Colombia, Sebastiana Silva petitioned the local government in Popayán for help in gaining the return of her son, who was forced to work as a domestic servant, a then not uncommon arrangement for poor children. She demanded his return, but the family refused, 'as if we still were in the barbarous times in which the government allowed the slavery of men. Today, thankfully, we have a republican and democratic government that will not allow such monstrosities.'[77] Silva was a poor, illiterate woman and her invocation of slavery—along with her family's situation of forced domestic service—suggests she was Afro-Colombian. She cleverly manipulated the discourse of American republican modernity, equating slavery with barbarism and calling on the authorities to live up to its own claims to legitimacy. In this sense, the petitions of subalterns 'heard' the elite discourse of European backwardness and insisted that the principles of democracy and republicanism be upheld in ways meaningful for them. Many of the poor and working class were able to take advantage of this discourse, asserting claims that are now well-documented in the literature.[78] The words and deeds of petitioners in Mexico and Colombia betray another serious problem with much of the postcolonial and decolonial theoretical literature that denies that 'decolonization' among subalterns was possible in the nineteenth century. That literature relies almost exclusively on elite writings. When we shift our focus back to popular groups, different visions of nation, citizenship and colony become much clearer.[79]

The political aspirations of Mexico's and Colombia's subalterns suggest we should take care when assuming nations functioned the same in postcolonial environments in the 1850s as in the 1950s. Subaltern Studies scholars, when discussing postcolonial India, note that the nation became more of a unit of control and political manipulation than a vehicle for emancipation, representation, or equality. Chatterjee argues that the concept that the subaltern majority 'had all become citizens of the republic' was a mere 'fiction.'[80] The new postcolonial nations, it rather quickly became clear, would not serve as vehicles for citizenship for the subaltern majority; nationalist elites would seize the nation for their own goals and interests. Guha notes how, in the struggle for the nation, elites always fell back on excluding and disciplining subaltern actors when their mobilization appeared to threaten elite interests. Elites 'construed and idealized as the interest of the nation' their own class interests and disciplinary projects.[81] However, this failure of the nation was not due to subaltern apathy or hostility toward the nation (although this emerges as a theme in much of the Subaltern Studies literature). Chatterjee notes that when interviewed in the 1970s, the most striking note among those subalterns who had fought for Indian independence was the 'despair and bitterness in their voices' over the failure of the nation.[82] While this disenchantment with the postcolonial nation apparently happened strikingly quickly in India, in Mexico and Colombia a similar process took over half a century to come to a head. Until the 1880s, in Latin America the nation was still rather up for grabs (elites did not yet control the idea of the nation), in part because the ex-colonial state was too weak or, rather, too dependent upon the subaltern classes. The nation did not fail because of the inherent limitations of citizenship or subaltern disinterest, but because elite state makers knowingly feared the exercise of these rights. By the 1880s elites were finally powerful enough to restrict them, and thereby attract capital investment for export-oriented development schemes (a story I do not have space to pursue here).[83]

In the ex-colonial republican decades prior, however, the nation was not yet seen to be a hostile or imposed means of elite control but a community of rights and promise that many subalterns could eagerly embrace. In this regard, it is notable that even regular soldiers in the Americas could assume that they might inspire Europe to seize the republican banner of revolution and decolonize itself. And indeed, there is evidence suggesting that Hispanic American conceptions of modernity and revolution reached Europe during this period.

The Garibaldinos were soldiers who had fought with the 'Hero of Two Worlds' during his sojourns in Brazil and Uruguay (1836–1848). Notably, most of Garibaldi's comrades did not accompany him from Europe. Most were Italian, Spanish, and French immigrants already settled as permanent residents in the Americas, while others were native-born Creoles; still others were originally from Africa, victims of the slave trade. Upon Garibaldi's departure from Montevideo to return to Europe, the vast majority of his soldiers stayed behind in their new (or old) home, and they now referred to their 'Italian Legion' as the 'Italian-Oriental Legion' since Uruguay was then known as the Banda Oriental, or Eastern Bank of the River Plate that divided Uruguay from the Western Bank, or Argentina.[84] These soldiers who remained to make their lives on the Rio de la Plata requested in 1852 that the national government recognize their Legion's standards, earned in the past civil war, citing their 'service to the Republic.' The Legionnaires wished to send their battle flags to Genoa, as an 'example for the Italian democrats.' For while their compatriots had been fighting despotism for over three centuries, 'this banner will teach them that against the tyrant's bayonets . . . free men and true republicans can triumph.'[85]

Writing from the small town of Buga, Colombia, Juan de Dios Restrepo evoked this Hispanic American sense of a wide struggle for decolonization in these terms:

> The situation of America is dire; *the fight is between the colonial system and the modern liberal spirit*, between the paganism of the Roman priests and the evangelical Christian idea, between those that dream of re-establishing slavery, privilege, monarchy, theocracy and those that believe that all of those abominations should remain in Europe.[86]

Restrepo's views challenge many current assumptions about the location of modernity and democracy.[87] Indeed, many mid-nineteenth-century Colombian and Mexican understandings of an ex-colonial future won in the Americas directly call into question some of the founding assumptions of postcolonial and decolonial theory. Recycling the old 'same male, new rider' trope, Robert Young claims, for example, that Latin America's nineteenth century was still dominated by a colonial mindset, where 'a sense of political and economic powerlessness, and corresponding lack of cultural identity' reigned, and where for subalterns 'things changed very little with independence.'[88] I do not wish to suggest that empire did not leave powerful legacies of inequality and exploitation, but I am arguing that many Mexican and Colombians believed they were leading a project that could solve these problems on a global scale. These plans and hopes did not fail *only* because of their own inadequacies or lacunae. To be sure, the ex-colonial republican projects sometimes failed due to their own internal contradictions, including the racism and classism of elites, the incompatibility of elite liberalism and popular liberalism, and the limits that these imposed upon the legal concept and everyday practice of citizenship. The primary reason for their failure in the late nineteenth century, however, was the drive for capitalist investment supported by a Europhile positivism emanating from the new centers of the North Atlantic.

Whose Failure?

Does postcolonial and decolonial theory decenter and provincialize Europe's privileged position? Or do these theoretical idioms serve to reify Europe? The ahistorical treatment of 'the West' as world history's all-powerful hero or villain has grave implications that go far beyond the historiographical and theoretical debates of academics. The limitations of the postcolonial and decolonial recipes, exemplified by Said and Mignolo, is that while justly critiquing those accounts that ignore extra-European or non-Western ideas and practices they still assume, against the historical evidence, that certain ideas of freedom, rights, or democracy are 'Western.'[89] In his discussion of Joseph Conrad, Edward Said presents a now standard, 'postcolonial' vision of world history. Said critiques but also concedes to a seemingly timeless Europe certain 'Western' creations which in fact were not Western at all. He argues that Conrad, while he criticized the arrogance of imperialists, was simply unable to imagine any non-European response to imperial power: 'All Conrad can see is a world totally dominated by the Atlantic West, in which every opposition to the West only confirms the West's wicked power. What Conrad cannot see is an alternative to this cruel tautology.'[90] Like many postcolonial theorists who have followed in his footsteps, Said assumes that in the nineteenth century the dichotomy between 'us' Western imperialists and 'them' colonized natives was well established everywhere.[91] But this is pure fiction. Said's loose use of the term 'the West' is telling here. He condemns Conrad for not allowing any response to the West but assumes that such a response will necessarily have to be non-Western. More than anything else, this view reflects his rather ahistorical view of the 'integrities' and 'resistance' of Asian, African, or American indigenous cultures.[92] Beyond his anachronistic and binary projection of 'the West' back onto the nineteenth century, Said's formula gives too much credit, in any case, to a mythical 'West.' The postcolonial theoretical formula of 'the West' ignores the actual historical agency of nineteenth-century Hispanic Americans, who fit uncomfortably into the ready categories of 'East' or 'West,' 'imperialist' or 'colonized.' Said skirts the issue here by creating a mythical 'Atlantic West' for Conrad.[93] The Garibaldinos were not trapped by Said's late-twentieth-century postcolonial views, however. If they were indeed the Atlantic vanguard of 'the West,' then Europe was surely the home of Oriental despots.

The Mexican case illustrates this point. In Maximilian's execution and Mexico's republican triumph we see how in Europe a few enlightened democrats held that the Americas (and not only, as occurred much later, Anglo America), not Europe, would lead the way forward toward a new global civilization.[94] In a letter to 'The Republican French Workers,' revolutionary writer Féliz Pyat saluted Juárez for joining the global pantheon of republican heroes. For Pyat, Juárez's execution of Maximilian avenged the lost republics of France and Rome. He mocked Europeans' gasping at Juárez's supposed barbarism, declaring that the Mexican President had given a 'lesson in justice' to degenerate European civilization, providing an example that Europeans would do well to follow. 'Your thunderclap, emanating from the Andes,[95] has shaken the world,' Pyat noted, adding hopefully that perhaps 'in a France regenerated by Mexico, there might also be justice.'[96] The radical French adventurer Gustave Cluseret rebuked his countryman for invading Mexico. He celebrated the Americas as 'the living and universal protestation of the free human species against crowned oppressors.' In America, he believed, there would be a 'fusion' of races to create 'the future type of humanity, the FREE MAN,' while Europe would only stagnate in its decrepitude.[97] Mexico had been subjected to 'the invasion of the Russians of the west, of a new Attila coming to destroy republican civilization in the name of monarchical barbarity.'[98] He urged Mexicans to resist the French, for he believed 'the European system' could not survive alongside the American system. 'It must kill us or die.'[99]

The war between Mexico and France illuminated the stark political contrast between the Old and New Worlds, manifesting the progress the New had made in creating a more egalitarian civilization. Italian workers from Genoa (where the Uruguayan Garibaldinos had sent their battle flags decades before) also hoped to imitate the Mexicans. They saluted Mexico for Maximilian's defeat: 'One more gift that the New World has sent us.' They only hoped that 'in our Italy just one ray of that splendid light that shines over the peoples of the American continent would appear.'[100] The Association of Militant Democracy of Brussels declared that Mexico was the star that would guide other peoples, and assured Juárez that, when the moment was right, they would not hesitate to act against their own tyrants, 'imitating your valor.'[101] With the war's end, radical Europeans knew the true home of civilization lay across the sea.

Victor Hugo and Garibaldi wrote to Juárez asking him to spare Maximilian because they were opposed on principle to capital punishment. Hugo, in his praise of Juárez's victory, admitted that it was the Americas that would show barbarous Europe the true meaning of both democracy and civilization: 'You have just interred monarchies underneath democracy. You have shown them its power; now show them its beauty! . . . Show the barbarians civilization.'[102] Garibaldi praised Juárez and Mexico as a whole, for being the 'Illustrious Champion of world liberty and human dignity.' Mexico's defeat of 'European despotism' served not just the New World, but 'all of humanity.'[103] In a similar vein, the Spanish republican Emilio Castelar credited the Americas with destroying retrograde ecclesiastical privileges, promoting equality, abolishing slavery, and promoting freedom of thought. 'American democracy,' he wrote, 'so assailed, had lent great services to liberty and civilization.'[104] Castelar thus recognized that republican decolonization was a world-wide problem, but one in which the Americas were leading the way.[105]

In *Provincializing Europe*, Dipesh Chakrabarty decries the limits of a European politics that denies the communal and spiritual ethos of the non-European world, but seriously errs in ascribing such institutions and concepts as democracy, history, equality, and human rights to his hyperreal 'Europe.'[106] Mid-century orators and writers did not take Europe to be the origin and promoter of equality or rights but instead the single biggest obstacle blocking the creation of a more just and equitable world. If, as Mark Thurner suggests in his introduction to this volume, we rewrite the history of decolonization to include the Latin American past, then we would do well to include Europe in the story as well. This Europe, however, is not only a metropolitan fountainhead of modernity, history, democracy, imperialism, and just about everything else, but instead a bloody and backward stage where revolution faltered, the nation failed, and the emancipatory potential of modernity was realized first not at home—where 'internal colonialism' ruled—but in her ex-colonies.

Notes

1. *La Alianza de la Frontera* (Chihuahua), September 4, 1862; *El Monitor Republicano* (México), January 8, 1848; *El Siglo Diez y Nueve* (México), August 15, 1848. This chapter draws upon material previously published in James E. Sanders, *The Vanguard of the Atlantic World: Creating Modernity, Nation, and Democracy in Nineteenth-Century Latin America* (Durham: Duke University Press, 2014).
2. Walter D. Mignolo, *Local Histories/Global Designs: Coloniality, Subaltern Knowledges, and Border Thinking* (Princeton: Princeton University Press, 2000), 133.
3. Zvi Ben-Dor Benite, 'Modernity: The Sphinx and the Historian,' *The American Historical Review* 116 (June 2011), 638–646.
4. Dipesh Chakrabarty, *Provincializing Europe: Postcolonial Thought and Historical Difference* (Princeton: Princeton University Press, 2007).
5. *La Chinaca* (México), June 30, 1862.
6. Speech of Manuel Merino, Chihuahua, September 15, 1868, in *La República* (Chihuahua), September 18, 1868.
7. *El Voto del Pueblo* (Guadalajara), June 29, 1862 reprinted in 'Elecciones,' *La Alianza de la Frontera—Suplemento* (Chihuahua), July 29, 1862.
8. 'El Voto del Pueblo,' *La Libertad de Durango*, July 6, 1862 reprinted in *La Alianza de la Frontera* (Chihuahua), August 28, 1862.
9. *El Caucano* (Cali), November 3, 1864.
10. Postcolonial critics tend to critique modernity as Eurocentric and violent, but to accept that modernity is fundamentally European. They also tend to assume that nineteenth-century Hispanic Americans absorbed Europe's ideas, and that these were not challenged until the mid-twentieth century. Both assumptions are mistaken. See Bill Ashcroft, 'Modernity's First-Born: Latin America and Post-Colonial Transformation,' in Alfonso de Toro and Fernando de Toro, eds., *El debate de la postcolonialidad en Latinoamérica: Una postmodernidad periférica o cambio de paradigma en el pensamiento latinoamericano* (Madrid: Iberoamericana, 1999), 18. Other scholars have questioned these views, however. See Nicola Miller and Stephen Hart, eds., *When Was Latin America Modern?* (New York: Palgrave Macmillan, 2007); and especially Guy Thomson, 'Mid-Nineteenth-Century Modernities in the Hispanic World,' in Miller and Hart, eds., *When Was Latin America Modern?*, 69–90. I am not interested here in what modernity 'really' means, but in how actors in the past employed the concept and what it meant to them. See Frederick Cooper, *Colonialism in Question: Theory, Knowledge, History* (Berkeley: University of California Press, 2005), 3–32, 113–149.
11. Emphasis mine. *El Ferrocarril* (Santiago) reprinted in *La Nación (Montevideo)*, December 19, 1860.
12. Speech of Manuel Merino, Chihuahua, September 15, 1868, in *La República* (Chihuahua), September 18, 1868.
13. Speech of Gabino Ortiz to National Guard, Morelia, January 5, 1862 in *La Guerra* (Morelia), January 10, 1862.
14. Ibid.; see also Fernando López-Alves, 'Modernization Theory Revisited: Latin America, Europe, and the U.S. in the Nineteenth and Early Twentieth

Century,' *Anuario Colombiano de Historia Social y de la Cultura* 38:1 (2011), 256.
15. Speech of Juan Cervin de la Mora to the Battalion of Artisans, Morelia, January 5, 1862, in *La Guerra* (Morelia), January 24, 1862.
16. *La Guerra* (Morelia), December 27, 1861.
17. Speech of Gabino Ortiz to National Guard, Morelia, January 5, 1862 in *La Guerra* (Morelia), January 10, 1862.
18. Federico Flores, 'La América se salvará,' *El Comercio* (Lima), July 13, 1864.
19. Héctor F. Varela, '*El Americano*: Sus prospectos y su misión,' *El Americano* (Paris), March 7, 1872.
20. Speech of Jesús Escobar y Armendáriz, Villa del Paso del Norte, September 16, 1867, *La República* (Chihuahua), November 8, 1867.
21. *El Republicano* (México), March 28, 1846.
22. Dipesh Chakrabarty, 'Postcoloniality and the Artifice of History: Who Speaks for "Indian" Pasts?' *Representations* 37 (Winter 1992), 17; Carlos J. Alonso, *The Burden of Modernity: The Rhetoric of Cultural Discourse in Spanish America* (Oxford: Oxford University Press, 1998), 32; see also Walter D. Mignolo, *The Idea of Latin America* (Oxford: Blackwell, 2005), 57–58. For a critique of Chakrabarty, see Fernando Coronil, *The Magical State: Nature, Money, and Modernity in Venezuela* (Chicago: University of Chicago Press, 1997), 13–14.
23. Francisco Bilbao, 'El evangelio americano,' in Manuel Bilbao, ed., *Las obras completas de Francisco Bilbao* (Buenos Aires: Imprenta de Buenos Aires, 1865), v. 2, 419.
24. Francisco Bilbao, 'Emancipación del espíritu en América,' in Bilbao, ed., *Las obras completas de Francisco Bilbao*, v. 2, 545–551.
25. *El Voto del Pueblo* (Guadalajara), June 29, 1862 reprinted in *La Alianza de la Frontera—Suplemento* (Chihuahua), July 29, 1862; see also *La Chinaca* (México), June 5, 1862; *El Aguijón* (Guanajuato), October 8, 1871.
26. See also Laurent Dubois, *A Colony of Citizens: Revolution and Slave Emancipation in the French Caribbean, 1787–1804* (Chapel Hill: University of North Carolina Press, 2004), 4–5; Cooper, *Colonialism in Question*, 21.
27. *El Aguijón* (Guanajuato), October 8, 1871.
28. *El Grito de Guerra* (Guanajuato), February 1, 1863.
29. Juan González Urueña, 'El verdadero objeto de la intervención,' *La Guerra* (Morelia), January 31, 1862.
30. *La República* (Chihuahua), November 22, 1867.
31. *El Caucano* (Cali), November 3, 1864.
32. Speech of Manuel Merino, Chihuahua, September 15, 1868, in *La República* (Chihuahua), September 18, 1868.
33. Speech of Mariano Murillo, Chihuahua, September 15, 1862, *La Alianza de la Frontera—Suplemento* (Chihuahua), September 23, 1862; for debates on Spanish colonialism and nationalism, see Christopher Schmidt-Nowara, *The Conquest of History: Spanish Colonialism and National Histories in the Nineteenth Century* (Pittsburgh: University of Pittsburgh Press, 2006).
34. Governor of Pasto to Secretary of Hacienda, Pasto, December 18, 1852, Archivo General de la Nación (Bogotá, Colombia), Sección República, Fondo Gobernaciones—Pasto, tomo 8, 539.
35. Speech of Juan de la Mora to the Battalion of Artisans, Morelia, January 5, 1862, *La Guerra* (Morelia), January 24, 1862.
36. Rebecca Earle, *The Return of the Native: Indians and Myth-Making in Spanish America, 1810–1930* (Durham: Duke University Press, 2007), 19; see also, Juan A. Ortega y Medina, 'Indigenismo e hispanismo en la conciencia historiográfica Mexicana,' in Roberto Blancarte, ed., *Cultura e identidad nacional* (México: Fondo de Cultura Económica, 1994), 44–72.

37. Ramón Mercado, *Memorias sobre los acontecimientos del sur, especialmente el la provincia de Buenaventura, durante la administración del 7 de Marzo de 1849* (Cali: Centro de Estudios Históricos y Sociales Santiago de Cali, 1996 [1855]), vii.
38. Ibid., xviii, xcv.
39. José Hilario López, *Mensaje del Presidente de la Nueva Granada al Congreso Constitucional de 1852* (Bogotá: Imprenta del Neo-Granadino, 1852), 1; Broadside in Biblioteca Nacional (Bogotá, Colombia), Reparación.
40. *La Bandera Nacional* (Matamoros), July 13, 1864.
41. Ibid.
42. Justo Sierra, 'Conservadores y reaccionarios,' *La Libertad* (Junio 12, 1878) in Justo Sierra, *Obras completas del Maestro Justo Sierra, v. 4: Periodismo político* (México: Universidad Nacional Autónoma de México, 1948), 149.
43. Mignolo, *Local Histories/Global Designs*, 133. For the sense of possibilities in the mid-century Americas, see James Dunkerley, *Americana: The Americas in the World, Around 1850* (London: Verso, 2000).
44. For quote, see Robert J. C. Young, *Postcolonialism: An Historical Introduction* (Oxford: Blackwell, 2001), 11.
45. Speech of Jesús Escobar y Armendáriz, Villa del Paso del Norte, September 16, 1867, *La República* (Chihuahua), November 8, 1867.
46. *La Guerra* (Morelia), December 27, 1861.
47. Stuart Hall, 'The West and the Rest: Discourse and Power,' in Stuart Hall, David Held, Don Hubert and Kenneth Thompson, eds., *Modernity: An Introduction to Modern Societies* (Cambridge: Polity Press, 1995), 184–227; Aníbal Quijano, 'Coloniality and Modernity/Rationality,' *Cultural Studies* 21 (March–May 2007), 168–178.
48. See Walter D. Mignolo, *The Darker Side of Western Modernity: Global Futures, Decolonial Options* (Durham: Duke University Press, 2011), xx–xxiii.
49. Bilbao, 'Emancipación,' 420; for Hegel, see Susan Buck-Morss, *Hegel, Haiti, and Universal History* (Pittsburgh: University of Pittsburgh Press, 2009).
50. S. Cosío, *La República* (Zacatecas) reprinted in *La República* (Chihuahua), May 10, 1867.
51. Benedict Anderson long ago insisted on the world-historical role of Hispanic America in pioneering the nation form. However, his work focused almost exclusively on Creole elites. Benedict Anderson, *Imagined Communities: Reflections on the Origin and Spread of Nationalism*, 2nd ed. (London: Verso, 1991).
52. Latin American Subaltern Studies Group, 'Founding Statement,' *Boundary 2* 20 (Fall 1993), 117; Ania Loomba, *Colonialism/Postcolonialism* (London: Routledge, 1998), 197–203.
53. Partha Chatterjee, *The Nation and Its Fragments: Colonial and Postcolonial Histories* (Princeton: Princeton University Press, 1993), 3–4.
54. Ranajit Guha, 'On Some Aspects of the Historiography of Colonial India,' in Ranajit Guha and Gayatri Chakravorty Spivak, eds., *Selected Subaltern Studies* (New York: Oxford University Press, 1988), 43. Indeed, the more obvious failure of the nation by the 1970s propelled the development of Subaltern Studies itself. Gyan Prakash, 'Subaltern Studies as Post-Colonial Criticism,' *The American Historical Review* 99 (December 1994), 1476.
55. Mark Thurner makes a similar point in his 'After Spanish Rule: Writing Another After,' in Mark Thurner and Andrés Guerrero, eds., *After Spanish Rule: Postcolonial Predicaments of the Americas* (Durham: Duke University Press, 2003), 21–22. For Independence, see Anderson, *Imagined Communities*. For the nation as distant for subalterns, see E. Bradford Burns, *The Poverty of Progress: Latin America in the Nineteenth Century* (Berkeley: University of California Press, 1980); David Bushnell and Neill Macaulay,

The Emergence of Latin America in the Nineteenth-Century (Oxford: Oxford University Press, 1988) and John Lynch, *The Spanish American Revolutions, 1808–1826* (New York: W.W. Norton & Company, 1986). Even some scholars engaged with postcolonial studies argue that 'the post-independence Spanish overseas provinces in the Americas failed to create a feeling of nationalism.' J. Jorge Klor de Alva, 'The Post-Colonization of the (Latin) American Experience: A Reconsideration of "Colonialism," "Postcolonialism," and "Mestizaje,"' in Gyan Prakash, ed., *After Colonialism: Imperial Histories and Postcolonial Displacements* (Princeton: Princeton University Press, 1994), 251.

56. For example, Bushnell argues, 'Centuries of subordination to the Spanish state and church as well as to the small upper class of European descent had instilled in the Indian and mestizo peasantry an instinctive deference . . .' David Bushnell, *The Making of Modern Colombia: A Nation in Spite of Itself* (Berkeley: University of California Press, 1993), 78. Many writers assume Indians' disinterest in independence and nation, claiming without foundation these things were elite and 'Western' constructions. Mignolo, *Local Histories*, 137–144. Klor de Alva, 'The Postcolonization,' 266.
57. Cabildo pequeño de indígenas of Yascual to President of the Provincial Legislature, Túquerres, October 8, 1852, Archivo Central del Cauca (Popayán, Colombia) (hereafter ACC), Archivo Muerto, Paquete 48, Legajo 4, no page number. [191b].
58. Testimony of Governor Bautista Pechene, Popayán, August 18, 1856, ACC, Archivo Muerto, Paquete 62, Legajo 45, no page number. [232a].
59. Governors of Pitayó, Jambaló, and Quichayá to Governor of the State, Jambaló, August 1, 1859, ACC, Archivo Muerto, Paquete 74, Legajo 51, no page number. [256a].
60. Members of the cabildo pequeño de indígenas and adults of the village of Sibundoy [over 60 names, majority signed with an X] to Citizen President of the State, Sibundoy, November 8, 1874, ACC, Archivo Muerto, Paquete 129, Legajo 45, no page number; see also, The cabildo pequeño de indígenas de Santiago de Pongo to Honorable Deputies, Santiago de Pongo, August 8, 1869, ACC, Archivo Muerto, Paquete 103, Legajo 3, no page number; Governor and Regidor of the pequeño cabildo de indígenas of Rioblanco to Jefe Municipal, Popayán, October 4, 1878, ACC, Archivo Muerto, Paquete 140, Legajo 62, no page number. [393a].
61. The Undersigned, Citizens of the Republic of New Granada [three pages of names] to Legislators of the Republic, María, February 20, 1855, Archivo del Congreso (Bogotá, Colombia) (hereafter ACON), 1855, Cámara, Proyectos de Ley Negados VI, 156.
62. Residents of Cabal Parish [over 75 names, majority signed for by others] to Honorable Representatives and Senators of Congress, Cabal, May 1, 1849, ACON, 1849, Senado, Leyes Autografas II, 175. [1184a].
63. The Assembly of Padres de Familia of the Aldea de Chinchiná to Citizen Legislators of the Republic, no place or date on letter but received in Bogotá on February 2, 1856, ACON, 1856, Cámara, Solicitudes IV, 20. [1212a].
64. Residents of San Juan [24 names, all signed with an X] to Citizen Senators and Representatives, no place or date on letter [1852], ACON, 1852, Senado, Proyectos Negados II, 19. [1179b].
65. The bogas of the Dagua River [over 115 names, all but 7 signed for by others] to Citizen President of the State, Cali, May 15, 1878, ACC, Archivo Muerto, Paquete 144, Legajo 64, no page number. [451b].
66. Inhabitants of the San Julián hacienda [over 25 names, all but a few signed for by another] to Governor of the Province, San Julián, October 15, 1853, ACC, Archivo Muerto, Paquete 55, Legajo 92, no page number. [212c].

114 *James Sanders*

67. Jorge Klor de Alba asserts that nineteenth-century Latin America was not a postcolonial environment. This would be an interesting academic argument, except that most everyone in nineteenth-century Latin America, elites and subalterns alike, thought they were living in a postcolonial environment. Klor de Alva, 'The Postcolonization,' 247, and Loomba, *Colonialism/Postcolonialism*, 9–12.
68. Hobsbawm, *Nations and Nationalism*, 19, 22.
69. Ibid., 73.
70. See Mark Thurner, *From Two Republics to One Divided: Contradictions of Postcolonial Nationmaking in Andean Peru* (Durham: Duke University Press, 1997); Eric Van Young, *The Other Rebellion: Popular Violence, Ideology, and the Mexican Struggle for Independence, 1810–1821* (Stanford: Stanford University Press, 2001); Brian DeLay, *War of a Thousand Deserts: Indian Raids and the U.S.-Mexican War* (New Haven: Yale University Press, 2008); Alfonso Múnera, *El fracaso de la nación: Región, clase y raza en el Caribe colombiano (1717–1810)* (Bogotá: Banco de la República, 1998); Romana Falcón, ed., *Culturas de pobreza y resistencia: Estudios de marginados, proscritos y descontentos, México, 1804–1910* (México: El Colegio de México, 2005).
71. Residents of Tumaco [over forty-five names] to Citizen President of the Union, Tumaco, August 30, 1878, Archivo del Instituto Colombiano de la Reforma Agraria (Bogotá, Colombia) (hereafter INCORA), Bienes Nacionales, Tomo 14, 947. [149a, 286c].
72. José del Carmen Castillo, Juan de los Santos Cuabí and Victoriano Rialpe [written for him] to the President, Tumaco, 12 December 1875, INCORA, Bienes Nacionales, Tomo 10, 49. The above petitioners described themselves as farmers and 'poor laborers.' Subalterns regularly cited the fact they lived under democratic or republican governments to be sufficient reason for the authorities to accede to their demands. See 'The Democratic Society of Jambaló to Superintendent of Public Instruction,' Jambaló, October 30, 1878, ACC, Archivo Muerto, Paquete 128, Legajo 34, no page number; 'President of the Democratic Society to State President,' Cali, September 14, 1877, ACC, Archivo Muerto, Paquete 137, Legajo 7, no page number; *El Guaitara* (Pasto), October 5, 1864; 'President of the Pereira Town Council to National Congress,' Pereira, February 18, 1874, ACON, 1874, Cámara, Proyectos Pendientes III, 186; 'Pedro Torres to Secretary of Government,' Pasto, May 25, 1874, ACC, Archivo Muerto, Paquete 106, Legajo 81, no page number; 'Indian residents of Cajamarca to State President,' Cajamarca, July 30, 1871, ACC, Archivo Muerto, Paquete 112, Legajo 18, no page number. [146a, 149a].
73. The pequeño cabildo of Indians of Mocondino to State President, Pasto, February 18, 1866, ACC, Archivo Muerto, Paquete 94, Legajo 54, no page number; Members of the pequeño cabildo of Indians of Yumbo to Municipal President, Yumbo, June 9, 1869, Archivo Histórico Municipal de Cali (Cali, Colombia), Archivo del Concejo Municipal, Tomo 156, 161; The indigenous cabildos of Guachucal and Colimba to Legislators, Guachucal, August 12, 1873, ACC, Archivo Muerto, Paquete 124, Legajo 60, no page number. [309a, 673c, 384a].
74. The undersigned members of Cali's Democratic Society to State President, Cali, June 1, 1877, ACC, Archivo Muerto, Paquete 137, Legajo 7, no page number [421d]. For more on the importance of land in Colombian society, see Catherine LeGrand, *Frontier Expansion and Peasant Protest in Colombia, 1830–1936* (Albuquerque: University of New Mexico Press, 1986).

75. Indigenous residents of Cajamarca Aldea to Cauca State President, Cajamarca, July 30, 1871, ACC, Archivo Muerto, paquete 112, legajo 29, no page number.
76. The undersigned residents of Paso del Bobo to [the President], Paso del Bobo, October 1, 1859, Archivo General de la Nación (México, México), Instituciones Gubernamentales: Época Moderna y Contemporánea, Administración Pública Federal Siglo XIX, Fondo Justicia, Justicia, v. 621, expediente 24,155.
77. Sebastiana Silva to Jefe Municipal, Popayán, October 13, 1874, ACC, Archivo Muerto, paquete 129, legajo 39, no page number.
78. For a review of the literature, see James E. Sanders, 'Popular Movements in Nineteenth-Century Latin America,' in Ben Vinson, ed., *Oxford Bibliographies: Latin American Studies* (Oxford: Oxford University Press, 2014).
79. This trend away from the subaltern was noted by Sarkar. Sumit Sarkar, 'The Decline of the Subaltern in Subaltern Studies,' in Vinayak Chaturvedi, ed., *Mapping Subaltern Studies and the Postcolonial* (London: Verso, 2000), 300–323. Mark Thurner makes a similar point about relying on elite narratives in Thurner, 'After Spanish Rule,' 29. Acree discusses the importance of 'everyday reading' and moving beyond the study of 'high literature.' William Garrett Acree, Jr., *Everyday Reading: Print Culture and Collective Identity in the Río de la Plata, 1780–1910* (Nashville: Vanderbilt University Press, 2011).
80. Partha Chatterjee, *Wages of Freedom: Fifty Years of the Indian Nation-State* (New Delhi: Oxford University Press, 1998), 16; Gyan Prakash, discussing how postcolonial criticism entered Indian historiography, assumes 'the persistence of colonialist knowledge' in postcolonial India, where it was 'authorized by colonialism and authenticated by the nation-state.' For Prakash, the postcolonial nation failed to build new forms of knowledge. Gyan Prakash, 'Postcolonial Criticism and Indian Historiography,' *Social Text* 31–32 (1992), 9, 17.
81. Ranajit Guha, *Dominance Without Hegemony: History and Power in Colonial India* (Cambridge: Harvard University Press, 1997), 151.
82. Chatterjee, 'The Wages of Freedom,' 4.
83. For the effects of this reorientation of modernity, see Barbara Weinstein, *The Color of Modernity: São Paulo and the Making of Race and Nation in Brazil* (Durham: Duke University Press, 2015).
84. *El Conservador* (Montevideo), April 19, 1848.
85. Draft of letter from Italian Legion to Uruguayan National Government [undated, 1852], Museo Histórico Municipal (Montevideo, Uruguay), Archivo y Biblioteca Pablo Blanco Acevedo, Colección Museo Histórico Nacional, Tomo 1283.
86. Emphasis mine. Emiro Kastos [Juan de Dios Restrepo], 'La Guerra,' Buga, January 13, 1864, *El Caucano* (Cali), January 21, 1864. See also, *El Ciudadano* (Popayán), June 17, 1848.
87. For modernization theorists, see William H. McNeill, *The Rise of the West: A History of Human Community* (Chicago: University of Chicago Press, 1991),731; John M. Headley, *The Europeanization of the World: On the Origins of Human Rights and Democracy* (Princeton: Princeton University Press, 2008), 4–5; see also, Felipe Fernández-Armesto, *The Americas: A Hemispheric History* (New York: The Modern Library, 2003), 133–134; Alvaro Vargas Llosa, *Liberty for Latin America: How to Undo Five Hundred Years of State Oppression* (New York: Farrar, Straus and Giroux, 2005), 28–33; Lawrence E. Harrison, *The Pan-American Dream: Do Latin America's Cultural Vales Discourage True Partnership with the*

United States and Canada? (Boulder: Westview Press, 1997); Howard J. Wiarda, *The Soul of Latin America: The Cultural and Political Tradition* (New Haven: Yale University Press, 2001), 7; W. Raymond Duncan, *Latin American Politics: A Developmental Approach* (New York: Praeger, 1976), 17–18; Glen Dealy, 'Prolegomena on the Spanish American Political Tradition,' in Howard J. Wiarda, ed., *Politics and Social Change in Latin America: The Distinct Tradition*, 2nd ed. (Amherst: University of Massachusetts Press, 1982), 163–183.

88. Young, *Postcolonialism*, 194. Ironically, when discussing nineteenth-century opposition to colonialism, Young focuses on European thinkers not Hispanic Americans whom, he assumes, were only interested in Europeanizing themselves. Young, *Postcolonialism*, 88–100, 194.
89. Mignolo, *The Darker Side*, 2–3, 14, 259; Mignolo, *Local Histories*, 296–297, 317–318; Chakrabarty, *Provincializing Europe*, 4; for a critique of such postcolonial assumptions, see Sebastian Conrad, 'Enlightenment in Global History: A Historiographical Critique,' *The American Historical Review* 117 (October 2012), 1005–1006.
90. Edward W. Said, *Culture and Imperialism* (New York: Knopf, 1993), xviii; see also, xix, 24–30, 146, 165–166. Paul Armstrong also notes Conrad's contradictory politics of critiquing imperialism while fearing revolution, although he is largely concerned with metaphysical questions. Paul B. Armstrong, 'Conrad's Contradictory Politics: The Ontology of Society in *Nostromo*,' *Twentieth Century Literature* 31 (Spring 1985), 1–21.
91. Said, *Culture and Imperialism*, xxv; see also, 52, 108, 223, 228, 263–264. See also, Mignolo, *The Darker Side*; Mignolo, *Local Histories*.
92. Said, *Culture and Imperialism*, xviii; see also Loomba, *Colonialism/Postcolonialism*, 12.
93. For exclusion from the 'West,' see Jorge Cañizares-Esguerra, *Puritan Conquistadors: Iberianizing the Atlantic, 1550–1700* (Stanford: Stanford University Press, 2006), 224–230. For extra-European democratic innovation, see Hilda Sabato, 'La reacción de América: La construcción de las repúblicas en el siglo XIX,' in Roger Chartier and Antonio Feros, eds., *Europa, América y el mundo: Tiempos históricos* (Madrid: Fundación Rafael del Pino, 2006), 263–279; Dubois, *A Colony of Citizens*; Nick Nesbitt, *Universal Emancipation: The Haitian Revolution and the Radical Enlightenment* (Charlottesville: University of Virginia Press, 2008); Sanders, *The Vanguard of the Atlantic World*.
94. Manuel de Silva to Benito Juárez, Sevilla, July 12, 1867, *Diario Oficial del Gobierno Supremo de la República* (México), August 24, 1867.
95. The 'Andes' was then still used as a generic name for the bifurcating mountain ranges that run the length of the Western Hemisphere, from Argentina to Canada. The name thus glossed what is today called the Sierra Madre and the Rocky Mountains as well as the Andes proper.
96. Félix Pyat, 'Salutación de los Obreros Republicanos Franceses, al Presidente Benito Juárez,' *La República* (Chihuahua), October 11, 1867.
97. G. Cluseret, *Mexico, and the Solidarity of Nations* (New York: Blackwell, 1866), 90.
98. Ibid., 94.
99. Ibid., 109.
100. The Association of Genoese Workers, 'Felicitaciones á México,' *La República* (Chihuahua), October 25, 1867.
101. Asociación de la Democracia Militante to Ciudadano Juárez, Brussels, September 25, 1867, *La República* (Chihuahua), December 20, 1867.
102. Victor Hugo to Benito Juárez, Hauteville-House, June 20, 1867, *El Boyacense* (Tunja), September 7, 1867; also in *El Globo* (México), August 8, 1867.

103. J. Garibaldi, 'Un saludo á México,' Castelleti, June 5, 1867, *La República* (Chihuahua), August 9, 1867.
104. Emilio Castelar, 'Política de Napoleón en America,' *La Bandera Nacional* (Matamoros), May 14, 1864.
105. Ibid.; see also Charles A. Hale, 'Emilio Castelar and Mexico,' in Iván Jaksic, ed., *The Political Power of the Word: Press and Oratory in Nineteenth-Century Latin America* (London: Institute of Latin American Studies, 2002), 128–141.
106. Chakrabarty, *Provincializing Europe*, 4; For critique, see Cooper, *Colonialism*, 121–122, 140; Coronil, *The Magical State*, 13–14. Similarly, Chakrabarty ascribes 'historicism' to nineteenth-century Europe, but Thurner demonstrates that historicism emerged earlier in Hispanic America. See Mark Thurner, *History's Peru: The Poetics of Colonial and Postcolonial Historiography* (Gainesville: University of Florida Press, 2011), 257.

6 Second Slavery and Decolonization in Brazil

Barbara Weinstein

Over the last two decades a new narrative of the nineteenth-century Atlantic world has emerged. This narrative acknowledges the vanguard role of the Iberian empires turned postcolonial nations in the emergence of modern political concepts, and foregrounds the prominent participation of subaltern groups, including indigenous peoples and enslaved and freed Africans in the rise of modern notions of political community, citizenship, and freedom. At the same time, historical research on labour regimes has registered the constitutive role of slavery (especially those in Brazil, Cuba, and the US South) in the rise and spread of capitalism during the same period.[1] As Brazilian historians Márcia Berbel and Rafael de Bivar Marquese noted in a 2007 essay, 'the nineteenth century [marked] a conjuncture that brought about a fundamental change in the historical structures of colonialism *and* black slavery.'[2] Despite this temporal convergence, the new political history and the historiography of 'the second slavery' have moved, for the most part, on separate tracks. The privileging of economics by second slavery historians tends to set them apart from the new political history. At the same time, second slavery historians ironically find themselves in close company with the culturalist approaches of 'decolonial' criticism and its failure narrative. Thus, the claims of such critics as Jorge Klor de Alva and, more recently, Walter Mignolo, to the effect that Latin America has never been postcolonial and has yet to be decolonized, find a sympathetic echo among the historians of slavery, who likewise point to the 'colonial legacy' or stubborn persistence of forms of forced labour and the ethno-racial hierarchies they entail.[3] In this sense, cultural studies that critique (always failed and postponed) decolonization and historical studies of the second slavery coincide on several key points. In those locales where the second slavery flourished, forms of coercion and distinctions based on race and origin, associated with colonial rule, were intensified if not reinvented. These practices delayed independence altogether (as in Cuba) or produced a 'transition' that not only failed to remove colonial elites but reinvigorated their power and prosperity, thereby impeding decolonization, and possibly creating an even more onerous 'colonial' condition for the (non-white) majority of the population.

Working within this shared narrative of failed decolonization, several leading historians of postindependence politics in Brazil have contended that the transition to an independent empire under a constitutional monarchy enhanced the power of a planter elite whose interests curbed any significant movement toward social or political change. Rendered in this fashion, Brazilian history is not part of the new story of the nineteenth-century Atlantic world that recognizes Latin America as an important laboratory for postcolonial experiments. Indeed, a quick scan of Brazil in the mid-nineteenth century would seem to provide the 'best case' scenario for the claim that formal independence in Latin America did not imply decolonization. The attenuated Brazilian transition from colony to nation, with the transfer of the Portuguese Court to Rio de Janeiro (1808) as the salient episode, and with minimal armed struggle and popular mobilization, appears to be the case *par excellence* for the persistence in Latin America of a colonial legacy without decolonization. After all, it was not just the local, Creole representatives of the imperial culture who seized power; it was the very people who ruled at the epicentre of the empire. The favourites of the Portuguese Court (whether Peninsular or American born) received large tracts of land in the hinterlands of Rio de Janeiro, the Portuguese empire's New World capital. These elites were positioned to be among the primary beneficiaries of the opportunities generated by the unmet global demand for sugar in the decades following the Haitian revolution. They would later flourish as the first cohort of slaveowners in Brazil to take full advantage of the rapidly expanding worldwide market for cheap coffee. Already in the early 1820s, this slaveholding elite, together with some of their counterparts in the northern provinces, pushed for a constitution that concentrated power in the monarchy and privileged order over rights.[4] Two decades later, amidst booming coffee profits, they used their position to consolidate their power under Conservative rule, now known as the 'Tempo Saquarema.'[5]

Despite the obvious disjuncture between the new narrative of decolonization in political history and the second slavery literature, here I will suggest that Brazil presents a strong case for merging the approaches and problematics of these two historiographical turns. In short, I will contend that Brazil formed part of a wider Latin American movement of decolonization that set it apart, for example, from the short-lived US Confederacy.

More Than Fear: Slavery After Haiti in Cuba, the US South and Brazil

To consider Latin America's first postcolonial moment together with the history of the second slavery, we need to move beyond the focus on fear as the defining element in the disposition of slaveholding elites in the years following the Haitian Revolution. To be sure, the proceedings of the 1823 Brazilian constitutional assembly demonstrate that even several decades later elite representatives still appeared deeply disturbed by the events in Saint-Domingue. But these constitutional debates can be read in several ways. Rafael de Bivar Marquese, a historian working with the concept of the second slavery in Brazil, reminds us that we have to distinguish between genuine fear of a Haitian-style rebellion and the opportunistic use of that threat.[6] In her brilliant study of Haiti and Cuba during and after the Haitian Revolution, *Freedom's Mirror*, Ada Ferrer argues that the emphasis on the fear that Haiti generated among slaveholders has obscured the opportunities that it afforded to those very same slaveholders. As the world's leading sugar and coffee producer went offline at the precise moment when demand was burgeoning, a representative of the landed class in Cuba, a colony whose proximity to Haiti should have filled the elite with terror, announced in 1793: 'There can be no doubt. The hour of our happiness has arrived.'[7]

This 'hour of happiness' might well be read as confirmation of 'the second slavery' thesis and at the same time may call some of its assumptions into question. Although the concept of 'the second slavery' was coined by Dale Tomich, a historical sociologist of the Caribbean, the best-known work in this vein concerns the US South. Drawing upon Eric Williams' *Capitalism and Slavery*, second slavery historians argue that slavery gave rise to global capitalism. In other words, slavery was not just compatible with capitalism but was constitutive of it, perhaps even (in Edward Baptist's case) the *vanguard* of capitalist expansion.[8] Far from regarding slavery and coerced labour as a relic of the past or a precapitalist mode of production, they see it (especially in its nineteenth-century guise) as the cutting edge of modernity. In its routinization and intensification of the labour process, the fostering of new technologies and capital accumulation, slavery was a ubiquitous feature of capitalist economies. Unlike dependency and world-systems theorists, second slavery historians have no narrative of underdevelopment, no notion of periphery.[9] What drove the masters was the accumulation of wealth, plain and simple. There was nothing genteel or seigneurial about their attitude towards their property, whether in land or in slaves. Eager to make as much money as possible off the world's craving for more cotton, more sugar, or more coffee, they converted forest to farmland and people to chattel on an unprecedented scale, experimented with new techniques and machinery, and consolidated political structures that simultaneously conceded them enormous power and influence within their own domains and furnished them the juridical and policing apparatus of the state to guarantee their control of their land and their labour force.[10]

Unlike the United States, Cuba remained a colony with no significant anticolonial movement until the 1860s. For the island's elite, the opportunities afforded by the opening in the sugar trade appear to have outweighed all other considerations. Certainly, they shored up aspects of the island's security, but they made no move to limit the influx of enslaved Africans or to systematically improve conditions on the sugar estates. They did encourage Spanish immigration, however, in part to prevent the development of the lopsided racial demographics associated with prerevolutionary social conditions in Saint-Domingue. Keen to protect their newfound prosperity, they distanced themselves from the turmoil unleashed by the anticolonial movements springing up on the mainland.

The fortunes of cotton planters in the US South were not so directly impacted by the Haitian revolution. Nevertheless, the success of a mass slave rebellion close to US shores combined with new ideas about slavery and freedom (including the concept of free soil) shaped aspects of the southern cotton boom and its politics.[11] Perhaps most significant was the acquisition of the immense Louisiana territory from Napoleon by the US government. This game-changing acquisition would have been much less likely had France retained control of Saint-Domingue. It not only allowed the southern planters to expand the slave plantation economy, but also led some to imagine a hemispheric, slavery-based empire.[12] At the same time, the lessons of Haiti made it difficult for southern planters to coalesce around the reopening of the transatlantic slave trade, since a 'black majority' was cited as one of the reasons for the slaves' success in Saint-Domingue. Despite this fear, expansionist factions within the South pressed for reopening the trade.[13] As it turned out, by the time the cotton economy reached its heyday in the 1810s–1850s, the great majority of slaves in the US South were American born. The South's white majority and the accumulating store of wealth derived from the cotton trade meant that the slave states could build a robust ex-colonial American identity based on slavery and white supremacy. Essential to this identity was the definition of certain portions of the population, slave and free, as residing permanently beyond the boundary of citizenship.

When compared to the cases of Cuba and the US South, the case of Brazil is particularly complex and ambivalent. After all, no other ex-colony became the centre of the empire to which it had once belonged. At the time, no ex-colony had become independent without significant armed conflict. None could boast a head of state who was the scion of the royal family of its former metropolis. And no other independent Latin American *nation* (Cuba remained a Spanish colony until the end of the century) experienced such a dramatic reinvigoration of its slave regime in the years following independence. Within a decade or two of independence most of the former Spanish American colonies, where slaves were minorities, had begun the process—though typically a very gradual one—of slave emancipation. Brazil made the transition to independence with slaves forming by far the single largest category of its population.[14] The post-Haiti boom in Brazil rejuvenated the northeast sugar economy and drove the coffee boom in the southeast. Brazilian traffickers imported some 700,000 enslaved Africans in the three decades immediately following independence.[15]

Brazil thus presents an especially interesting case as it combined the political experience of independence with a massive influx of enslaved workers whose status further complicated efforts to construct Brazilian national identity. Given these circumstances, it is not surprising that for many years the dominant scholarly narrative of independence foregrounded Portugal's decline and subordination to the British Empire, such that Brazil was a classic case of 'same mule, new rider.' Brazil passed from colony to neocolony; political power shifted from the representatives of Portugal and their slaveholding favourites to the representatives of the white protonobility in the Brazilian Emperor's court; meanwhile, most of the Brazilian population—slaves, free and freed persons, indigenous peoples, poor whites—found themselves on the margins. To be sure, this scenario also dominated the earlier historiography of independence in Spanish or Hispanic America, as John Lynch's classic study, *The Spanish American Revolutions*, makes clear.[16] Nevertheless, I would argue that given Brazil's peculiar features, the colonial to neocolonial, 'one elite for another' narrative endured the longest in its national historiography. On a more global level, this narrative was assisted by Benedict Anderson (whose account, Thurner points out, was indebted to Lynch[17]) who dispatched the conundrum of Portuguese America's postcolonial unity (in contrast to Spanish America's fragmentation) with a reference to José Murilo de Carvalho's argument that the Brazilian elite had been socialized at the University of Coimbra in Portugal and not in American universities, as in Hispanic America.[18] Ironically then, Brazil's 'success' at remaining intact as an independent, imperial nation becomes evidence of its 'failure' to decolonize.

The New History of Postcolonial Brazilian Empire

The last two decades have seen a gradual unravelling of the master narrative of failed Latin American decolonization, even in 'best case' Brazil. The contention of an earlier historiography that independence was a non-event is no longer tenable, at least for the moment. Whereas historians writing in the 1960s and 1970s emphasized the shift from colonialism to neocolonialism and the failure of independence to shake up the social order,[19] recent research has examined more closely and seriously the challenges posed by the process of gaining and consolidating independence.[20] The critique has included a reassessment of Roberto Schwarz's famous claim, with reference to liberal, democratic ideologies in Brazil, that such modern, European 'ideas were out of place' in a peripheral or dependent, slave-based society.[21] Rejecting such normative, dependency readings of Latin American political discourse, historians have sought instead to understand the particular modes and means of Brazil's modern nationhood.

As Kirsten Schultz argues in *Tropical Versailles*, the transfer of the imperial capital and its court from Portugal to Brazil involved much more than mere relocation.²² The tropical move led to a serious questioning of the very bases of imperial rule and monarchical authority. It created a transatlantic context in which a modern concept of constitutional monarchy (with its implied transformation of subjects into citizens) became increasingly viable and urgent. At the risk of oversimplifying, the tropicalization of the Braganza court also made manifest the palpable ambiguities of the metropole–colony distinction of the period or, in today's culturalist jargon, the 'colonizer/colonized' antinomy. In this regard, Iara Lis Carvalho Souza has traced the way in which rituals of rule during the reign of Dom Pedro I (1822–1831) initially drew upon premodern notions of the king's persona as the embodiment of empire. In response to increasing, anti-Portuguese unrest, however, this old representation of the empire gave way to a modern set of symbols and commemorations that disembodied the empire/nation.²³ In short, new work suggests that the empire was 'Brazilianized' in ways reminiscent of other postcolonial regimes around the world.

Other recent work explores the invention of a Brazilian (as opposed to Portuguese) past and identity in the decades following independence. In *Cores, marcas e falas*, Ivana Stolze Lima traces the idea of Brazil as a 'mixed' nation back to the earliest years following independence, demonstrating the ways in which literary works and theatrical productions portrayed the hybrid features of the Brazilian population as its distinguishing, and positive characteristic.²⁴ Lilia Schwarz's *The Emperor's Beard* details the many efforts in the 1840s and 1850s by the Instituto Histórico e Geográfico Brasileiro (which included among its members the Emperor Dom Pedro II) to document the indigenous genealogy of the Brazilian people. The Institute sought to construct a heroic 'American' history of the Brazilian nation, a mission that culminated in the widely read and performed Indianist novels of José de Alencar (*Iracema, O Guaraní*). The editors of the short-lived journal *Nitheroi* advocated the cultivation of a modern national spirit that 'would consist of transforming Brazil's [cultural] subordination to Portugal, and promoting the triumph of a national literature, which in the Brazilian case ought to take account of the poetic abilities of the Indian.'²⁵

Perhaps the most significant break with the neocolonial narrative of the earlier historiography is the new emphasis on the subaltern as *political* actor as well as greater attention to a range of middling groups that cannot be easily classified either as popular or elite. Whereas earlier works depicted an elitist political system that left no room for popular *political* action, thereby relegating collective protest to the realm of prepolitical or social resistance, recent work insists not only that popular groups (slaves, free labourers, foot soldiers, etc.) participated in public life, but that they were aware of and even shaped the political events and ideological trends of the age. Indeed, many were astutely alert to the radical potential of certain 'liberal' ideas. These more recent studies focus on popular denunciations of the Portuguese born and their disproportionate presence and authority within the new Court of the Brazilian empire, and their prominent role in commerce.[26] These popular agitations are now read as part of the nationalist political contests of the era, and as reflecting anti-Portuguese, decolonizing sentiments shared by some members of the elite.

In his 1986 study of slave rebellion in Bahia, João Reis detailed the many acts of protest by underpaid soldiers and dissatisfied plebeians. Some of these protests targeted Portuguese merchants and innkeepers, denouncing them as responsible for high food prices and other outrages. Portuguese residents of Bahia were robbed, injured, and even murdered.[27] Hendrik Kraay, also writing about Bahia, includes a rich account of the political and social turbulence of the period from independence to the mid-1830s. His study explores the role of the military in politics during the transition from colony to nation, and the importance of the armed forces in creating a space for political activity initiated by people of colour.[28] Gladys Sabina Ribeiro's pathbreaking study, *A Liberdade em construção* (2002) maps the clashes between the Portuguese and people of colour in nineteenth-century Rio, and shows how these conflicts both reflected and induced tensions at other levels of Brazilian society.[29] Hebe Mattos's *Escravidão e cidadania no Brasil monárquico* considers the efforts of free people of colour to distance themselves politically and juridically from those 'Brazilians' who marked the outer limits of national belonging based on slavery. They insisted on the 'deracialization' of slavery, that is, delinking slave status from skin colour and political status from descent. The Brazilian Constitution of 1824 makes no mention of race or skin colour regarding citizenship, and Mattos contends that free people of colour jealously guarded against the slightest effort to revive and recodify colonial hierarchies based on race, colour, or 'blood' (*mancha de sangue*). Indeed, in sharp contrast to their US southern counterparts, Brazilian elites by and large refrained from defending slavery on overtly racial grounds precisely because it would have so enraged free people of colour, many of whom were actively engaged in the political life of the new nation, including a significant segment who were men of property and standing.[30] The militancy of free people of colour on such matters did not necessarily extend to the institution of slavery itself, which went largely unquestioned until well past the mid-nineteenth century. Thus, free people of colour, a substantial fraction of whom were slaveholders themselves, asserted their rights as citizens and resisted the racialization of political status, thereby affirming the propertied limits of citizenship.[31]

A Necessary Evil?

How can we make sense of the voracious efforts of second slavery masters to maximize their gains from the booming global commodity markets (first sugar, then coffee) by sustaining the flow of human chattel from Africa to the Empire of Brazil, while also acknowledging the frequently expressed sentiment that slavery and the slave trade were remnants of the colonial past incompatible with a modern, sovereign nation? Further, how can these notions be squared with the recent historiography of the subaltern and middle sectors?

As I have argued elsewhere, in Brazil linking slavery with the colonial past did not generate a significant antislavery discourse until well into the second half of the nineteenth century.[32] However, and unlike the US South, no strong proslavery argument emerged in Brazil during this period, with most of slavery's active defenders framing it as a necessary evil. This weak defence of slavery is striking since a very substantial portion of the Brazilian free population had a direct stake in it. As recent research has demonstrated, slave ownership was widely distributed in Brazil during the decades after independence, with many individuals of limited wealth or income owning one or two slaves (many were ex-slaves or descendants of slaves themselves).[33] Yet despite the substantial number of Brazilians with a stake in slavery, large or small, it was rare to hear the guardians of the slaveholding order utter the kind of vigorous, root-and-branch defences of human bondage that were circulating in the US South, where by the 1830s slavery was widely touted as a 'positive good' and where colour lines hardened to a degree unprecedented in the New World.

Given the pervasive presence of slavery in Brazilian society, it is interesting to consider the serious objections registered by prominent statesmen-intellectuals during the debates over citizenship and the slavery question in the 1823 Constituent Assembly. In the critique prepared for presentation to the assembled, several speakers not only denounced the evils and horrors of slavery but detailed its economic liabilities as well. According to João Severiano Maciel da Costa, future councillor of state, slavery was part of an *old colonial system* that would foster an agricultural economy dependent upon foreign demand, while the eminent politician and political economist José da Silva Lisboa warned that the continued existence of slavery would mean prolonged reliance on *primitive methods* of production.[34] In other words, in dramatic contrast to what some second slavery historians might predict, they portrayed slavery as a drag on Brazilian economic progress and the opposite of modernity. To be sure, there was little risk of slavery being abolished at this time; most of the delegates in the assembly undoubtedly took its continued existence for granted. But the typical response to such criticisms was always to portray slavery as a 'necessary evil.'

In this regard, the opinions about slavery expressed within the Chamber of Deputies during the debates in the mid-1820s over the question of abolishing the transatlantic commerce in slaves, raised mainly due to pressure from the British, are even more striking. Even those speakers who vigorously defended the slave trade and slavery typically did so on purely pragmatic grounds. At no point did anyone offer a moral or philosophical defence of the slave trade or slavery. Instead, Raymundo José da Cunha Matos, secretary in perpetuity of the Sociedade Auxiliadora da Indústria Nacional (a planters' association), protested that the impending abolition of the slave trade would 'cause enormous harm to national commerce,' would 'destroy agriculture, the vital foundation of our people's existence,' would be 'a cruel blow to state revenues,' and would be 'premature.'

To be sure, these were all spirited arguments in favour of maintaining an appalling form of commerce, but they were not the basis for a permanent commitment to a slave-based economic and social order nor a compelling moral vision for the Brazilian nation. In this regard, it is worth noting that Cunha Matos felt obliged to preface these objections with the following statement:

> I am in no way proposing to defend the justice and eternal convenience of the commerce in slaves for the Brazilian Empire: I would not fall into the unpardonable absurdity of supporting in today's world and in the midst of the top-ranking intellects of the Brazilian nation a doctrine that is repugnant to the enlightened men of this century and that contradicts generally accepted philanthropic principles.

Cunha Matos was referring to the slave trade, not slavery, but it is impossible to read this description of the trade and its fundamental incompatibility with enlightenment and progress without hearing implications for slavery itself—and this from one of the few avid *defenders* of the slave trade in the Chamber of Deputies.[35]

Aside from concerns about the economic implications of Brazil's continuing dependence on slave labour, there was the challenge that the slave population, and especially those recently brought from Africa, posed to the construction of a stable and secure national order, an anxiety that the memory of events in Saint-Domingue surely exacerbated. In the decision to deny political rights to enslaved and freed Africans, we can see how citizenship was racialized without recourse to explicit colour lines. Whereas at the time of independence, residents of Brazil born in Portugal were automatically eligible for the status of citizen, while future European immigrants were expected and even encouraged to seek naturalization, speakers at the Constitutional Assembly characterized Africans as stateless peoples and heathens who would remain forever outside the charmed circle of Brazilian citizenship.[36]

Using Brazilian versus African place of birth as the dividing line between potential citizens and permanent outsiders obviated the need for any explicit reference to colour, something that would have surely alienated influential figures among Brazilian-born *Pardos*.[37] But even if the emphasis on African birth rather than blackness enabled the incipient fiction of Brazil as a colour-blind society, it raised other issues with respect to the viability of the new nation. For one, it created the unwelcome prospect of a permanently 'alien' population embedded within the nation whose various means of resistance and rebellion, real and imagined, could present an ongoing threat to national strength and stability. Whether slaves struggling for their freedom or free persons chafing at their indeterminate civil status, the numerous people of African descent in the new Brazilian nation were rightly seen by those in power as a potential challenge to the existing order.

Schultz notes that the same antislavery treatises that critiqued slavery's retarding effects on the nation's economic progress devoted even more space to the negative *political* consequences of continued reliance on (African) slave labour. José Bonifácio, the 'Patriarch' of Brazilian independence, put it most vividly when he denounced the 'commerce in human flesh' as 'the cancer that gnaws at the entrails of Brazil.' Similarly, Silva Lisboa worried that it 'prevented the formation of a homogeneous and compact nation,' and Maciel da Costa claimed that 'the indefinite multiplication of a heterogeneous population' posed an 'imminent and inevitable threat [to the] security of the state.' Such heterogeneity, José Bonifácio noted, was hardly regarded as a problem under colonial rule; indeed, Portuguese imperial interests 'wanted [us to be] . . . a mixed and heterogeneous people, without nationality, and without brotherhood, so as to better enslave us.'[38] In other words, it was the very condition of independent nationhood that made these questions of vital concern to at least some of the delegates.[39]

In highlighting these remarks, my intention is not to dispute Marquese's claim that 'control over the apparatus of the State by a *new* seigneurial class permitted the vigorous expansion of slavery in Brazil.'[40] He and other historians working in the second slavery vein rightly see the transition from colony to nation as entirely auspicious for the emerging coffee-planter elite and an unalloyed advantage for their slavocratic ambitions.[41] Nonetheless, this view ignores the challenges involved in the expansion of an enslaved population in a nation where whites were in the minority, and where the substantial political presence of freepersons of colour limited recourse to explicit, *de jure* forms of white supremacist rule. It also ignores the anxieties of Brazilian politicians and literati about the new nation's standing as a slaveholding and minority-white nation on a British-dominated world stage. Moreover, one can detect in the various commentaries by defenders and detractors of slavery during this period a sense that national sovereignty would never be attained as long as enslavement remained the dominant mode of labour extraction in Brazil. Even the three 'experts' on slavery and labour management quoted by Marquese as examples of the rational capitalist approach to slave plantation economics peppered their prose with disclaimers about slavery (described as a violation of natural right, as a lamentable necessity in an under-populated nation, and as creating the 'sad condition' of the captive) that would be unimaginable in an analogous treatise by a defender of slavery in the antebellum US South.[42]

Whereas southern US planters were busy making it virtually impossible or even illegal to free individual slaves, the rate of manumission in nineteenth-century Brazil was extraordinarily robust for an economy hungry for additional labour. According to the 1872 census, after a half-century of independence by far the largest single category in Brazil was that of free people of colour, a demographic sector almost three times the size of the enslaved population even though abolition still lay some sixteen years in the future. Elite anxieties about the African 'strangers' in their midst surely contributed to the acquiescence to British demands for ending the slave trade. A growing emphasis on the need to 'creolize' the slave population, a process that produced a whole new set of challenges from slaves who increasingly saw themselves as Brazilians, is also evident. South of Rio, the association of slavery with colonialism and backwardness undergirded Paulista self-fashioning as 'progressive planters' eager to throw off the 'chains' of slavery and shift to (white) wage labour, a posture that set the stage for the São Paulo–dominated First Republic.[43] Indeed, despite substantial evidence of the coffee planters during the Conservative period presenting themselves as the foundations of order and prosperity, with slavery a means to civilize and Christianize Africans, a steady stream of opinion in Brazilian politics and culture continued to see slavery as an impediment to the formation of a modern, progressive society that could claim a place at the table of sovereign nations.[44]

The second slavery historiography emphasizes the need to think of slavery as a global phenomenon and rightly notes certain common features in the political economy of nineteenth-century slavery in Cuba, the United States, and Brazil.[45] This perspective has also produced a tendency to treat the southern US experience as a historical template for understanding the relationship between slaveholding, political discourses, and the emergence of a national state. Despite sharing certain features with the slavocratic order of the US South, the more demographically diverse Brazilian case reveals the impediments to constructing a sovereign nation on a slave foundation, and not only because of 'external' pressures to end the slave trade, and then slavery itself. With men of colour playing key roles in the limited but crucial struggles for independence, challenging the prominence of the 'Portuguese' in the immediate postindependence decades, and with massive arrivals of Africans creating the spectre of a united black population with no allegiance to the Brazilian nation, it was never possible to create a Brazilian analogue of the 'White Man's Republic' that emerged in the United States and that, as an ideological project, has proved so alarmingly durable. Instead, the ambiguities produced by the strained marriage of the post-Haiti slave-based economy with the political demands of the ex-slave, indigenous, and mixed race lower and middle classes, created new possibilities and anxieties in Brazil characteristic, perhaps, of the postcolonial condition in nineteenth-century Latin America at large.

Notes

1. See Peter Guardino, *'The Time of Liberty': Popular Political Culture in Oaxaca, 1750–1850* (Durham: Duke University Press, 2005); James E. Sanders, *The Vanguard of the Atlantic World: Creating Modernity, Nation, and Democracy in Nineteenth-Century Latin America* (Durham: Duke University Press, 2014); Anne Eller, *We Dream Together: Dominican Independence, Haiti, and the Fight for Caribbean Freedom* (Durham: Duke University Press, 2016); Scott Eastman and Natalia Sobrevilla Perea, eds., *The Rise of Constitutional Government in the Iberian Atlantic World: The Impact of the Cádiz Constitution of 1812* (Tuscaloosa: University of Alabama Press, 2015). A small sample of the second slavery literature would include Dale W. Tomich, *Through the Prism of Slavery: Labor, Capital, and the World Economy* (Lanham, MD: Rowman & Littlefield, 2003); Sven Beckert, *Empire of Cotton: A Global History* (New York: Alfred A. Knopf, 2014); Dale W. Tomich, ed., *Slavery and Historical Capitalism during the Nineteenth Century* (Lexington, MA: Lexington Books, forthcoming).
2. Márcia Regina Berbel and Rafael de Bivar Marquese, 'The Absence of Race: Slavery, Citizenship, and Pro-Slavery Ideology in the Cortes of Lisbon and the Rio de Janeiro Constituent Assembly (1821–4),' *Social History* 32:4 (November 2007), 416.
3. Most prominent among those literary or cultural studies scholars who see decolonization as something yet to occur in Latin America are J. Jorge Klor de Alva and Walter Mignolo. See, for example, Klor de Alva, 'The Postcolonization of the (Latin) American Experience,' in Gyan Prakash, ed., *After Colonialism: Imperial Histories and Postcolonial Displacements* (Princeton: Princeton University Press, 1994), 241–75; Walter Mignolo, *The Darker Side of Western Modernity: Global Futures, Decolonial Options* (Durham: Duke University Press, 2011).
4. Evandro Charles Piza Duarte and Marcus Vinícius Lustosa Queiroz, 'Just for English Eyes: Citizenship in the Brazilian Constituent Assembly of 1823 and the Tensions of Portuguese Empire in the Black Atlantic' (unpublished paper).
5. Ilmar Rohloff de Mattos, *O tempo Saquarema: A formação do Estado imperial* (São Paulo: Hucitec, 1987).
6. Rafael de Bivar Marquese, 'Escravismo de independência: a ideologia da escravidão no Brasil em Cuba e nos Estados Unidos nas décadas de 1810 e 1820,' in Istvan Jancsó, ed., *Independência: história e historiografia* (São Paulo: Hucitec, 2005), 809–827.
7. Ada Ferrer, *Freedom's Mirror: Cuba and Haiti in the Age of Revolution* (New York: Cambridge University Press, 2014), 4–5.
8. See Edward E. Baptist, *The Half Has Never Been Told: Slavery and the Making of American Capitalism* (New York: Basic Books, 2014).
9. For an insightful discussion of the second slavery scholarship in the US context, see James Oakes, 'Capitalism, Slavery, and the Civil War,' *ILWCH* 89 (Spring 2016), 195–220.
10. See, for example, Baptist, *The Half Has Never Been Told*; Walter Johnson, *River of Dark Dreams: Slavery and Empire in the Cotton Kingdom*

(Cambridge, MA: Belknap Press, 2013); Rafael de Bivar Marquese, *Feitores do corpo, missionários da mente: senhores, letrados e o controle dos escravos nas Américas, 1660–1860* (São Paulo: Companhia das Letras, 2004).
11. On Haiti as a source of free soil ideology, see Ada Ferrer, 'Haiti, Free Soil, and Antislavery in the Revolutionary Atlantic,' *American Historical Review* 117:1 (February 2012), 40–66.
12. On the Louisiana Purchase as a ramification of the Haitian Revolution, see Steven Hahn, *A Nation Without Borders: The United States and its World in an Age of Civil Wars, 1830–1920* (New York: Viking, 2016), 24–25.
13. On nodes of southern support for re-opening the slave trade, see Hahn, *A Nation Without Borders*, 203.
14. On the link between independence and emancipation, see Barbara Weinstein, 'The Decline of the Progressive Planter and the Rise of Subaltern Agency: Shifting Narratives of Slave Emancipation in Brazil,' in Gilbert Joseph, ed., *Reclaiming the Political in Latin American History: Essays from the North* (Durham: Duke University Press, 2001), 81–101.
15. On the illegal (but tolerated) slave trade, see Sidney Chalhoub, *A força da escravidão: Ilegalidade e costume no Brasil oitocentista* (São Paulo: Companhia das Letras, 2012), 45–69.
16. John Lynch, *The Spanish American Revolutions, 1808–1826* (London: W.W. Norton & Company, 1973).
17. See Mark Thurner, 'After Spanish Rule: Writing Another After,' in Mark Thurner and Andrés Guerrero, eds., *After Spanish Rule: Postcolonial Predicaments of the Americas* (Durham: Duke University Press, 2003), 12–57.
18. Benedict Anderson, *Imagined Communities: Reflections on the Origin and Spread of Nationalism* (London: Verso, 1983), 51, n. 19.
19. The classic work in this vein is Fernando Novais, *Portugal e Brasil na crise do antigo sistema colonial, 1777–1808* (São Paulo: Hucitec, 1979).
20. For an excellent sample of more recent work on the question of independence, see Istvan Jancsó, ed., *Independência: história e historiografia* (São Paulo: Hucitec, 2005).
21. Schwarz articulated this argument in *Ao vencedor as batatas: forma literária e processo social nos inícios do romance brasileiro* (São Paulo: Livraria Duas Cidades, 1976). A very early critique of this position is Maria Sylvia de Carvalho Franco, 'As idéias estão no lugar,' *Cadernos de Debate* I—História do Brasil (São Paulo: Brasiliense, 1976). For a more recent critique of this debate, see Elias Palti, 'The Problem of "Misplaced Ideas" Revisited: Beyond the History of Ideas in Latin America,' *Journal of the History of Ideas* 67:1 (2006), 149–179.
22. Kirsten Schultz, *Tropical Versailles: Empire, Monarchy, and the Portuguese Royal Court in Rio de Janeiro, 1808–1821* (New York: Routledge, 2001).
23. Iara Lis Carvalho Souza, *Pátria coroada: o Brasil como corpo político autônomo, 1780–1831* (São Paulo: Ed. UNESP, 1999).
24. Ivana Stolze Lima, *Cores, marcas e falas: sentidos da mestiçagem no Império do Brasil* (Rio de Janeiro: Arquivo Nacional, 2003).
25. Lilia Moritz Schwarcz, *The Emperor's Beard: Dom Pedro II and the Tropical Monarchy of Brazil* (New York: Hill and Wang, 2003), 94.
26. Gladys Sabina Ribeiro, *Liberdade em construção: Identidade nacional e conflitos antilusitanos no primeiro reinado* (Rio de Janeiro: Relume Dumará/ FAPERJ, 2002).
27. João José Reis, *Slave Rebellion in Brazil: The Muslim Uprising of 1835 in Bahia* (Baltimore: Johns Hopkins University Press, 1993), 38.
28. Hendrik Kraay, *Race, State, and Armed Forces in Independence-Era Brazil: Bahia, 1790s-1840s* (Stanford: Stanford University Press, 2001). See also his

Days of National Festivity in Rio de Janeiro, Brazil, 1823–1889 (Stanford: Stanford University Press, 2013).
29. Ribeiro, *Liberdade em construção*.
30. Hebe Maria Mattos, *Escravidão e cidadania no Brasil monárquico* (Rio de Janeiro: Jorge Zahar, 2000).
31. The distinction between the rights of people of colour and the condition of the enslaved was not easily maintained, since freed persons laboured under the constant threat of re-enslavement. See Chalhoub, *A força da escravidão*, 227–276. The position of free persons here is reminiscent of the Ecuadorian mestizos described by Andrés Guerrero in 'The Administration of Dominated Populations Under a Regime of Customary Citizenship: The Case of Postcolonial Ecuador,' in Mark Thurner and Andrés Guerrero, eds., *After Spanish Rule: Postcolonial Predicaments of the Americas* (Durham: Duke University Press, 2003), 272–309.
32. Barbara Weinstein, 'Slavery, Citizenship, and National Identity in Brazil and the United States South,' in Don Doyle and Marco Antonio Pamplona, eds., *Nationalism in the New World* (Athens: University of Georgia Press, 2006), 248–271. I am using the concept of a 'weak argument' not in the sense of 'ineffective,' but rather meaning that the argument is temporary and 'defensive' rather than 'offensive.'
33. See Zephyr L. Frank, *Dutra's World: Wealth and Family in Nineteenth-Century Rio de Janeiro* (Albuquerque: University of New Mexico Press, 2004).
34. For an excellent discussion of Silva Lisboa's complicated position on slavery and a future Brazil without slavery, see Robert Paquette, 'José da Silva Lisboa and the Vicissitudes of Enlightened Reform in Brazil, 1798–1824,' in Paquette, ed., *Enlightened Reform in Southern Europe and its Atlantic Colonies, c. 1750–1830* (Farnham and Burlington, VT: Ashgate, 2009), 383–387.
35. Brasil (Governo), *Anais da câmara dos deputados*, July 3, 1827, 21.
36. Duarte and Queiroz, 'Just for English Eyes,' 15–18.
37. 'Pardo' (brown) was typically used by and for free people of colour regardless of their actual skin colour since blackness was associated with enslavement. Hebe Mattos, *Das cores do silêncio: os significados da liberdade no sudeste escravista, Brasil século XIX* (Rio de Janeiro: Nova Fronteira, 1998), 104.
38. Kirsten Schultz, 'Brazilian Independence, Citizenship, and the Problem of Slavery: The Assembléia Constituinte of 1823,' paper presented at the symposium 'Revolution, Independence and the New Nations of Latin America,' Irvine, CA, March 23–24, 2003, 12–15.
39. Note that the references cited by Ivana Stolze Lima to Brazilians being 'mixed' implied that mixture was the dominant quality, not a source of diversity or heterogeneity.
40. Marquese, *Feitores do corpo*, 262.
41. Other contributions to the second slavery literature on Brazil include Ricardo Salles, *E o Vale era escravo: Vassouras, século XIX. Senhores e escravos no coração do Império* (Rio de Janeiro: Civilização Brasileira, 2008), and Tâmis Parron, *A política da escravidão no Império do Brasil, 1826–1865* (Rio de Janeiro: Civilização Brasileira, 2011).
42. Marquese, *Feitores do corpo*, 268–292.
43. Alfredo Bosi, 'Sob o signo de cam,' in *Dialética da colonização* (São Paulo: Companhia das Letras, 1992), 246–272.
44. Two quite different studies of the coffee planters of the Paraíba Valley, both of which emphasize the coffee planters' successful construction of an orderly slaveholding culture, are Salles, *E o Vale era escravo*, and Jeffrey D. Needell, *The Party of Order: The Conservatives, the State, and Slavery in the Brazilian Monarchy, 1831–1871* (Stanford: Stanford University Press, 2006).

45. In the case of Cuba, it is instructive that the episode typically cited as the inaugural moment of the anticolonial struggle, the Grito de Yara (1868), involved a slaveholding sugar planter, Carlos Manuel de Céspedes, not only declaring war on the Spaniards but liberating his slaves in the process. Whether it was the shadow of Haiti, or the many slave uprisings and conspiracies in Cuba itself, or sheer military necessity, Céspedes clearly deemed the retention of chattel slavery and the fight against Spanish rule as incompatible projects. See Ada Ferrer, *Insurgent Cuba: Race, Nation, and Revolution, 1868–1898* (Chapel Hill: University of North Carolina Press, 1999), 21.

7 The Lost Italian Connection

Federica Morelli

The Hispanic American and Italian independence movements were intimately connected. Both sought to excise Spanish rule in the territories they sought to liberate and unite. The foundational, transoceanic connections of the 1820s that linked the two were, however, lost to view when a longstanding, anti-Hispanic sentiment was rekindled by late-nineteenth-century Italian nationalists. Like many other European nationalists of the period, the Italians came to view Latin America as unfit for independent nationhood. Political instability in the decades following independence from Spain fuelled a narrative of failure in Europe. Italian historiography finished the job, erasing most of the traces of the early connection. Although a new historiography has begun to recover the complexity of those lost connections, the enduring tendency to view independence and decolonization in teleological, national terms continues to hinder understanding of the transatlantic reach of 'the first wave of decolonization.'

The Constitution of Cadiz and Federalism in Hispanic America and Italy

In the first Risorgimento, Italian interest in Spanish America was particularly strong. Indeed, the Hispanic American experience, and in particular the Constitution of Cadiz, was initially perceived as a model to learn from. At that time, the concept of independence for Italians did not necessarily imply that the nation must free itself from an imperial power. Instead, the concept was associated with political and cultural 'regeneration,' as the same term *Risorgimento* suggests, and this concept could be accommodated under a federalist model. Although federal constitutions were debated earlier in the United States and France, in the Hispanic and Italian case the key precedent or model was not Philadelphia or Paris but Cadiz. This constitution was sworn into law across Spanish America, the Caribbean, and the Philippines (which all thereby became 'Ultramarine Spain'). It reemerged again in the writing of independent constitutions for the new republics of South America in the 1820s. In Italy, the Cadiz Constitution circulated widely soon after its declaration in 1812 and it became the banner of revolutionaries in Naples and Turin in 1820 and 1821. Its checks on monarchical power, the broad definition of citizenship and nation, and its defence of Catholic religion and ancient institutions, all ensured its enthusiastic reception in Italy.

The Cadiz Constitution briefly established a transoceanic 'Spanish nation' of citizens consisting of all the adult males of the Empire with, after much debate and American opposition, the exception of those of African descent. This radical substitution of 'the Spanish Nation' for the 'Hispanic Monarchy' did not imply a new order of the territory, which continued to be constituted of the chartered territorial subjects inherited from the Bourbon regime of the eighteenth century (*audiencias*, provinces, intendencies, municipalities, parishes). The Cadiz idea of an imperial nationhood under a constitutional monarch and that maintained territorial integrity and internal political structure fitted well with the one that many Italian patriots shared in the 1820s.

Many Italian patriots shared with Hispanic Americans a federalist reading and application of the Cadiz Constitution. For instance, Luigi Angeloni supported a 'confederation of republics' along the same lines advanced by Americans during and after independence from Spain.[1] The federalist interpretation began during the constitutional debates in Cadiz of 1810–1812,[2] when Hispanic American delegates opposed the more centralist vision of the Peninsular delegates.[3] Two essential features of the Cadiz constitution left open federalist opportunities for successor regimes.[4] First, the vague limits of the territorial spaces of each 'republic' or jurisdiction. In America, this uncertainty produced instability and allowed for the confederation of administrative units.[5] Second, the Cadiz Constitution granted to local institutions considerable powers, contributing to the dramatic fragmentation of jurisdictions.[6]

The strong autonomy of local institutions established in Cadiz drew the attention of Italian patriots, especially of Piedmontese and Neapolitans who, in 1820, created liberal regimes inspired by the same constitution.[7] They considered the Cadiz Constitution the best instrument to overcome the administrative centralization imposed by Napoleon and then by the absolutist restoration. It would return to the provinces and municipalities the room for political manoeuvre that they had lost. The resentment against the French model that had dispossessed the municipalities of their traditional powers constituted one of the main causes of the Neapolitan rebellion in 1820.[8]

Echoing the American readings of the Cadiz Constitution, Bartolomeo Fiorilli, a Neapolitan exile in Spain, underlined the need for local autonomy in Italy, noting that 'sovereignty lies essentially in the towns [pueblos] and not in the nation.'[9] As the historiography on the Spanish American independence has clearly demonstrated, this antinomy between 'nation' (which in the 'Spanish Monarchy' was transoceanic) and the 'towns' (*pueblos*), persisted in the constitutional debates in some parts of Latin America into the middle decades of the nineteenth century.[10]

Italian–American Connections in the 1820s

The 1820s represented a period of setbacks for the Italian regeneration. The failure of the 1820–1821 'revolutions' in Turin, Milan, and Naples marked the end of a generation's dreams of introducing a Cadiz-inspired, liberal federation among the Italian states. Amid failure and indeed the collapse of the revolution at home, international events became once again the source of inspiration and theme of discussions among Italian intellectuals. The failed revolutions of the 1820s had been led by former Napoleonic civil servants and army officers apparently nostalgic for the achievements of Bonaparte, or by backward-looking aristocrats anxious to regain their pre-revolutionary stations.[11] In short, federalism during the Restoration has been dismissed as the preferred option of the Italian oligarchy, who wished to maintain their regional power bases and thus were hostile to any idea of united nationhood based on popular sovereignty.[12] These views are linked to the idea that Risorgimento federalism was fundamentally anti-democratic in nature, an interpretation which seems to be confirmed by Filippo Buonarroti and Giuseppe Mazzini, who, like Bolivar, saw unity as the only means to defeat the aristocracy. New research on the reception of the Cadiz Constitution, however, suggests that the appeal of federalism was not nostalgic or backward-looking, but instead rather more democratic and international than previously thought.

In the late eighteenth and early nineteenth centuries, the contested meanings of the terms 'independence' and 'nation' were very much in flux on both sides of the Atlantic. The Junta of Quito declared in 1811 that it was 'absolutely free from the dependence, vassalage, and power of any foreign government, and subordinated only to the supreme and legitimate authority of our King Ferdinand VII.'[13] Here, independence glossed the desire not to be dependent on any foreign government while affirming allegiance to a distant monarch forced into French exile. The US Declaration of Independence reflects a similar notion of independence, being not only a declaration of freedom from all foreign powers but a recognition of interdependence. As David Armitage has demonstrated, 'independence' at this moment reflected the concept of the liberty of a state or political community to act freely with respect to other states or external authorities, including the ability to make agreements to limit voluntarily its own liberty.[14] Behind this concept of liberty was the notion of 'the Law of Nations' elaborated by the Swiss jurist Emer de Vattel, whose book *Le Droit de Gens* (1758) circulated widely both in Europe and America. Vattel compared political communities or states to free individuals living in a state of nature. Since men were originally free and independent, so too were the political communities they created by consent; 'the law of nations,' he wrote 'is nothing but the natural law applied to nations.' Thus, the guerrilla and mercenary war fought against Bonaparte's forces in the Iberian Peninsula was soon called a 'war of independence' although of course Spain was never a French colony, even under Bourbon rule. Instead, Bonaparte was a foreign tyrant and 'Anti-Christ' whose removal would restore a previous 'Spanish liberty.'

During the first three decades of the nineteenth century in Hispanic America, political communities on several levels could and did define themselves as 'independent' even if they formed part of greater associations such as monarchies, viceroyalties, or confederations. The political crisis of the monarchy produced a fragmentation of sovereignty, such that in the short run colonial administrative units did not necessarily become unified, national territories, as Anderson assumed.[15] More basic units, often called *provincias*, *pueblos*, and *republicas*, represented by various kinds of *cabildos*, or councils, exercised de facto, often highly democratic forms of citizenship and independence well into the nineteenth century. In turn, these provinces and pueblos could unite to form larger, regional units in moments of crisis and civil war, increasingly frequent in the post-independence decades. In Mexico, Central and South America, inter-provincial and inter-state confederations were formed and reformed, consolidated or disbanded.[16] Some hardened into national states; others did not. The shifting borders of Latin American states and provinces during this period reflected the dynamics of local sovereignties born, in part, of a Cadiz-inspired, federalist independence, and in part in response to increasing militarization and the need for local defence.

Although Italian historians have more recently restored the importance of the early years of federalism in Italy, the tendency is still to underplay the international political dimension.[17] Concepts of Italian 'resurgence' elaborated in the 1820s rarely presupposed a unified Italian nation-state covering the entire peninsula. Santangelo, who promoted the 1821 revolution in Naples and then joined the liberals in Spain and in Spanish America, claimed that in Italy there were not one, but many nations.[18] Like their Hispanic American counterparts, many Italian intellectuals of the period supported federalism as the most appropriate model to grant individual and collective rights as well as to defend political communities against external threats. Finally, they would advocate for an inclusive, federal nation based on political commitment rather than on linguistic or cultural differences. These Cadiz- and Hispanic American–inspired characteristics of the first Risorgimento were, however, progressively treated as expressions of backwardness and romanticism. The Italian historiography also focused on the presence of Italian heroes—above all Garibaldi—in the Americas rather than on the influence of Cadiz and Latin America on Italian political culture.[19]

An important exception is the work of Lucy Riall. Riall has documented the importance of Garibaldi's experiences in South America for his own personal and political evolution, freeing it from the mythologized prison to which it had been assigned by Italian romanticism. Garibaldi's political ideas, most notably his lasting belief in the virtue of dictatorship in time of war, derived from his observations on politics and the conduct of war in South America. Many of the battles over the political forms of nation-building and the struggles between conservatives and liberals which Garibaldi was to become involved in on his return to Italy, he first encountered in republican circles in Montevideo. Finally, it was in Rio Grande and Uruguay that Garibaldi learned to fight.[20] Another important exception to the rule is Maurizio Isabella's work on political activists who left Italy after the collapse of the Napoleonic regimes in 1814 and the suppression of liberal political movements in 1820–1821. Isabella has shown that the cross-cultural exchanges and writings of these critical-minded intellectuals contributed decisively to Italian Risorgimento nationalism.[21]

During this early period of the 'First Risorgimento,' hundreds of Italians left the peninsula to join foreign uprisings or fight wars of independence in southern Europe (Spain and Greece) and in America, giving rise to a global movement of solidarity that benefited the Latin American cause of independence. It was in this context of displacement and solidarity that Latin America became newly relevant to the Italian Risorgimento. Together with hundreds of British and Irish fighters, large numbers of Italian volunteers, many of whom were former Napoleonic soldiers or officers, joined the independence campaigns of patriotic forces in South America and Mexico.[22] Among the most famous of these was the Piedmontese Carlo Castelli, who joined Bolívar in Haiti in 1816 and was promoted to General in 1830.[23]

Another notable Piedmontese volunteer was Giuseppe Avezzana. Avezzana joined Colonel Riego in Spain, sailed to Louisiana, and from there to Mexico, where he defended Tampico against Spanish aggression in 1829. Later he fought in the Mexican Civil War supporting Santa Ana against Bustamante. He returned to Genoa amidst the risings of 1848 and soon became one of the most important officers of the urban insurrection of 1849. Another important ex-Napoleonic officer in Bolivar's forces was Agostino Codazzi. After the defeat of Napoleon in 1815, Codazzi joined other ex-soldiers drifting around Europe and the Near East in search of employment, eventually undertaking commercial ventures in the Ottoman Empire. In 1817, he sailed to Baltimore with his friend Costante Ferrari. They travelled to Texas, Mexico, Central America, and the Caribbean, finally arriving in New Granada where they joined Bolivar's camp. After the wars, Codazzi became an important political figure in Venezuela and Colombia. He made the first detailed topographic maps of both countries, guiding the work of the Colombian Corographic Commission.[24]

The intellectual connections between the Italian diaspora and Latin America were further enhanced by the circulation of printed material. Despite official censorship, echoes of the events in Latin America reached the Italian peninsula through the press. In some cases, Italian journalism reported on the political and economic conditions of Latin America, often with information gleaned from the French press. The Milanese review, *Annali Universali di Statistica*, is a case point.[25] Its editorial staff consisted of former Napoleonic civil servants who did not hide their sympathies for the new republics. Italian intellectuals not only were informed about the events taking place on the other side of the Atlantic; they also followed debates among Hispanic American patriots, and in some cases participated in those debates. In turn, many of the Italian exiles wrote about Latin American events in Europe, whether from direct experience in America or thanks to documents they received from their overseas contacts.

Such intellectual exchanges frequently took place outside Italy in the metropolitan centres of Paris, London, and Brussels. Italian exiles in England, France, and Belgium had direct contacts with Hispanic American diplomatic representatives of the new republics in Europe, such as Emmanuel de Gorostiza, Vicente Rocafuerte, and José Mariano Michelena. Disputes between federalists and centralists reverberated in the Spanish émigré journals in London and in the publications of prominent Hispanic American liberals in Europe such as Vicente Rocafuerte, author, with the editorial support of the Spanish exile José Canga Argüellas, of a passionate defence of American federalism against Bolivar's centralizing constitution of 1826.[26] Italian exiles followed these debates.[27] The circulation of ideas among Italians and Americans was further encouraged by epistolary exchanges, such as that between Giuseppe Pecchio, exiled in Spain, and José Cecilio del Valle.[28]

Other Italian intellectuals made their way to the Americas. The Neapolitan Pietro de Angelis settled in Buenos Aires in 1827, where he became a supporter of Juan Manuel de Rosas, President of the United Provinces of Río de la Plata. Claudio Linati, Orazio Santangelo, and Fiorenzo Galli, for instance, moved to Mexico and became directly involved in the clash between *Yorkinos* and *Escoceses* lodges before returning to Europe.[29] Siding with the radical faction of Yorkinos in the pages of *El Iris* or in later articles and publications, the Italians supported the view that sovereignty resided in the people and that federalism could consolidate the nation and defend individual rights. Among the Yorkinos, Lorenzo de Zavala was the Mexican politician most closely connected with the Italian exiles. Through Zavala, Santangelo and the other exiles met other radical politicians.[30] Another Italian, Giacomo Costantino Beltrami, travelled extensively in Mexico in 1824 and 1825. His *Le Mexique*[31] positively compared the Mexican federalist model to the Achaean League.[32] Orazio Santangelo was another Italian federalist deeply involved in Mexican political debates.[33]

The writings of these exiled Italian federalists in America and Europe generally celebrated the liberal nature and federal constitutions of the 'independent, industrial, and commercial republics' of the Americas, deeming them to be the only ones compatible with the spirit of modern civilization. They therefore advocated an American-inspired federalism for a future independent Italy.[34] Following the post-independence debates and experiences of the Hispanic American republics, they came to support the view that sovereignty lay in the people, and that federalism alone could defend both individual and collective rights.

The example of the new Hispanic American republics encouraged among Italian observers a notion of nationhood that was based not on race or ethnicity, but on granting citizenship to almost the entire adult male population. This Cadiz-inspired model of an inclusive nation is strikingly illustrated by Claudio Linati in his famous collection of engravings describing the new Mexican state, published in Brussels in 1828. Linati was an ex-officer of the Napoleonic army who, after having participated in various liberal movements in Italy and Spain, was exiled to Mexico in 1825, where he obtained citizen status and established Mexico's first lithographic press. He also co-founded and edited *El Iris*, a periodical that published the first political cartoons in Mexico. Linati praised the ethnic variety of the country and the Creole role in independence. However, the most striking element in his representation of the nation was the presence of foreign volunteers. Through a number of engravings, he celebrated the contribution of Italian volunteers to the establishment of the Mexican Republic, arguing that foreign volunteers such as Count Giuseppe Stavalo and General Vicente Filisola were indeed part of the nation since they had linked its emancipation to the worldwide struggle for independence.[35]

Other Italian exiles questioned the linguistic basis of a successful national identity, an idea then widely disseminated in Europe. In his *Dei futuri destini dell'Europa* (1828), Vitale Albera, (exiled to Geneva and Brussels after having participated in the Piedmontese revolution), claimed that in an age of proliferating exchanges between nations, language and culture were losing importance. The newly established Hispanic American republics were proof that linguistic homogeneity in a continent did not preclude the birth of separate nations, a point observed by Benedict Anderson in *Imagined Communities*.[36] For Albera, 'the principle of keeping one language to the exclusion of all others belongs to the time of hostility and political intolerance.' He was convinced that 'each and every national spirit stems from the people's government and from their institutions.'[37]

The Resurgence of Anti-Hispanism

Anti-Spanish sentiment in Italy has been widely noted and examined in the Italian historiography.[38] Nevertheless, only in rare exceptions has the history of this sentiment been connected to changing interpretations of Latin American independence in Italy. Many Risorgimento intellectuals would come to blame the 'Spanish occupation' or rule of Italian territories for the political, cultural, and economic decadence of the peninsula. Whereas in the early modern period the anti-Spanish attitude sought to delegitimize the Spanish power in Italy, during the nineteenth century it became a key component of the Italian nationalist imaginary. Intellectuals such as Sismondi, Botta, and Balbo joined the theme of decadence to the end of sixteenth-century 'Italian liberty,' producing a master narrative that has long underwritten Italian historiography. In the nineteenth century, anti-Spanish sentiment became not only an emotional trait of Italian identity but also a storyline that explained the Italian past as a struggle between foreign tyranny and native liberty.[39]

The Spanish Black Legend and the so-called 'Dispute of the New World,' reconstructed by Antonelli Gerbi in his well-known work, shaped the image of independent Latin American republics as deformed by the stubborn colonial legacy of Spanish despotism. This was coupled with an earlier image of the presumed natural and physical inferiority of the American continent, established by northern European philosophes such as Buffon and De Pauw, and later transformed by Hegel into a spiritual incapacity to progress.[40] Whereas the sixteenth- and seventeenth-century anti-Spanish Black Legend was essentially linked to the Reformation, with the eighteenth-century Age of Enlightenment dispute it assumed an essentially cultural character. In the nineteenth century, it morphed into a political disability that condemned the Latin American republics to chaos and failure. This last notion also applied to the Italian south, and indeed to Spain itself. In short, the transatlantic 'colonial south' was no longer a federalist model of independence to be imitated.

Conclusion

The strong connections between the Italian and Hispanic American independence movements reveal not only the importance of transoceanic networks and exchanges but also a shared history of Spanish rule. In the early phase, the Napoleonic invasions and the Constitution of Cadiz created shared conditions that were ripe for a decolonizing or liberating federalism that might guarantee a measure of 'independence' within larger spheres of interdependence. Italian and Hispanic American exiles exchanged notes and experiences in Europe and the Americas. During the early 1820s Hispanic America became a model for Italian revolutionaries. By the 1830s, the instability of the Spanish American republics as well as Giuseppe Mazzini's hostility to federalism, eroded Italian admiration for Latin America. However, it was the advent of cultural and linguistic nationalism in the following decades that completely transformed the image of Latin America in Europe. Italian and European liberals now saw Latin America as a degenerate and passive continent, inadequate to the task of modernity, due to its Spanish colonial legacy.

Notes

1. Luigi Angeloni, *Sopra l'ordinamento che aver dovrebbero i governi d'Italia* (Paris, 1814).
2. *Diario de Sesiones de las Cortes Generales y Extraordinarias* (Madrid, 1872), 2590–2591, 2618.
3. Manuel Chust, *La cuestión nacional americana en las Cortes de Cádiz, 1810–1814* (Valencia and Mexico: UNED, Fundación Instituto Historia Social and Instituto de Investigaciones Históricas, UNAM, 1999).
4. Clément Thibaud, 'En busca de la república federal: el primer constitucionalismo en la Nueva Granada,' in Antonio Annino and Marcela Ternavasio, eds., *El laboratorio constitucional iberoamericano, 1807/8–1830* (Frankfurt and Madrid: Iberoamericana-Vervuert, 2012), 35–54.
5. Federica Morelli, '¿Constitución imperial o jurisdiccional? La dimensión atlántica de la carta gaditana,' in Roberto Breña, ed., *Cádiz a debate: actualidad, contexto y legado* (Mexico City: El Colegio de México, 2014), 85–106.
6. Antonio Annino, 'Soberanías en lucha,' in Antonio Annino and François-Xavier Guerra, eds., *Inventando la nación: Iberoamérica siglo XIX* (Mexico City: Fondo de Cultura Económica, 2003), 152–184; Federica Morelli, *Territorio o Nación. Reforma y disolución del espacio imperial en Ecuador, 1765–1830* (Madrid: Centro de Estudios Políticos y Constitucionales, 2005); Jordana Dym, *From Sovereign Villages to National States: City, State, and Federation in Central America, 1759–1839* (Albuquerque, NM: University of New Mexico Press, 2006); José Antonio Serrano Ortega and Juan Ortiz Escamilla, eds., *Ayuntamientos y liberalismo gaditano en México* (Mexico City: El Colegio de Michoacán, 2007).
7. Maria Sofia Corciulo, 'La costituzione di Cadice e le rivoluzioni italiane del 1820-21,' *Le Carte e la Storia* 2 (2000), 18–29; Gonzalo Butrón Prida, *Nuestra Sagrada Causa. El modelo gaditano en la revolución piamontesa de 1821* (Cádiz: Ayuntamiento de Cádiz, 2006).
8. Alfonso Scirocco, 'Il problema dell'autonomia locale nel Mezzogiorno durante la rivoluzione del 1820-21,' in *Studi in Memoria di Nino Cortese* (Roma: Istituto per la Storia del Risorgimento Italiano, 1976), 485–503.
9. Bartolomé Fiorilli, *Causas filosófico-políticas de la caída del Reino constitucional de las Dos Sicilias* (Barcelona: Imprenta de la viuda Roca, 1821).
10. Javier Fernández Sebastián, *Diccionario Político y social del mundo iberoamericano. La era de las revoluciones, 1750–1850* (Madrid: Centro de Estudios Políticos y Constitucionales, 2009), 1115–1250.
11. Alberto Maria Banti, *La nazione del Risorgimento. Parentela, santità e onore alle origini dell'Italia unita* (Torino: Einaudi, 2000).
12. See, for example: Marco Meriggi, 'Centralismo e federalismo in Italia. Le aspettative preunitarie,' in O. Janz, P. Schiera and H. Siegrist, eds., *Centralismo e federalismo tra Otto e Novecento: Italia e Germania a confronto* (Bologna: Il Mulino, 1997), 49–63; Vittorio Criscuolo, *Albori di democrazia nell'Italia in rivoluzione, 1792–1802* (Milan: Franco Angeli, 2006), 103–122.
13. 'Acta del Gobierno de Quito en que se constituye como soberano y sanciona su independencia de España,' Archivo General de Indias, Quito 276, fls. 259r–259v.
14. David Armitage, *The Declaration of Independence: A Global History* (Cambridge, MA: Harvard University Press, 2008).
15. Benedict Anderson, *Imagined Communities: Reflections on the Origin and Spread of Nationalism* (London: Verso, 1983).
16. On the territorial effects caused by the crisis of the Spanish monarchy in America, see Maria Teresa Calderón and Clément Thibaud, *La Majestad*

de los pueblos en la Nueva Granada y Venezuela, 1780–1832 (Bogotá: Universidad Externado de Colombia/IFEA, Taurus, 2010); Morelli, *Territorio o Nación*; José Carlos Chiaramonte, *Ciudades, provincias, estados. Orígenes de la Nación Argentina, 1800–1846* (Buenos Aires: Ariel, 1997); Antonio Annino, 'Cadiz y la revolución territorial de los pueblos mexicanos, 1812–1821,' in Antonio Annino, ed., *Historia de las elecciones en Iberoamérica* (Buenos Aires: Fondo de Cultura Económica, 1995), 177–225.
17. Maurizio Isabella, *Risorgimento in Exile: Italian Émigrés and the Liberal International in the Post-Napoleonic Era* (New York: Oxford University Press, 2009), 17–18.
18. Orazio de Santangelo, *Las cuatro primeras discusiones del Congreso de Panamá tales como debieran ser* (Mexico City, 1826), 46.
19. See, for example, an international conference held in Genoa in 2005, *Tracce del Risorgimento italiano in America Latina*. See also: *Giuseppe Garibaldi. Liberatore globale tra Italia, Europa e America* (Ancona: Affinità Elettive, 2007); Pietro R. Fanesi, *Garibaldi nelle Americhe. L'uso politico del mito e gli italoamericani* (Rome: Gangemi, 2007).
20. Lucy Riall, *Garibaldi: Invention of a Hero* (New Haven: Yale University Press, 2007), 37–56.
21. Isabella, *Risorgimento in Exile*.
22. Salvatore Candido, *Combattenti italiani per la rivoluzione bolivariana: corsari e ufficiali* (Naples: Edizioni Scientifiche Italiane, 1983).
23. Marisa Vannini, *Carlos Luis Castelli: Vida y Obra Del General de División Carlos Luis Castelli, Ilustre Prócer de la Independencia* (Caracas: Cámara de Comercio, Industria y Agricultura Venezolana-Italiana, 1988).
24. Agostino Codazzi, *Le Memorie* (Milan: Istituto Editoriale Italiano, 1960). On the work of Codazzi in Colombia, see Nancy Appelbaum, *Making the Country of Regions. The Corographic Commission of Nineteenth-Century Colombia* (Chapel Hill: University of North Carolina Press, 2016).
25. Aldo Albonico, 'La Gran Colombia in una rivista milanese coeva. Gli 'Annali universali di statistica,' in Id, *L'America Latina e l'Italia* (Rome: Bulzoni, 1984), 61–72.
26. Vicente Rocafuerte, *Cartas de un Americano sobre las ventajas de los gobiernos republicanos federativos* (London: Imprenta Española de M. Calero, 1826).
27. Isabella, *Risorgimento*, 48–49.
28. Ibid.
29. Erika Pani, 'Gentlihomme et révolutionnaire; ciyoyen et *étranger suspect*. Orazio de Attellis, marquis de Santangelo, et les républiques américaines,' in Clement Thibaud, Gabriel Entin, Alejandro Gómez, and Federica Morelli, eds., *L'Atlantique révolutionnaire. Une perspective ibéro-américaine* (Paris: Perséides, 2013), 115–130.
30. Orazio de Attellis Santangelo, *Statement of Facts Relating to the Claim of Orazio de Attellis Santangelo, a Citizen of the United States, on the Government of the Republic of Mexico* (Washington: Peter Forge, 1841).
31. Giacomo Costantino Beltrami, *Le Méxique* (Paris: Crevot, 1830).
32. Ibid., 232–233.
33. O. Santangelo, 'Situation politique du Mexique,' *L'Abeille* 24 (October 1835), 3, cited in Isabella, *Risorgimento*, 56.
34. Claudio Linati, 'Etat de l'Instruction en Amérique,' in 'Claudio Linati,' *Memorie parmensi per la storia del Risorgimento* 4 (1935), 24–28.
35. Claudio Linati, *Costumes civils, militaires et religieux du Mexique dessinés d'après nature* (Bruxelles: Lithographie Royale de Jobard, 1828).

36. Anderson, *Imagined Communities*.
37. Isabella, *Risorgimento*, 107.
38. Ricardo García Carcel, *La leyenda negra. Historia y opinión* (Madrid: Alianza Editorial, 1992); Aurelio Musi, ed., *Alle origini di una nazione. Antiespagnolismo e identità italiana* (Milano: Guerini e Associati, 2003).
39. Banti, *La nazione del Risorgimento*.
40. Antonello Gerbi, *La disputa del Nuovo Mondo. Storia di una polemica, 1750–1900* (Naples-Milan, Ricciardi, 1955).

Contributors

Lina del Castillo is Associate Professor of Latin American History at the University of Texas at Austin. She is the author of *Crafting a Republic for the World: Scientific, Geographic and Historiographic Inventions of Colombia* (Lincoln: University of Nebraska Press, 2018).

Marixa Lasso is Associate Professor of History at the Universidad Nacional de Colombia. She is the author of *Myths of Harmony: Race and Republicanism during the Age of Revolution in Colombia* (Pittsburgh: University of Pittsburgh Press, 2009) and *Erased: The Untold Story of the Panama Canal* (Cambridge: Harvard University Press, 2019).

Federica Morelli is Associate Professor of History at the University of Turin. She is the author of *Territorio o Nazione. Riforma e dissoluzione dello spazio imperiale in Ecuador, 1765–1830* (Soveria Mannelli: Rubittino, 2001) and *L'indipendenza dell'America spagnola. Dalla crisi della monarchia alle nuove repubbliche* (Firenze: Mondadori, 2015).

Francisco Ortega is Associate Professor of History at the Universidad Nacional de Colombia and Senior Researcher at the Centro de Estudios Sociales (CES). He is co-editor of *Conceptos fundamentales de la cultura política de la independencia* (Bogotá: Universidad Nacional de Colombia, 2013).

James Sanders is Professor of Latin American History at Utah State University. He is the author of *The Vanguard of the Atlantic World: Creating Modernity, Nation, and Democracy in Nineteenth-Century Latin America* (Durham: Duke University Press, 2014) and *Contentious Republicans: Popular Politics, Race, and Class in Nineteenth-Century Colombia* (Durham: Duke University Press, 2004).

Todd Shepard is Arthur O. Lovejoy Professor of History at Johns Hopkins University. He is the author of *The Invention of Decolonization: The Algerian War and the Remaking of France* (Ithaca: Cornell

University Press, 2006) and *Sex, France, and Arab Men, 1962–1979* (Chicago: University of Chicago Press, 2017).

Mark Thurner is Professor of Latin American Studies at the University of London. He is the author of *History's Peru: The Poetics of Colonial and Postcolonial Historiography* (Gainesville: University Press of Florida, 2011), *From Two Republics to One Divided: Contradictions of Postcolonial Nationmaking in Andean Peru* (Durham: Duke University Press, 1997), and co-editor of *After Spanish Rule: Postcolonial Predicaments of the Americas*, (Durham: Duke University Press, 2003).

Barbara Weinstein is Silver Professor of History at New York University. She is the author of *The Amazon Rubber Boom, 1850–1920*, (Palo Alto: Stanford University Press, 1983), *For Social Peace in Brazil: Industrialists and the Remaking of the Working Class in São Paulo, 1920–1964*, (Chapel Hill: University of North Carolina Press, 1996) and *The Color of Modernity: São Paulo and the Making of Race and Nation in Brazil*, (Durham: Duke University Press, 2015).

Index

Abascal, José Fernando (Viceroy of Peru) 33
Adams, John Quincy 70, 71, 74n32, 76n74
Age of Revolution 1, 5–6, 48, 74n35, 77–79, 90, 91n1, 94n44, 129n7
Albera, Vitale 139
Alencar, José de 123
Algeria 3–5, 7n5, 26, 102
Amphictyonic Congress 51, 69–70
Anderson, Benedict 1, 5, 7n2, 44n4, 48, 72n1, 112n51, 112n55, 122, 130n18, 136, 139, 141n15, 143n36
Aranda, Pedro Pablo Abarca de Bolea, Conde de 13–14, 22n30
Areche, José Antonio de 28
Atlantic world 4, 21n13, 36, 44n12, 73n24, 97–99, 110n1, 118–119, 129n1

Barlow, Joel 54–56, 60, 71, 73n21–24, 74n31–32, 74n35, 74n43, 75n50
Beltrami, Giacomo 138, 142n31
Bentham, Jeremy 4
Bermudez, José Francisco 82
Bilbao, Francisco 98, 101, 11n23–24, 112n49
Black Legend 7, 29, 52, 57, 66, 140
Bolívar, Simón 25n60, 39, 46n48, 50–51, 62–72, 76n71, 76n73, 80–89, 93n14, 93n26, 135–138
Bonaparte, Joseph (José I) 16, 33
Bonaparte, Napoleon 135–136
Bonn, Moritz 2
Bourbon reforms 10, 21n13, 28, 31–32
Brazil 6, 33, 37, 42, 44n5, 48, 59, 71, 72n8, 91n1, 106, 115n83, 118–131
Britain vii, 4, 7n8, 17, 29, 50–51, 59–60, 71, 86, 89

Brussels 109, 116n101, 138–139
Buenos Aires 17, 24n41, 24n46, 40, 50, 58, 61–62, 70, 91n1, 92n10, 138
Buffon, George Louis Leclerc Comte de 78

Caballero, Manuel 81
Cadiz, Cortes and Constitution of 10, 12, 16, 19, 33–35, 45n33, 69, 129n1, 133–136, 140, 141n3, 141n5, 141n7, 142n16
Caracas 13, 40, 62, 66, 75n62, 76n73, 78, 80–81, 91n1, 92n6, 93n15
Cartagena de Indias 17, 80–85, 91n1, 93n14, 93n32
Castelar, Emilio 109, 117n104–105
Castelli, Carlo 137, 142n23
Catherine the Great 57
Chakrabarty, Dipesh x, xin6, 98, 109, 110n4, 111n22, 116n89, 117n106
Charles III 5
Charles IV 13, 16
Charles of Hesse, Prince 57–58
Chatterjee, Partha 105–106, 112n53, 115n80, 115n82
Chile 38, 46n48, 61, 70–71, 96, 98
citizenship ix, xin5, 34, 43, 62, 79–88, 92n3–5, 102–107, 118–126, 129n2–4, 131n31, 131n38, 134, 136, 139
Clavigero, Antonio 78
Cluseret, Gustave 108, 116n97
Codazzi, Agostini 137, 142n24
Colombia 5–6, 35, 43, 48–95, 100–114, 137, 142n24–25
colonialism (coloniaje) viii, x, 2, 5–6, 7n4, 7n8, 8–9, 18, 22n25, 27, 33, 36, 41–42, 44n5, 44n7, 46n52, 49,

Index 147

90, 95–104, 110, 111n26, 111n33, 112n52, 113n55, 115n80, 116n88, 118, 122, 128, 129n3
colonial system (sistema colonial) x, xin7, xiin8, 2, 5, 17–19, 26–27, 33–43, 45n37, 46n53, 99–101, 107, 125, 130n19
colonies (colonias) x, xin7, 2–19, 21n5, 27–37, 41, 44n10, 45n34, 46n41, 55, 78, 91, 92n7, 100, 110, 121, 131n34
Columbia 5, 48–59, 64–66, 70–72, 73n22–23, 73n29, 74n35
Columbus, Christopher 49–57, 62, 65–66, 71–72, 73n21, 73n27, 74n32, 74n35, 74n47
constitution (constitución) 3, 8, 14–17, 23n32, 23n34, 24n46, 32–33, 50, 66, 133; *see also* Cadiz, Cortes and Constitution of
constitutional monarchy 35, 38, 41, 59, 96, 119, 123; *see also* Cadiz, Cortes and Constitution of
Cuba 25n59, 46n41, 55, 59, 70–71, 78, 94n53, 118–121, 128, 129n6–7, 132n45
Cunha Matos, José da 126

da Silva Lisboa, José 125–127, 131n34
decolonial theory viii–x, 6, 27, 44n4, 95, 101–102, 105, 107, 112n48, 118, 129n3
decolonization vii–xi, xin1–2, xin5, 1–6, 7n1, 7n5, 7n9, 7n11, 19, 26–27, 38, 43, 43n2–3, 48, 72n2–3, 77, 91, 95–109, 118–122, 129n3, 133
decolonize (descolonizarse) vii–xi, xin1, xin5, 2, 5, 18, 26–27, 38–43, 48, 51, 95–101, 106, 118, 122
De Pauw, Cornelius 78, 140
De Pradt, Dominique-Georges-Frédéric Dufour 4, 11, 21n15, 32, 36–37, 42, 45n31, 45n34–39, 46n40–42, 47n60
Diderot, Denis 4, 28, 52–53, 72n7
Dom Pedro I 123
Dom Pedro II 130n25
Dwight, Timothy 56

Ecuador 48, 131n31, 141n6
Escobar y Armendáriz, Jesús 98, 101, 111n20, 112n45

Europe x, xin6, 5–7, 7n5, 7n10, 15, 21n14, 27, 33, 36–37, 52, 70, 91, 95–109, 110n10, 110n14, 117n106, 131n34, 133–140

federalism ix, xi, 5, 42–43, 48–49, 55–56, 71, 133–140, 141n12
Ferdinand VII 16–17, 33–36, 62, 135
Fiorilli, Bartolomeo 134, 141n9
Flores, Federico 97, 111n18
Flórez Estrada, Álvaro 19, 25n57
Fonfrède, Henri viii, xin3, 2, 4, 26, 44n2
France vii–x, 4, 7n5, 26, 33, 43n2, 48, 50, 58–61, 85–86, 96–99, 108–109, 121, 133, 138

Gálvez, José de 11, 14, 21n20, 28
Garcilaso de la Vega, Inca (Gómez Suárez de Figueroa) 14, 59, 75n49
Garibaldi, Giuseppe 106, 109, 136–137, 142n19–20
Garibaldinos 96, 106, 108–109
Genoa 49, 106, 109, 137
George III 62, 75n60
Gerbi, Antonello 23n38, 45n16, 92n4, 140, 143n40
Godoy, Manuel 13, 22n30
González Urueña, Juan 99, 111n29
Guatemala 70
Guha, Ranajit 7n8, 102, 105, 112n54, 115n81
Gustavus III 57

Haiti viii–xi, xin7, 6, 50, 61, 70, 77–78, 84–87, 92n5, 93n34–37, 112n49, 116n93, 119–121, 129, 129n7, 130n11, 130n12, 137
Hamilton, Alexander 56
Herder, Johann Gottfried 4
Hobsbawm, Eric 104, 114n68
Hugo, Victor 109, 116n102
Humboldt, Alexander von 18–19, 25n56

Inca(s) 14, 30–31, 38, 48, 59, 66, 75n49
independence viii–x, xin2, 2, 5–8, 13, 17–19, 20n3, 24n39, 26–43, 44n8, 46n41, 50–71, 74n45, 75n63, 76n69, 76n74–75, 77–90, 91n1, 92n12, 93n29, 93n37, 97–107, 112n55–56, 114n70, 126–128,

Index

129n1, 130n14, 130n20, 130n28, 131n38, 133–140, 141n14
India 3–5, 7n7–8, 36, 53, 61, 102–106, 112n54, 115n80–81
Indies (Indias) 8, 20n3–12, 21n12–19, 23n37, 24n42, 29–33
Ireland 100
Italy 3–7, 29, 98, 100, 109, 133–140

Jamaica 25n60, 51, 55, 66, 76n71
Jefferson, Thomas 61
Juan, Jorge 30
Juárez, Benito 108–109, 116n94–96, 116n101–102

Kant, Immanuel 4
Kennedy, Dane 1, 7n1, 7n5, 7n11, 43n2, 72n2
Klor de Alva, Jorge 44n5, 113n55–56, 114n67, 118, 129n3

Las Casas, Bartolomé 52
Lima 18, 24n41, 26–43, 43n1, 46n45–49, 47n56, 111n18
Linati, Claudio 138–139, 142n34–35
Louisiana 50, 58–61, 121, 130n12, 137
L'Overture, Touissant 86
Lynch, John 113n55, 122, 130n16

Maciel da Costa, Joao Severiano 125–127
Marquez, Remigio 83–84
Maximilian I 96–97, 108–109
Mazzini, Giuseppe 135, 140
Mercurio Peruano 28–33, 45n17–20
Mexico (New Spain) 8, 12, 17, 19n1, 24n39–41, 24n50, 25n50, 28, 36–37, 42, 46n41, 60, 70, 91n1, 92n10, 96–109, 114n70, 116n97, 116n100, 117n103, 117n105, 136–139, 141n6, 142n30
Mignolo, Walter viii, x, xin2, 44n4–5, 95, 101, 107, 110n2, 111n22, 112n43, 112n48, 113n56, 116n89, 116n91, 118, 129n3
Milan 135, 138
Miranda, Francisco de 49–76, 80
Monteagudo, Bernardo xi, 35–43, 45n31, 45n39, 46n45–54, 47n57–59
Montesquieu, Charles-Louis de Secondat, Baron de La Brède et de 11, 21n14, 30, 38–41, 46n55
Murilo de Carvalho, José 122

Naples 5, 45n33, 134–136
Napoleon III 99, 101
Nuix, Juan 29, 44n12

Ortiz, Gabino 97, 110n13, 111n17

Padilla, José Prudencio 84–85, 93n32
Paine, Thomas 32–33, 45n22
Palti, José Elías 40, 44n5, 47n56, 92n12, 130n21
Panama 48–51, 58, 61, 65–71, 75n62, 76n73, 76n77, 142n18
Paris 4, 23n31, 50, 60, 65, 86, 98, 133, 138
Peralta Barnuevo, Pedro de 30
Peru x–xi, 2, 7n6, 23n32, 26–48, 54, 70, 92n10, 97–99, 114n70, 117n106
Philadelphia 56, 65–66, 69, 76n75, 133
Philippines 24n45, 25n59, 133
Pitt, William 59, 61
Popham, Sir Home Riggs 61–62
postcolonial theory ix–x, xin6, 4, 6, 22n25, 27, 44n5, 95, 101–108, 110n4, 110n10, 111n22, 112n44, 112n52–55, 114n67, 115n79–80, 116n88–92, 129n3
Puerto Rico 25n59, 46n41

Quito 54, 135, 141n13

Raynal, Guillaume Thomas François 4, 11, 21n15, 28–31, 36, 45n37, 52–53, 72n7–9, 73n10–16
republicanism 7–12, 37–72, 77–105
Restrepo, José Manuel 85, 93n32–33
Revillagigedo, Count (Viceroy of New Spain) 8, 12, 19n1
rights of man 16, 85
Rio de Janeiro 119, 129n2, 130n22, 130n28, 131n33
Risorgimento 133–143
Rivero y Ustariz, Mariano de 31
Robertson, William 11, 21n15, 28–31, 44n11, 53–57, 73n17
Rome 65, 88, 108
Rosas, Juan Manuel de 91n10, 138
Rousseau, Jean-Jacques 22n25, 32, 38–41

Said, Edward 107–108, 116n90
Sánchez Carrión, José Faustino viii–xi, 2, 18, 26, 28, 35–43, 46n48

San Martín, José de 35, 39, 46n41, 46n48–49
Santa Anna, Antonio López 101, 105
Santangelo, Orazio 136–138, 142n18, 142n29–30, 142n33
Schwarz, Roberto 44n5, 122–123, 130n21
second slavery 6, 72, 118–143
Sierra, Justo 101, 112n42
Silva, Sebastiana 105, 115n77
slavery 35, 39, 51, 61, 70–91, 100–109, 118; *see also* Second slavery
Smith, Adam 4
Sociedad Patriótica 40–41, 46n45, 80–81
Spain ix–x, 4–5, 7n6, 8–18, 26–42, 46n41, 50–52, 57, 59–62, 70, 72n9, 82, 90–91, 100, 133–144
Steward, Maria W. 89

teleology ix, 6, 52, 79
Teresa de Mier, Fray Servando 17, 24n46–47, 70

Thornton, William 50–51, 65–72, 75n66
Torquemada, Juan de 14
Tupac Amaru II 58–59, 73n24
Turin 134–135

Ulloa, Antonio de 30
Unanue, José Hipólito 30–34, 40
United States 42, 49–61, 65–72, 75–78, 84–91, 96–97, 102, 115n87, 120, 128, 130n12, 131n32, 133
Uruguay (Banda Oriental) 96, 106–109, 115n85, 137

Varela, Héctor 98, 111n19
Vastey, Baron Pompée Valentín de x, xi, xin7, xiin8
Venezuela 48–51, 58, 61, 64–69, 75n63, 78–82, 93n22, 93n26, 111n22, 137, 141n16
Vico, Giambattista 5

Washington, George 55–56, 62
Wheatley, Phyllis 56